Praise for *"I SANG THAT..."*

"If one is looking for a tour guide to navigate working in the studio or on the road during the 60s and 70s, Sally Stevens would be your perfect choice. There was nothing Sally couldn't do in the studio. She brought talent, professionalism and magic to every session. She was one of the most successful backup singers that I had the privilege to work with.

Sally was a huge asset while we were on the road together. She not only brought the best out of herself in every single performance, but she pushed the other singers to make their most beautiful sounds.

In her spare time, Sally wrote her own songs and poems. She traversed every area of the music business and brought much happiness to those lucky enough to know her.

While I was scoring *Butch Cassidy and the Sundance Kid*, Sally was vital in helping me achieve the vision of how I wanted the score to sound, and I couldn't have recorded "South American Getaway" without her.

My journey with Sally Stevens – I wouldn't have missed it for the world. Hats off to you, Sally- you've done it all!"

- **Burt Bacharach, Composer/Songwriter/Multi-Oscars & Grammys Awards Winner**

"Have you ever wanted to peek behind the scenes of the music industry, and even hear the voices behind the voices? This music maven's love of her life in music is beyond illuminating. It's edifying. She is the real deal and she shows us what it is to walk her walk with delight, passion, talent, and positivity. This book is more than a gem. It's a primer on how to live in your passion. Sally Stevens shows us how."

- **Laura Munson, *New York Times* bestselling author and founder of Haven Writing Programs**

"I SANG THAT..."

"I SANG THAT..."

From *The Sound of Music* to *The Simpsons*
to *South Park* and Beyond...

A Memoir From Hollywood

by

Sally Stevens

atmosphere press

DEDICATION

I would like to dedicate this book to all the wonderful singers and musicians that make up the mostly invisible and often unrecognized music community here in Hollywood—to those amazing singers who came before me, who graciously helped me to learn and progress, and who smoothed the bumps in the road a bit -- to those wonderful colleagues I got to sing with through the years, side by side-- and to all the talented young people still to come, who aspire to one day be a part of the Hollywood musical community. May you find your way, may you have the good fortune to be at the right place at the right time so your talents can be discovered, and may you enjoy a long and rewarding music-making journey. May the scoring stages here in Hollywood survive the changes in our business, and may you all, as I did, get to one day stand on those stages where Judy Garland sang "Over The Rainbow"—where composers like John Barry, Elmer Bernstein, Burt Bacharach, Tyler Bates, Alf Clausen, Bill Conti, Mychael Dana, Michael Giacchino, Jerry Goldsmith, James Horner, James Newton Howard, Walter Murphy, Alfred Newman, David Newman, Lionel Newman, Thomas Newman, Alex North, John Powers, Marc Shaiman, Lalo Schifrin, Alan Silvestri, and John Williams (in alphabetical order) and so many others—brilliant composers who came before and after—conducted the orchestras and voices that breathed life into their music and delivered such emotion to the images on screen for the filmmakers of Hollywood, all through the decades.

TABLE OF CONTENTS

INTRODUCTION

One day, during the period of the coronavirus pandemic that hit the world early in 2020 and brought activities to a screeching halt, I came across a box of sheet music I'd stored away—scribbled lead sheets of songs I had written back in the late sixties and seventies. Some of them were completed and I had actually recorded demos of them. Some were almost complete, but had a few missing bars of lyrics, or the pencil scribblings were so faded that I couldn't quite make them out.

I've spent hours during this last year sitting at the piano playing through those songs, trying to remember what person or what heartbreak inspired each one. I've gotten mad at myself for not working harder at them, for not believing more in myself and my ability to do that.

There's a little framed art piece hanging on the entryway hall of my house next to my front door. In black letters, painted artistically on a background that looks like it's made of sackcloth, are the words of its thought-provoking message: "I am lost. I have gone to look for myself. If I should return before I get back, please ask me to wait. Thanks."

I see that little sign every time I leave my house, and I ponder upon its meaning. Why did I feel that message was so clearly for me? Was it a moment of clarity? Did I somehow lose myself along the way? Did I end up on the path I had not intended to travel? I spotted that little sign maybe ten years ago, when I was shopping in a neighborhood gift shop. It struck home immediately but I wasn't sure exactly why. I just knew I had to buy it. Maybe writing these pages will help me figure it all out.

The songwriting began for me decades ago when I was still in junior high school. It was partly self-expression and partly a conscious creative endeavor. That was when I began to think seriously about wanting to make a living in the music business. Though I'd sung with a little band of guys from my high school who performed for dances at the Elks Lodge, my first real professional audition happened one day in 1957 during my last year in high school. It was through the kindness of a lighting man who had been on the road with my father when he was road manager for Holiday on Ice that I got a chance to audition for one of the afternoon TV talk shows produced in Los Angeles. The lighting man had remembered my father talking about his daughter who wanted to be a singer, and he was now working at CBS TV on the afternoon show. The band was looking for a singer, and my dad had successfully convinced the lighting man that I was pretty good, so he somehow managed to get me involved in the auditions.

I couldn't believe this really was happening. At that point I was still pretty shy, so I lived somewhere between adequate self-confidence and total fear and paranoia. Part of me must have thought that I might somehow, at seventeen years of age, be good enough to get hired on a network TV show. The other part of me was scared to death I wouldn't be able to pull it off.

I wish I could tell you the name of the show, but it has long escaped my memory, along with the name of the song I sang. I was terribly nervous, and on top of just being nervous about the singing, I had never driven into "the city" from the little town of Tujunga where we lived.

CBS Studio was, and still is, at the corner of Fairfax Boulevard and Beverly Boulevard, sort of on the west edge of Hollywood. Tujunga is in the low hills at the far north end of the San Fernando Valley. There was no Siri in those days to tell you where to turn, nor any Google Maps on the dashboard. So my mother wrote out careful instructions for me, and I tried to follow them. I don't think she was terribly happy about this audition that my father had helped arrange. Cautionary lights were blinking on and off in my mother's mind.

I pulled up to the guard gate at the CBS lot and told the guard I was there for an audition. He had my name on his list, and eventually I found my way through the hallways to the right studio. The musical director of the show was standing down at the front of the auditorium. I made my way through the empty aisles and he waved me over to the bandstand. "What are you singing for us?" he asked. I handed him my music. He handed the music to the piano player as I walked up onto the little stage into position in front of the standing mic. The piano player started the intro, and I sang my song, nervous but still persevering.

When I finished, the musical director walked over to me, handed me back my sheet music, and said, "Honey, why don't you find a nice boy and get married?"

The drive home was painful in a different way than the drive into town had been. I was no longer nervous, just disappointed, depressed, and pretty discouraged.

But here's the thing. I did eventually find *three* "nice boys," and I married them all, sequentially of course. And somehow along the way I stumbled into working successfully in the music business as a singer, vocal contractor, and lyricist for film and TV scoring, sound recordings, concerts, and commercials—with and for some of the best people in the business— for the next sixty years. I've been blessed to sing on so many projects over these years, as either soloist or as part of a choir or small vocal group. You've heard many of them, I suspect, but they were for the most part uncredited, which is the custom for us "session singers" here in Hollywood. I'll share some of those specifics with you as we travel together through these pages.

The journey through all those years, between the tragic events of that day at CBS and today, has been a fascinating and blessed one. Perhaps I should dedicate this book to those three *sequential* husbands I mentioned earlier, and to that unknown music director at CBS who unwittingly provided the initial challenge to do it all.

CHAPTER 1

AN OVER-THE-SHOULDER LOOK BACK—2016

It is early spring, 2016, and I am driving down the busy main street of Studio City, California, in pouring rain, the beginning of what was projected to become and in fact did become the most severe storm to hit Los Angeles in twenty years. I am on my way to meet a friend for lunch. The local NPR station is playing on the car radio, and I hear the wrap-up of an interview recorded a few years earlier with a woman jazz pianist and singer who has just passed away on *this* day at the age of ninety-two. Naturally, that catches my attention.

Hmmm. Ninety-two. I, myself, on the day of this broadcast, am seventy-seven. In fifteen years, if I am lucky, I will be ninety- two. And if the next fifteen years fly by as quickly as the last fifteen, they will be over in an instant. *Fuck*, I say to myself. (I can talk that way when I'm driving alone in my car.) And I say it because I think, *wow*. I can actually admit that there will be a time when I no longer exist.

It's hard to think about death. It's hard to even be realistic about time, about one's age, about the appropriateness of one's life at any particular age. What will I do with the gift of those next fifteen years? Age seems to dictate so much, especially in the business I've been part of all these years. Age has proven to be, in most cases, famously restrictive in our business.

And then I laugh out loud. Because three days earlier, I had just performed on camera for the Grammy Awards broadcast, this seventy-seven-year-old woman, along with five other considerably younger, talented, sexy singers, singing backup for Sturgill Simpson, the singer-songwriter who was nominated for, and won, Best Country Album of the year.

In our business, a seventy-seven-year-old female backup singer rarely ends up on camera at the Grammys. The job admittedly came about as so many things in life do, in an "out of the blue" way. A dear singer friend, Renée Armand, who relocated years ago to the music community in Nashville, Tennessee, happened to be asked by the musical director for Sturgill's albums and concerts (who also lives in Nashville), if she could recommend someone in LA to work with Sturgill on the Grammys. Bless her heart, she suggested he get in touch with me.

When he called, I warned him that I was an antique, just so he wouldn't embarrass himself or Sturgill. I also sent a recent photo, and a paragraph or so about what I had been doing most recently, which included several film score sessions and working on the music for *Family Guy* and *The Simpsons*. He wasn't scared off by the photo apparently, and we proceeded with the project.

This is a picture of me with two of the lovely singers, when we got together in our dressing room floating above the seats in the Convention Center where the Grammys were held. It's not fair of me to jump into this story at this point in time, but you have to start someplace, right? And it's probably hard for you, the reader, to figure out the connection between the California rainstorm of the decade, the Grammy Awards, and my considering the years between seventy-seven and ninety-two. So let me explain just a bit more.

Music has been my life for six decades. You've never heard of me, and I suspect that's part of why the journey's lasted this long. So, naturally, I identified a bit with this jazz singer who had just passed away at ninety-two years of age. I had seen her perform live about fifteen years ago at a little club in New York City, and I so admired the fact that she was still out there in the world. I've managed to stretch my own career a bit past the norm. There are many other very talented singers who also have done what I've done for a living, but for some unknown reason I seem to have made it last a bit longer than average. I've seen many changes in our business, some due to technology, some due to expanding production centers, changing styles—all kinds of changes.

So, I'm driving in the car, in the rainstorm of a century, cautioning myself that the end is near, that I'm dangerously close to that ninety-two-year-old singer myself. And suddenly I awaken to the fact that at least in this moment, I'm about as plugged into today as anyone could be. I say to myself, *go with it, be grateful. Realize how special this is. You just wrapped up a week of singing on camera for the Grammys behind the artist nominated for Country Album of the year, in a crowded stadium as the exciting events unfolded, standing on stage with two lovely young ladies and this sexy, handsome country singer, and no one minded that you're past retirement age.*

But of course, I am, way past. And I realize that if one is going to try to write about the long-lasting adventures of this

SALLY STEVENS

life in music, one better *do* it, before the brain cells evaporate.

My second passion has always been writing, and I've focused on that every summer for the last twenty-one years, doing writing workshops at the University of Iowa. As my writer friends in those workshops learned how I've made my living over the last many decades, they often said, "Oh, you have to write a book!" Eventually, I realized there's a lot I *would* like to share about the world I have loved so much, as I wandered through it.

So on that day in 2016 as I drove through the rain, I told myself I'm still pretty busy with the singing. I wrapped up the conversation with myself and put the book writing on hold for a while. I'll make some notes, keep the journals going. I'll get to it.

Eventually, as I drove along, the story of the recently deceased jazz singer ended, the rain stopped, the storm passed, and life continued. I had lunch with the friend I was on my way to meet, and I pushed away the idea that time was running out.

But suddenly, now, it's two years later. The world is morphing, has morphed. There are realities to face. And man, I didn't see this one coming. About to hit eighty, going around a curve pedal to the metal, and you come face to face with the fact that it isn't exactly a curve. It's more of a winding road, slowing down to a dead end.

I've been so damn lucky, I don't want the road to end. I've loved doing what I do for a living. More even than that, I realize I have *become* what I do for a living. Without it, I'm fearful that I will have no identity. I will not exist as a whole, valid person in the world.

Over the course of the last sixty years, I've sung on the sound stages of film studios in Hollywood, in the TV studios, in the recording studios, on the stage at the Hollywood Bowl and the Greek Theatre, and on concert stages all over the world. Of course, they never would have let me onto those stages or near those microphones but for the celebrities, the famous artists I was singing with. I was, for the most part, carefully positioned just outside the spotlight that shone on *them*. I just sort of borrowed their identity for a few minutes, when I stepped up to perform for the audience who obviously had come to see *them*. But the connection with the audience is an emotional one, whether you're standing on a live stage or in the vocal booth of a recording studio with only the producer or composer as your audience. And you really experience that connection, in the moment when you stand there alone in the spotlight sharing your part of the story.

Session singers, which is what we are called, are for the most part invisible to the public, whether we're recording a solo or singing as part of a choir. We mostly work off-camera and the advantage of that, for me, has proven to be that people might not notice it when you're about to hit eighty. Or if they have, they haven't mentioned it. We work through vocal contractors who are also singers but assume the additional role of casting director or choral director, putting together the right voices for the sound the composer needs. The work of vocal contractor (which early on I never wanted to do, fearing it was too "political" a role) began for me almost twenty-five years into my work as a singer. It allowed me to continue singing but also to work more closely with the composer or the producer on the project, to feel more a part of the creative process. And on a business level, it expanded my responsibility within the business. The vocal contractor must look out for the singers they hire. They must see that the proper paperwork is filed, that the contracts are filled out correctly, that the right amount is charged. This is all done through the union that has jurisdiction over the particular job. The two unions, the Screen Actors Guild, which covered theatrical films, prime time television, and TV commercials, and the American Federation of Television and Radio Artists, which covered sound recordings, network TV (daytime soaps, news, etc.), and radio commercials, merged in 2012 and are now SAG-AFTRA.

I fully acknowledge that the vocal contracting part of what I have done is really what stretched the years of my career. And the "invisibility" allows you to sneak in a few more adventures, until you stop being able to do well what you have done well all your life. That hasn't happened just yet for me, or if it has, no one has noticed it. But I'm trying to be watchful. I hum all the time, I vocalize every day, and so far, the vibrato (which I never had much of anyway) hasn't gotten out of control as sometimes happens with age. My tone is good, froggy-ness not too prevalent.

Session singers sometimes end up on camera at the Oscars or Grammys or Emmys, or on stage performing with an artist, not necessarily featured. But we get to see up close the personal side of those famous, talented artists that the public knows only from their performances. And *they* know us, they see us. We sometimes get to interact with them, to work at their direction, to understand and respect them in a different way. I want to share the journey, the inside view, the personal side of a very public business. And I also want to share all the things that I suspect everyone in the world wants to share— the unique adventures of my own life.

That includes many things, of course. Those things we all have in common—the events our lifetimes encompass that become history to the next couple of generations. And it includes the other more unique, personal events that shape each of our own lives—the loves, the challenges, the fears, the triumphs, the families, and the professional journey.

CHAPTER 2
AN OVER-THE-SHOULDER LOOK BACK—2019

Now we move on, to the spring of 2019. I'd spent the last few days trying to pull myself out of a rare period of illness—nothing serious, a little temperature, a sore throat, runny nose...but feeling ill is so rare an event in my life these last few years that I definitely noticed! Had a couple of singing gigs that required more takes (re-singing with the fresh push of the "record" button) than usual, because of the sore throat. Gratefully, they did all work out.

And it's been raining again. A lot. It doesn't do that so often in Sunny California, so when it does, we notice. *Where's the sun?* we speculate. We need this rain, sure, but does it have to rush down my street flowing like a river? My dog and I are overdue for a walk.

So I've done what I rarely do. I've canceled social plans and appointments. I've hunkered down, and I've dealt with the current events in life. Some I can help with, some I can't. I have two beautiful granddaughters who, thankfully, I'm able to help financially with college and that transition from kid to young woman of the world. I can help sustain a friend or two who might reach out in time of need. Lately, it seems, maybe numerous friends. Which only makes me realize again, how blessed I have been.

But the truth is, at this late point in life, there are days when I feel quite alone. I have had plenty of opportunities to *not* be alone, like the three marriages to the nice boys I mentioned earlier. But obviously, they didn't go so well. About two years ago my first husband, the father of my daughter Susie, passed away after a long period of declining health, his absence leaving a big hole in my daughter's heart. My third husband passed away two years ago after a shorter period of declining health, about which his Christian Science background influenced his choice of just deciding not to deal with it. The middle husband, that "Peter Pan" kind of guy who wandered off to Copenhagen about twenty-five or thirty years ago and decided to stay...we are still in touch. We write each other sweet email notes every few days, across the miles.

But this has turned into a time when every once in a while, some little life event hits us on an unexpected emotional level. Yesterday, for instance, news unfolded through texts and emails that revealed developing family plans and decisions. My dear stepmom, who has over the years become my very best friend (my dad's fourth and most happy marriage and the mother of his other two children) will be moving to Atlanta with her son and his family. She's been a part of their family these last eighteen years or so here in California, and it's been a blessing for all of them. She and I, meanwhile, have had many visits here at my home. We've taken cruises and trips together and shared some wonderful adventures. And whenever my heart becomes overburdened with some situation, some problem, some hurt, I pick up the phone and call my best friend Dotty. She's the one who tries to convince me I didn't really screw up being a mother all that badly, that my daughter needs to "get over it." Stuff like that. She is probably way too forgiving of me, and holds a far too favorable, slightly unrealistic picture of who I am. And I didn't realize how much it would hurt to hear the news that she would be moving to the other end of the country.

"Atlanta, Dotty? Atlanta, Georgia? Oh my goodness. That's

so far away. Well, of course you'll still come to visit. It'll just be a plane ride instead of a train ride. And we have to start working on those plans for another cruise. I do understand—a tough decision for Bruce and Rene, but a good business decision, I know."

But when I hang up the phone the tears start to come.

It's moments like this when I get in touch with that little hidden part of me that's probably been driving the paths of my life these last seventy-five or so years. It's that part that was the little girl standing out on the curb in Glendale, watching her daddy with his second wife drive off, bravely waving *goodbye*, not knowing when she would see him again, and then turning to go back inside the empty house, where she was part of a family, but she wasn't.

I grew up in the Clarke house when my mother remarried. My name was still Stevens, and I'm glad of that. But a lot of the time, especially when I was little, I felt like an outsider. I think that's part of why I feel so uncomfortable still, at a social gathering, if I attend alone. It's like I've walked back into that house again, but it's a circle of people I'm not a part of. That of course was an assumption on my part and not necessarily true, but it became an organic part of my psyche early in life.

We do shape our own lives. The decisions we make become the borders within which we live. Usually, we could do better than we do. So, I've managed to wander through three marriages, maybe a few more really meaningful relationships that were destined to go up in a puff of smoke because the adored ones in those relationships were "8 x 10 glossies" like my own dear dad: handsome, smart, funny, tender, adorable—and totally unavailable.

My third husband, Jack, told me in strong terms several times years ago that my singer friends, the community I was part of, were "not your friends!" His implication was that they just kissed up to me because they wanted work calls. I was by then doing vocal contracting, so I might be the source of those work calls. The politics of our freelance business inevitably play a part in where our lives go, how our careers develop. But I have always felt, *had* always felt and still do, the warmth of those friendships and the fun that spending time with them brought to me. I did notice, after Jack and I divorced, how much less "social" one becomes when one ceases being part of a couple. So, sometimes when it seems like everyone has stepped away, I recall his words. He may not always have been the nicest guy, but I guess he was no dummy.

These last couple of years have brought unexpected and irrevocable *goodbyes* to loved ones that had been in my life from nearly the beginning. My dear childhood friend Margit lost her battle with Alzheimer's two years ago, and then last year my singer friend of fifty years, Carol Lee Lombard, went into the hospital for a relatively simple bit of surgery and never came out. Carol was one of the first people I met in the music business, and I worked side by side with her in the studios for years. We continued our friendship long after she stopped singing, into the later period of our lives. Shortly after we lost Carol, my dear high school friend Barbara Michaels, one of the most beautiful women on the planet, who had had a modeling career before she moved to the other side of the camera and became an assistant director, experienced a serious stroke that went undiscovered. Her daughter found her three days later in the lovely little condo where she lived, up at the top of a mountain in Bel Aire. Barbara succumbed after only a few more days had passed, and would not have wanted to continue as she was then. And at the beginning of 2021, my precious friend Ann White, who I sang with for decades in the studio, and traveled with during the Bacharach years, passed away at her home in Coarsegold, California, where she had retired with her husband Michel DeMers a few years earlier. My house is filled with little gifts Annie would bring me over the years when she visited, constant reminders of how dear our friendship was and how well she knew me.

And my dear friend Russ, my "significant other" for so many social events, movies and dinner outings, and daily phone calls during the pandemic, was sadly diagnosed at the beginning of 2021 with liver cancer, which took him from all of us, his family and friends who loved him. These were the heart connections for me. These were the people who understood where I came from, who were there all through the journey, and from their different points of view were ready with advice and encouragement. Regardless of these changes, life goes on until it doesn't. That's the fact that I'm becoming more aware of—that someday, life won't go on. I still have things I want to do, things I want to better understand about life, about myself.

The truth is, I look around my house in recent days, and ponder how in the world my daughter will ever deal with all the stuff I'm leaving behind. But I get away with murder hanging on to memorabilia and gifts that remind me of people, places, and times, because there's no one around who insists I clear the deck. I've lived alone for the last twenty-five years. Most of the time I like it. It's only when I feel a heart connection slipping away that I start to kick myself for having perhaps made a few wrong turns. And there are heart connections even at this late stage of life, romantic heart connections that sometimes we hold onto long after the chapter is closed. I think my self-doubt has played a hand in the failure of some of those romantic heart connections. I tend to project an unhappy ending so I don't have to be surprised by it. And ironically, of course, sometimes I therefore create it. I should have trusted more, and been more willing to risk the threat of disappointment. It probably has to do with believing or not believing in our own souls that we are actually lovable.

There's a gradual acceptance though, that I think innate intelligence or the hand of God allows us to experience around this time in life. The thing I've always dreaded, feared, refused to consider—I now must admit will, in fact, happen someday.

There may be more happy times, perhaps even more than I can imagine. And there will be an end. On the way to the end, there will be some changes. I see it happening to those friends I still have left. And though I don't like to admit it, they can probably see it happening to me.

CHAPTER 3
LET'S GET ACQUAINTED

On a quiet Saturday morning recently as I sipped my coffee, skimmed through the emails on the computer screen, and thought about what I hoped to get accomplished during the day, I heard a news announcement that pulled me immediately into the kitchen to the radio.

The announcer on public radio was sharing information about the recent passing of a very successful songwriter and singer, someone I had known in the seventies in California, but hadn't spoken to or thought of in decades. My reaction surprised me, because the tears quickly turned into sobs. The memories came back. I knew him only briefly, and at the time I'm sure I gave his presence in my life much greater importance than my own life had in his.

He was living and writing in Nashville, had several big hits by other artists, and to this day I cannot remember exactly how we met. It must have been on a session or at a singer event—possibly an AFTRA convention in our singer caucus meeting. We dated—not for long, as his days in Los Angeles were scattered and brief. And I think my tears this morning were not only caused by the news of his death, but by a very personal and painful look back into my own life as it was in the seventies. And to some of those things one eventually learns that perhaps they shouldn't have done.

I won't share the name of this person. He was handsome, he was a "southern gentleman" (to a degree—the gentleman part) and his actions were disappointing in the few brief moments that have stayed in my mind. He did like one of the songs very much that I had written at that time, "Love is a Mirror," and I was encouraged by that, coming from such a successful songwriter as he. I think the fact that he liked it was what gave me the courage to play it for Burt Bacharach, and it was the song that Burt had me play on the last night of our concert tour in South America, to the large audience in the stadium-like hall where we appeared. Burt even asked me once if the southern gentleman was going to produce it. I thought maybe he was kind of interested in it, and just let that possibility linger.

But it became obvious to me that the handsome southern gentleman had someone else in his life—someone with status and permanence—and yet, I let him into mine. After the tears began to dry this morning, I went online to read the obituaries and commentaries that were already in place, so quickly following his passing. The words others spoke about him were honoring, and told of his dignity, his integrity in that he never smoked or drank, and he never used cusswords. When I knew him, he was young, and no doubt a bit full of himself. And rightly so, as his success was blossoming. In the photographs of him from his later years, his smile had softened, his hair was grey, he looked less like the handsome young dude he had been, and he was rightly viewed as an icon within the community where his work was known and admired.

When I met him, I was *also* young. With luck, our characters do improve with age and apparently, his very much did. I don't mean to dishonor him, and I don't understand, still, why my emotional reaction was so strong upon hearing the news of his passing. The few detailed memories I still have of him are not sentimental or particularly loving. During the time we dated, I was in the midst of moving from one house to another.

My work had slowed down, and I had decided to sell the house where my daughter Susie and I were living in Benedict Canyon and move to the valley, to a less expensive neighborhood. But in the process, it became obvious that I could rent the house in Benedict Canyon for enough to pay for that mortgage plus the mortgage on the valley house. So I'd altered my plans slightly, but was nonetheless in the midst of the move.

The handsome southern gentleman had stayed overnight in the upstairs guest room the night before the move was to actually happen. I am not sure why I didn't see the impracticality of that plan, as I had been busy, trying to pack, to make it through the day. When I went in to wake him on moving day, he cheerfully informed me that he had been thinking about how much he would love a cheese omelet that morning, with maybe a little bacon on the side and some hot coffee . . . ? I, not so cheerfully, informed him that the movers would be arriving shortly, and that the cheese omelet would *not* be arriving. I pushed down my irritation at his total lack of sensitivity.

The only other specific memory I have of the southern gentleman is when, one morning as he was dressing and preparing to go back home, he asked me if I would take his tiny scissors and trim his ear hairs for him. He explained that his "lady" always did that for him. That was the first time I had heard of his lady. And the first and last time I've trimmed anyone's ear hairs.

Now, these are not the kind of memories that would normally trigger tears or heartbeats. But they were so consistent with another realization I had encountered in recent months regarding those songs I had come across from the late sixties and seventies. Some of them are really good. The lyrics are strong, the melodies lovely. But what I especially noticed was that almost every one of them was about lost love. They were about the "if you had come sooner" guy who wanders into someone's life at a time when there was no place for him to land. They were about "Michael" (this was an alias, of course). "Michael's eyes are deep and wise, Michael's heart is true—he can take the greyest skies and turn them suddenly blue—Michael can be anything that Michael wanted to be—the only thing he cannot do—is give his heart to me." Or "And all the women—he has looked for love with other women . . . he may still think of the other women . . . but time will surely be the test, the love he shared was not the best—with other women...And all the women-they could never see the goodness of him—all he needs is someone who will love him—this time more carefully he chose—he'll find I'm not like one of those—the other women."

Then there's the song called "The Leaving Day," which is basically about the end of love and the symbolic end of the world. "Sullen clouds suspended upon smiles can't touch the ground, for if they do the tears would spill, and every whippoorwill—would know the leaving day . . .'Goodbye my love, I never loved you anyway,' they have to say—'Goodbye my friend, my friendship for you wasn't real,' they have to feel." OMG. Happy little ditties.

When I had the opportunities to write lyrics for other composers, when there was a "framework," a main title for a film, or a source cue in some production and a message to be delivered, my lyrics were shaped to tell *that* story. When the lyrics just came from my own heart, from the emotions I was feeling in any given moment, they were all pretty downspirited.

I honestly don't clearly know the connection between all this and the tears that fell this morning for the southern gentleman the world lost a couple of days ago. Maybe the tears were also for me. The handsome southern gentleman was four years younger than I. Maybe the tears were just for a little dose of reality. The seventies are definitely gone. Soon—hopefully not too soon—the rest of us who traveled through the seventies will be gone as well.

CHAPTER 4
AN OVERVIEW, AS WE BEGIN

In just the course of the history I myself have lived through, our country experienced the first death by assassination in modern time, of the United States president, John F. Kennedy. It shocked a nation and changed life as we knew it. We watched the nation grow numb as we moved on, to witness the assassination of Martin Luther King Jr., and then of Bobby Kennedy. The numbing has intensified, until today we have mass shootings on school campuses because the NRA has convinced politicians through their large contributions that guns make a whole lot of sense, and the more bullets they can fire all at once, the more sense they make. They have even convinced them that grammar school teachers with guns would make campuses a lot safer for little kids. We've experienced a transition from the kind of men we knew as our presidents, the past leaders of our nation—persons of dignity, moral strength, intelligence, and ethics—to a president whose last gig was being a reality show host and now refuses to admit his "show" in the White House has been canceled. Time adjusts all insane things to normalcy. I rest my case.

But just so you know where I'm going eventually with this book you so kindly have decided to read, it's not really about guns, or politics, or the Episcopalian guy who ran off to Australia (we'll touch upon him later).

It's really about my own personal and diverse journey through the world of the music business. That journey has covered a lot of territory, working with people whose names you will recognize. It is a journey through a myriad of changes in technology, of different eras in terms of musical styles, artists, and methods of delivery, and it's a journey that spans six decades. That is what brings us to this slow winding in the road that I spoke of earlier. Even *I* know I can't expect it to go on forever.

Though I had lots of other jobs as a kid, in my adult life I have always worked as a singer. Midway in my career, the vocal contracting was added, and the choral directing. I had opportunities to write some lyrics for film, television, and sound recordings along the way. I sang on Frank Sinatra records back in the day; I sang with Danny Kaye on his TV variety show in the sixties; I wore pink sequins and feathers as a production singer in Las Vegas; I toured with Nat King Cole, Ray Conniff, and later, Burt Bacharach. I sang on major TV and radio commercials in the sixties and seventies, and on probably a thousand film and episodic TV scores over the years. As of this writing I still sing, and can be heard on the TV show *The Simpsons*, for which I also sang the main title thirty years ago that's still airing today, and on the main title for *Family Guy*, another show I've worked on since its inception. We have done some unusual music cues for that show, like "You Have AIDS" (that one was back a decade or so, and I'll tell you a heartwarming story about how it turned into a happy ending later in the book). It's been a pretty big leap from "How do you solve a problem like Maria?" (from "Maria," *The Sound of Music,* 1964) to earlier in 2018, in my seventy-ninth year, when I had the privilege of singing and contracting the choir for *Deadpool 2*. If you haven't seen that one yet, track it down! It's hysterically funny and there is even a PG-13 version out now. It's the first time I've ever been asked to give a cut-off as I conducted a serious professional choir, at

the end of a phrase like "You can't stop this Motherfucker."
The arts encompass many, many things.

So you see, for me, "It ain't over yet," as they say. But I
have hit that curve where you know the end is coming soon.
And before I forget all the details, I want to share them with
you. It's been quite a journey. I was Choral Director for the
Oscars for about twenty-three years, and have met and
worked with some of the world's most celebrated artists
there—Barbra Streisand, Madonna, Robin Williams, Marc
Shaiman, John Legend, Adele, Randy Newman . . . to name
only a few...in addition to working with the knowledgeable,
kind and experienced production staffs over the years. I've
sung for the Emmys and the Grammys broadcasts. Almost all
of these things have seemed to come out of left field, but it's
always fun to be there.

The recording musicians' and singers' community over the
years eventually became my family. Once in a while these
days, I admit to succumbing to an occasional moment of
depression when I find myself losing old friends, as inevitably
we do in this later period of life. Or sometimes feeling left out
of activities—of being not so much a part of the community I
was once at the core of that's now full of much younger people.
And okay, it hurts when I read on Facebook about the young
singer working on some glorious new film score with one of
my favorite composers, someone for whom I had sung and
booked the singers in past days. I miss those connections. I
miss what felt like special relationships with those composers,
and it's hard to accept that they have moved on as everyone
eventually does in this business, to younger colleagues. It
brings home the reality that we are all, for the most part,
disposable.

Because of my addiction to my union activities, which has
intensified over the decades, I still drag myself to committee
meetings, trustee meetings, etc., and sometimes seem to be
the only one still around who remembers where the rules

came from, or what they are. But that just may be my control issues kicking in. Though our original unions Screen Actors Guild and AFTRA have now merged, I began my work with the governance of both unions separately many decades ago. With AFTRA and SAG, I served on and chaired singer committees, helping to shape our new contracts at the end of each negotiating period. I served on the Local Boards, then the National Boards, and as a national officer in both unions. I'm still serving as a trustee of the SAG-AFTRA Health Plan and the AFTRA Retirement Fund. My attachment grew over the years as I realized what an important part of our lives the functioning of those unions was. They are what carries us through lulls in our work lives sometimes by way of the residuals checks that come as part of our contracted work. They provide health care and allow us to build pensions that later in life would assure our financial security and survival. And the more I learned about my own area of the business, the more I spoke out about problems that needed solving, about proposing waivers to accommodate changes in our business, etc. I grew to feel like a "mother hen" to my colleagues in our singer community. It was hard not to show up, not to speak out.

There's another aspect of life we haven't talked about. And it's really a much more important aspect than the music-related details. I am a mother. I have a beautiful, talented daughter and I am, and for many years have been, besieged with guilt, with regrets, about how I could have, how I should have, done a better job in that role when she was a child. I learned from her, late in both our lives, that she had felt invisible when she was little. I was working so much of the time, and I was torn between my love and responsibility for her and my own wish to rise to a successful level within the business that I was becoming part of.

I became a single mother after my divorce when Susie was about four-and-a-half-years old, and it then became my financial responsibility going forward to provide for us both. Additionally, I had become a mother at the age of twenty-one. I knew how to be a big sister. I knew how to be a babysitter. I thought I knew how to be a responsible mother. But I don't think I knew how to be an emotionally supportive mother yet, or how important it was to learn how. Without assigning blame, my own childhood was much similar to Susie's. My mom too became a single mother when I was a year and a half old. She also was gone during much of my early childhood life and I don't think I experienced the closeness, the affection, and love that a child needs in order to feel secure.

One day many years ago, after my divorce and my move with Susie to our little house in the hills of Benedict Canyon, my mother (who was by then a mother of six, and no longer singing in the studios, but had begun her second career as a high school teacher) came to visit. As we sat on the deck chatting away over our lunch, she suddenly began to cry.

"Sally . . ." she said tearfully, "I know I was gone so much when you were little, but I had to work—I needed to work in order to take care of us. I'm so sorry, and I don't want you to think I didn't love you."

I didn't know what had triggered her words that particular day, and I tried to assure her that I had had a happy life, that I knew things had been difficult, and that of course I knew she loved me. And I have tried to say those words my mother said to me to Susie, in various settings and in various ways, over these later years. It may have been too late. All I can do is pray that somehow, she knows that I love her, that I've always loved her, so much then and now. I can't go back and redo those years, and I am so proud of her, of who she became, in spite of the things missing in her childhood years. I have had to face the sad fact that in the process of working so intensely within the music business back in the sixties when sessions went on from nine in the morning till sometimes midnight, six or seven days a week, I grew to be a part of that community, a part of my "family" in the studios, but managed to put at risk my real family, my only daughter.

Eventually my daughter too became part of the "studio singer" community, and she's worked in the business very successfully as an adult, since the early days when she sang as part of a kids group for commercials and records. She has made her own way, and her own talents allowed her to continue on, to work in film scoring, television, and songwriting of her own. It's been a wonderful gift to share that world together. Susie also sings the main title of *The Simpsons,* along with me and Danny Elfman. She is an excellent singer and musician and her own talent earned her a place within the industry. But that doesn't make up for the early years, and it is still painful to look back on them. I am so conscious now of my daughter's loneliness and sense of abandonment as a child, that whenever I have to leave the house these days and say goodbye to my current significant other, my little dog Gracie, I see Susie in Gracie's sad little brown eyes.

In those days, as now, it was a very competitive business. It seemed that there was also a much greater volume of work than there is now; the industry was growing then, and if you were fortunate enough to find yourself in first position on the "A" team, you dared not miss a call, for fear of being replaced with someone who they might find they liked better. The Jack Halloran singers and later, the Ron Hicklin Singers, both of which I was blessed to be a part of, worked side by side with the Wrecking Crew, the versatile studio musicians who played on everything– every jingle, every film score, every hit record of the sixties and early seventies, and literally *became* the Monkees, the Association, the Beach Boys, etc. off-camera and hidden away carefully.

Because my work has been the most consistent part of my life, I've been reluctant to let go of it. It's survived through three failed marriages and twenty-five years beyond. So there was no "significant other" who I wanted to retire with later in life and just travel or pursue other dreams. Maybe I've paid too much attention to *it*, and not enough to the other things in my life. It drew my attention away from my child, and it took me out of town during much of my second marriage, which I know wasn't helpful. By the third marriage, if I'd been willing to spend more time "handling" the complicated man I lived with, that one might have survived. If I'd been a little more aware and protective of myself, that one probably never would have happened in the first place. More about that later too.

CHAPTER 5
THE FIVE-YEAR PLANS

Once upon a time, early in life, I had a series of five-year plans that projected forward how I might accomplish the things I loved. The first five-year plan focused on my marriage and my daughter Susie. But those plans also included giving myself a chance to pursue work as an actress, on camera, for commercials, and whatever else might pop up, because I didn't think any woman could break into the acting world after she hit twenty-five or so. I thought I'd try that while I was still young enough to make it as a visible being. As a child, Lucille Ball had been my hero and I think somewhere buried deeply in my psyche was the wish to be like her when I grew up, to be on screen and make people laugh. That plan, I realize now, was pure fantasy because I never had the belief in myself, the confidence at that early age to push forward in that direction, or the courage to risk. I did get a couple of commercial gigs that, interestingly, came along later in life—well, a little later anyway. I did a commercial on camera for Thrifty Drugstores, for Chuck Blore, a commercials producer in Hollywood for whom I also did a lot of voice-over and singing work.

I did another commercial later along the way, for some product that I can't remember, but the project involved flying to San Francisco for the filming. My second husband David and I had just begun to date about that time, and David drove me to the airport. When I showed up there with a good-looking young man, I noticed that the attitude of the director/ producer changed dramatically. He was all of a sudden not so friendly and complimentary as he had been at my audition, almost to the point of being rather dismissive and rude. When we got to San Francisco and began the shoot, he was at first a bit brusque. But the day went pretty well, he eventually became kinder, and even went out of his way at the end of the day to tell me that normally in the past, they always booked someone else to come in and do the close-up hand shots for the actress or actor displaying or using the product. There were hand model people that specialized in that. But he said this was the first time they were able to just shoot it all with me, including the hand modeling shots as we filmed the whole spot. That felt like a great compliment from him, and it felt like he was trying to make up for the rather rude behavior earlier in our travels. At the end of the day we did go to dinner, the gentleman and I, at a restaurant near the San Francisco wharf, but he was perfectly respectful and pleasant and kept his distance—which might not have been his original plan when he'd hired me.

In the eighties, I was hired as the on-camera TV spokesperson for KBIG radio, the station I had sung jingles for over several years. The TV spots made me a rather visible person in Los Angeles, and it was definitely the first and only time anyone recognized me out in public.

But there was one early audition I screwed up, one really important callback audition that could have expanded into a new direction. This involved an audition back in the sixties when the cable channels were just coming into play. I had an agent for on-camera commercials at that time, and they sent me on an audition for a new show about to go into production. The first audition went well—they were looking for a youngish woman to host what has now become the magazine show format—guests, conversations, like the morning shows do.

The audition was in a very unpretentious location, and the production guy with the clipboard was very friendly and kind, and helped me not be nervous. He was very encouraging during the first audition. And I guess it went pretty well, because I got a callback.

When I got there the next day, I discovered they had assembled three or four of us, chosen from the women who had auditioned the day before, and put us together to kind of sit at a table and interview each other. *Now*, I understand that the purpose was to see how well we did, making the other people comfortable, bringing them out in conversation and interacting. All of a sudden though, on that day, the other woman seemed very artificial to me, and I got very quiet and wasn't terribly responsive back and forth. I felt like the other ladies were showing off or were all full of themselves, playing against each other in some way. (That was my own inner-me creating the inevitable unhappy ending in advance.) At one point, the nice guy with the clipboard came over to me on a break, very troubled, and said "What's the matter with you? What are you doing?!" I just sort of shrugged, and we did another take spending a few more moments chatting at the table together on camera. I knew by the time I left that day that I had totally blown it. I still am not sure what happened, but most likely it was my insecure defensiveness taking over. Pretend there's something wrong with them, and then you can walk away believing those other girls were just all full of themselves, and you don't want to be like that, you don't want to be a part of that.

A few years later I saw that one of the women who had auditioned that day was now cast as hostess of a major cable show that had become quite successful. I'm sure the show we had auditioned for and that she most likely got hired for, was a very helpful step toward that goal. Good for her!

See, that's the helpful thing with singing in a group, or a choir. You just perform your part and focus on the choral director and the music in front of you. You don't have to interact with your fellow performers except on breaks and you don't have to compete with them on the job. Eventually, of course, I got a little better at the social and political aspect, but it's still not my strong suit. The personal connections, the friendships and interactions and supporting of one another, are very much a part of our community, and are a gift, as I learned later.

During the first of those five-year plans is when the session singing world began to open up, so I kind of drifted off the five-year plan approach. I'd thought I would move into the session singing at the end of the first five years, if I hadn't—you know—been "discovered" by then. But things had already taken a path in that direction, and I was making good head-way.

I originally had thought if neither of the first two five-year plans worked, then I would focus on fiction and poetry writing. I figured writing was something I could do into my grey-haired years and no one would mind.

My work as a vocal contractor eventually very much extended the singing work and my involvement with the business. I didn't just show up and sing the music someone put in front of me (though there's definitely nothing wrong with that). But I also got to help the composer find the right singers to sing those notes, and then I sang along too. I gained the knowledge eventually of understanding how to care for the singers I booked, to make sure they were paid properly and the paperwork was filed as it needed to be. And it gave me a chance to work with, to talk with, to help solve the challenges and needs of, and *learn* from people whom I never would have had a chance to even shake hands with otherwise. People like Danny Elfman, Alan Silvestri, James Newton Howard, James Horner, Marc Shaiman, and even John Williams and Steven Spielberg. I realize now, much later in life, that I never really had a "dream" when I started. Yes, I secretly wanted to be

Lucille Ball, and I wanted to write songs early in life. But I never created a plan or a roadmap for finding those dreams, and the eventual dream that I did live somehow just created itself along the way. One thing I know I learned was to never say *no* to an opportunity within the business. Fortunately, the opportunities that came my way were appropriate, but I really didn't know I could do them till I did them, like the early solo vocals in films like *Klute, Dirty Harry,* and others (yes, "I sang that . . ."). I didn't know that my "sound" was what they were looking for. But apparently, and thankfully, someone else did.

CHAPTER 6
GRANDMA, MRS. HOLLOWAY, AND THE SNAILS
(Thank You, Peter Fonda)

I'd been working on the memoir chapters on and off for several years, just diving into one subject or another at random, and had included a bit about my childhood on the earlier pages but didn't consider it of great interest to the reader. Then one morning, as I sat in a doctor's waiting room, I had an awakening.

I had just begun reading a book I'd purchased maybe fifteen years earlier that had gotten lost among the hundreds of books piled in disorganized stacks around my house. It was written by Peter Fonda, his own memoir entitled *Don't Tell Dad*. And as I read his pages, I realized how many details I had left out of my own childhood stories. The events on the pages of Peter's childhood and his early life in Brentwood, California, took place where my parents also lived when I was born, and there were things about the world of the forties and fifties that I had not bothered to write about because I took them for granted. But as I read them on Peter's pages, so many familiar memories and situations flooded into my mind, and it reminded me of how very different the world was then.

I've always had a special affinity for all things Fonda. Henry Fonda was one of my favorite actors in the era of his most shining stardom; his son Peter was, of course, super cool; and his daughter Jane was, to me, a strong, brave soul, a stunning actress and activist, and coincidently, had touched my life very indirectly in two different ways—or at least symbols of her presence had been in my life. I have lived in Studio City, California, now for twenty-five years, and nearby in the low hills off of Laurel Canyon there is a house a few dog-walks away from mine where Jane Fonda and Tom Hayden once lived with their family, back when they were a couple in the young, shared, politically passionate days of their lives. It is a charming, rambling, two-story house with rooms tucked away all over the hillside lot on which it sits. A composer friend of mine now lives across the street from that house, and when I visit, I still love looking at it, imagining the days when Jane and Tom lived there.

There was another locational connection with Jane Fonda back in the early seventies, in an old brick firehouse building in Venice, California, where she had the offices for her exercise and fitness businesses. My second husband David Ives was a photographer and we had found what seemed like the perfect charismatic space for his studio in that old building, just across the hall from Jane's office.

And of course, there were the solo vocal cues I got to sing in the score for those scary scenes of her Oscar-winning performance of *Klute*. That always felt like a connection, even though Jane, of course, wouldn't have known about it.

As I began to read Peter's beginning chapters, the memories he shared of his very early years made me think about some of my own very early years in a way I had not chosen to think of them until this morning, this reading. I don't know if I consciously chose to dismiss or forget them, if perhaps it seemed self-indulgent and melodramatic to think of my childhood in any negative ways. But all the elements of our childhood, the positive and loving and the less positive and more challenging, affect our personhood as we evolve into whoever we become through the years.

In his book, Peter talks about himself with Jane and his half-sister, Pan, living in Brentwood with their mother and their father, Henry Fonda, who at that time was beginning to experience the peak of his career. My father, similarly, had begun to work in films at the same time, as an actor and singer. His path never developed into one remotely resembling Henry's in terms of career progress or fame, but he did make a film, *Broadway Serenade,* in which he was cast as the romantic singing lead opposite Jeanette MacDonald, another big film star of the day. The film was about a Broadway singing star, and it included scenes from her onstage performance within the film, in which my dad, the handsome devil, was the actor who played her on-camera singing partner. And he could sing like the best of them. In recent years, thanks to a wonderful woman who writes about early film days, Laura Wagner, I've learned about so many on-camera roles he did that I had never known about because he had to step away from that part of his career and go off to war in 1942, and it just never came back together after his return.

In Peter's book he also talks about, as a three-year-old, seeing his father go off to war in 1943. My own father, heartbroken at my mother's decision to divorce, enlisted in the army when I was two years old. He was stationed in Germany until the end of the war, serving as a major in the United States Armed Forces. I remember his visits home only because there are photographs of us together, a little two-year-old standing beside the handsome, loving father in his uniform, holding my hand protectively.

Just the other day I came across the tiny leather-bound diary my father carried with him when he went off to war. It was written to me, and began as a sort of personal record of his military journey.

My father's own childhood was unusual. He had been separated from his birth mother as a toddler, and raised by

Grace, the woman I knew most of my life as my grandmother, but who was actually my father's aunt—and her husband Harry Stevens. His birth father, a young man who had been preparing for the Episcopal priesthood, was so jarred by the news that he was *also* about to become a father—something he was *not* prepared for—that he ran off to Australia, leaving my aunt Flossie (who was actually my grandmother) alone. Not a good condition in which to be left, as a single pregnant young woman in 1910.

My father accidentally learned of all this when he stumbled upon some papers in the attic, at fourteen years of age. The news caused him to run away from home briefly, but eventually he was found, and life resumed.

Because of this, my father throughout his life felt a great obligation to the people who had raised him, and who he knew and loved as his parents, but also to Flossie, who he had known as his aunt all those years. When he eventually settled in California, he brought them all out from Chicago where he had grown up, so he could take care of them. He and my mother, and Grace and Harry, my grandmother and grandfather, lived together after I was born in a charming, woodsy house in Studio City. I still drive by it often when I'm feeling homesick for a glimpse of the past, to see if the brick pathway through the front yard that my father built is still there. (It is.)

My grandmother was a strong woman, a most loving and nurturing grandmother to me, but apparently a somewhat controlling mother-in-law. Things did not go well. My mother told me that when she would get back from her trips to the grocery store, my grandmother would ask her for the change. Somehow, though grandma was not supposed to be in charge, she *was* in charge. And I guess my mother just couldn't deal with it.

On the first brief entry page of my father's little "off to war" diary is written, on August 26, 1942: *"Left Ken Murray Show."* He was working on Ken Murray's radio show at the time, and was really beginning to get established in Hollywood just before he went off to war. He had some pretty interesting projects on his resume, but by the time he got back from Germany, all the names on the doors of the studio offices had changed, and he was never able to get back on quite the same path he had begun.

The diary "off to war" pages continue, in his beautiful script, written to his little two- year-old child:

Dear Sally, today daddy left home at 6:45 a.m. Seems that Uncle Sam wants me. We came to the induction center, were examined, and took the oath. "I, Albert Kenneth Stevens, do promise to—and defend the United States of America from all her enemies, whosoever, so help me God." Daddy is now a soldier. While waiting to go to Fort MacArthur I met a boy, another V.O.C. who went to high school with me and I haven't seen since graduation day. Small world. Came to Fort Mac-Arthur and was assigned to Co. C. Learned after dinner, how to make beds. Did same, used same. Saturday, up at five a.m. Made beds, dressed and answered company call, rather sleepy. Got a hair "shave" and took I. Q. tests. I think I did okay. About 9 out of 50 boys not permitted to take 2nd test because of low I. Q. on the 1st one. Completed outfits then vaccination and "shots." Borrowed pants in order to get leave—no leave, so to bed, very sore arms. Sunday- Up at five a.m. Breakfast and got pass home to see you. Wonder what you'll say when you see me. Now I know. You said "You look like a Soldier boy. You sure are a funny daddy with a haircut."

And the rest of his little leather-bound diary could be a whole other book on its own. It's a treasure, and I'm grateful to have it.

When he was working on *Broadway Serenade* he had become good friends with one of the other actors in the film, Franklin Pangborn, and while I was about two years old, my father took me to visit him. Franklyn Pangborn lived in a beautiful old Mediterranean-style house, and as he welcomed us in, there was a step down into the living room, and the floors were very hard, shiny Spanish tile. I slipped somehow and cracked my head open on the edge of the tile step. There was blood everywhere, and my father rushed me out into the car and to the emergency room. I can remember sitting on an examination table as the doctor was sewing up the slash in my head. It hurt a lot, but I was not supposed to cry. My father got a box of caramel candies and had me offer them one by one to the nurses. I don't know if they make those little caramels any more. They were little square, individual-wrapped candies that came in a little cardboard tray of maybe ten or twelve. It was my dad's sweet way of trying to distract me from what was going on.

I was too young to really experience WWII, but I remember the newsreels at the movie theater in the forties. And I have vague memories of air raid drills, where we would sit in the dark, in the hallway at the center of my grandmother's house, till the "all clear" siren ran. The newsreels left a pretty strong impact on me. To this day, I admit it's a bit painful for me to hear a German accent.

After my parents divorced, my mother and I moved into a little duplex in Beverly Hills on Oakhurst Drive. That little one-story building is long-gone now, replaced by an elegant four-story condominium where the individual units probably cost more than the entire block did back in the forties. I remember the drives from Beverly Hills through Coldwater Canyon to the valley to visit Grandma and Grandpa Stevens, where I would spend many happy, well-cared-for weekends. I remember riding up that Coldwater Canyon Road in the pouring rain, when the huge, towering pine trees that still line that winding road through the magnificent residential neighborhood were at that time only about six or eight feet high, dripping with the rain. Now they are fifty or sixty feet tall, but we're all still here. We've just grown taller.

During my early childhood, my mother worked in the studios as a session singer/choral singer, much as I eventually would do. She sang with Walter Schumann, Gordon Jenkins, and Ken Darby, among other choral directors, and their voices were heard in the underscores of many films of the forties and fifties. She also, with voices sped up a bit, was one of the voices of the Munchkins, in *The Wizard of Oz*, in 1938. I love being able to share of her working on that film. It was such an iconic film, and I was proud that she was part of that amazing Hollywood film history.

In those days, the singers worked most often on weekly contracts, and they just sort of, as best I can understand, hung out on the studio lots, rehearsing with the musical director or choral director, and then playing bridge during the off-duty hours. This meant that my mother was gone most every day, and I was left in the care of Mrs. Holloway, who lived in a little Spanish-style house not far from our duplex. Mrs. Holloway was married to a retired Navy officer who spent most of his time in his own small office at the side of the house. He was also very involved with activities at the Mason's Hall. He wasn't very involved with the visiting toddler wandering around his house, who was cautioned not to disturb him.

My mother and I would walk the two or three blocks over to their house, and then she would come back after work and pick me up, and we'd walk home. Sometimes I slept overnight at Mrs. Holloway's, and I have clear memories of my mother leaning down in front of me as we stood on the sidewalk, discussing whether I should go home with her or stay at Mrs. Holloway's, or, perhaps just saying goodbye as she went off to work for the day.

Mrs. Holloway was a kind lady, not particularly emotional or affectionately demonstrative, but she took good care of me. She was a devout Catholic, and I often attended mass with her at Church of the Good Shepherd, an elegant old Catholic church that still stands on Santa Monica Boulevard in Beverly

Hills. It was intimidating, to a small non-Catholic child. Sounds echoed in its beautiful enormous space and candles burned off in the distance, as long-robed, white-haired gentlemen moved back and forth in front of the altar. Everything was in Latin in those days, and also in those days, it seemed like many of the movie stars, or at least the ones I knew about, were Catholic. So we would often spot one of them there at church, Loretta Young being the one we saw most frequently. That made going to church much more fun.

Beverly Hills and adjacent neighborhoods were, and still are for the most part, the neighborhoods of the stars. One day my mother and I were out shopping in the little stores, and we stopped for an ice cream sundae. As we sat enjoying our treats, in walked Margaret O'Brien with her grandparents. She was my idol, a movie star I had seen on screen at the movie theater. As they walked by our table Margaret stopped and actually spoke to me. She said in that same awe-filled, wide-eyed, breathy delivery she used for her on-screen lines, "That's a very pretty dress you're wearing." She looked into my eyes, and said it with the same emotional tone she would use if she were on the big screen looking into the eyes of her dying pet collie, saying, "I will never forget you, Lassie, and now we will die together, you and I . . ."

I could barely speak in response to Margaret, I was so overwhelmed. I mumbled, "Thank you," as they wandered on up to the counter to order their ice cream. I looked at my mother. She could tell I was overwhelmed. And it changed my relationship with that dress. It was one my grandma had made for me, and it was lovely like all of the dresses she made. But it had a "drop waist," and I thought it makes me look fat. I felt funny in it, I didn't like it, but I didn't want to hurt my grandma's feelings so I wore it sometimes.

But after Margaret gave it thumbs up, I never hesitated to be seen in it. And in retrospect, how lovely it was that someone—most likely her grandparents—had taught this child star to be sweet and go out of her way to be kind to some ordinary kid as she happened by.

The little girl who was to become in those days my best friend and closest companion, Helen Roehrer, lived just around the corner from Mrs. Holloway with her mother and father, who were both from Switzerland. Her father was a milkman for Arden dairies and in those days they still delivered fresh milk in glass bottles, door to door. I remember one day, as some sort of special occasion or anniversary of the company, he came through the neighborhood driving a horse and carriage milk delivery cart.

From Mrs. Holloway's house, I would walk around the corner to Helen's, holding my breath and hoping that she would be home. She was my only playmate, so I devoutly wanted to find her at home. If the garage door at her house was open and the car was gone, I would be sad and walk resignedly back to Mrs. Holloway's house. If the garage door was open and the car was parked inside, I would race up to the front door knowing Helen and her mother were home and we might play for a while. And if the garage door was *closed,* I couldn't know if the car was there or not, so that meant there was a fifty-fifty chance Helen was home, and I would bravely walk up to the front door with fingers crossed and ring the bell.

Next door to Helen's house lived Mr. Spencer, and somehow as a fringe benefit I had gotten to know Mr. Spencer. He was a white-haired, elderly gentleman and he used to make me little books, tiny blank paper pages stapled together, on which I could write stories or draw pictures. I think that's when the yearning in me to actually write stories or books was born.

It's funny, the details you remember from so long ago... there were some little concrete steps leading from the side of Mrs. Holloway's backyard down to the sidewalk, and lodged in the crevices of those steps I would find and capture tiny, tiny baby snails. I don't know how they got there, but they seemed magical to me, and I would gather them in glass jars with handfuls of grass from the lawn and they would become my pets. I don't recall ever seeing them grow to adulthood under my care, and it never occurred to me that their mothers might miss them. But snails still have a special place in my heart. If I walk now through my own garden after dark or along the path from the driveway and unknowingly step on one, the crunch of their fragile shell is deafening. I feel so bad that verbal apologies pour out, to the snail, to God, and to the universe in general. I've always felt this way about snails, but in more recent years I've expanded my sensitivities to bugs, flies, spiders . . . I see them in some magical way as just as connected to God as I am. If he didn't like them, he wouldn't have made them, so I should take care of them too. I carefully trap them in a glass, then slide a paper underneath and transport them out into the garden through the front door, hoping they somehow are able to reconnect again with family. This is, of course, unlikely. But maybe they can start a new family. I am not a vegetarian, so obviously I am a total hypocrite about all this. But I could never hunt with a gun, or catch a fish and not throw it back into the sea.

My father did eventually move on after the war, to many other interesting activities. He toured with Wayne King (the "Waltz King") as soloist; he did TV commercials and industrial films in Chicago; he did the Englander Mattress commercial "live" at the end of the nightly news broadcast in Chicago; and he had his own fifteen-minute radio show, sponsored by Oldsmobile. He toured with Sonja Henie's Ice Show as the band singer, and eventually took over managing the road company, moving on later to the Holiday on Ice traveling shows as company manager.

Then, when he married his fourth wife, my darling step-mom Dotty (who had been a featured skater in the Holiday on Ice show), they assumed management of the Osborn House, a charming old Victorian inn located in Windham, New York where guests from the city would come up in the summertime for holiday getaways. Dotty's parents and her aunt and uncle had established the inn, but by this time were really ready to retire. Dad supervised the kitchen, always having had an affinity for cooking, and then later in the evening he would sing across the street at the Bar & Grill with the band that played there for the dancing guests.

CHAPTER 7
THE GLENDALE YEARS

When I was five years old my mother remarried, to my stepfather Thomas Clarke, a singer who was also part of the studio singing community. Tom was a Christian Scientist, and our landlady at the duplex on Oakhurst was also a Christian Scientist, so the influence of the two had raised an interest in that faith with my mom. She eventually also became a devout Christian Scientist, and all her children (myself, my step-brother Mike and step-sister Vickie from Tom's first marriage, and the three children from that second marriage, Charles, Jon, and Lydia) were all raised in the faith. There was never any discussion of *not* attending Sunday school. It was a given. There are, by the way, many wonderful things of great value about the religion, though I no longer follow it. Mary Baker Eddy, its founder, was way ahead of her time. Many years later, following a scary emergency surgery wherein I had to undergo removal of a grapefruit-size tumor, peritonitis, and a total hysterectomy, I decided to take Christian Science class instruction, because I was so grateful for the kindness of the lovely practitioner, Frances Figgins, who was teaching the class. I met Frances through the church where I was serving as soloist at the time. In class instruction, which is a deeper level of study than just attending Sunday school or church services, one reads materials that the average Christian

Scientist might never read, and I remember writings of Mrs. Eddy's where she clearly stated that if one was experiencing such pain that they couldn't clear their thoughts or try to do healing metaphysical work for themselves, they should get a shot of morphine. Also if a broken bone needed setting, they should get it set. She also speculated about the fact that if a lobster, one of God's creatures, can grow an entirely new claw, why shouldn't we someday be able to grow a new arm, or a new organ? Well, tah-dah . . . stem cell therapies, welcome to Christian Science, or vice versa. I have observed metaphysical thought and scientific discovery growing closer together, year by year.

After my mother and Tom were married, they bought a lovely old two-story home in Glendale, California, where we all lived together, along with Tom's mother, E.E., who had moved down to Los Angeles from Portland, Oregon, to care for Tom's children when his ex-wife, Maudette, returned the unused portions of their childhood days. Maudette had taken them briefly to stay with her in Oklahoma after the divorce, but apparently that didn't work out well. So she had returned them and we were all together there in Glendale: Mom and me, Vickie and Mike, who were six and seven respectively when we merged households, my now stepdad Tom, and his mother, E.E.

My mother and I also had a cat named Oscar Wilde, who moved with us from the Oakhurst duplex to Glendale, but was missing one day. We were amazed but grateful when mother said that a phone call came, with the news that Oscar had found his way back to Beverly Hills, to the little duplex. I guess he preferred the Beverly Hills zip code. As I think about this now, I realize it was very possible that Oscar Wilde got eaten by one of the mountain lions that lived in the hills across the street from our house on Kenneth Road, and with that story about the phone call from Beverly Hills, my mother hoped to avoid breaking my heart. It would have been quite a walk for a kitty, all the way back to Beverly Hills.

E.E., in my opinion, got the best bedroom in the Glendale house. Her room had a huge walk-in closet and dressing room, plus a covered porch that extended off to the side of her room, overlooking the backyard. And the backyard was quite lovely. It had a three-car garage and laundry room to one side, and beyond that a grove of three avocado trees and a little chicken coop where the previous owners had raised ducks and chickens. They left the abandoned sliced-off heads lying about on the ground after hastily harvesting them, prior to their move.

To the left side of the porch view, there were gardens, grapefruit trees, and flowers, and the driveway which ran past the house, out through the deep front yard and between the two grassy lawns to the street. On one side of the driveway in front was a huge old tree, set a bit up off the ground with a low concrete wall around it to hold the soil and ivy in. My first new little brother, Charles, born when I was eight years old, was constantly compelled to climb up into that tree as soon as he was physically able, even before he could talk. On one perilous day, our parents had to call the fire department to get him down out of that tree. He continued always, through later life, to view the world from a higher place. I've always treasured his thinking, and his friendship.

Mike, Vickie, and I used to walk down Central Avenue each morning, past a block or so of residential houses, a couple of apartment buildings, a little dime store, and a neighborhood grocery store, to our grammar school, Eugene Field Elementary School. Eugene Field doesn't exist any longer, having given over its grounds to the creation of a large condominium complex decades ago. But in those days, it was a wonderful place to go to school. There were maypole dances in the spring, games on the asphalt schoolyard during recess, and Girl Scout meetings after school. I remember three teachers: Mrs. Rattray and Miss Poirier, who as I recall, had a very obvious crush on the third teacher, Mr. Kalinich. Funny how those things are discernable even to an eight- or nine-year-old.

In those early days, my mother had health issues that I was never totally clear about, but despite the Christian Science connection, I can remember going with her to some doctor's appointments at a little office on Western Avenue in Los Angeles, where she would sit in front of a machine of some sort. She held on to a couple of cords and then the doctor rubbed on a metal plate. Something would buzz, and it was some sort of diagnostic procedure, I have to assume. After that process was completed and evaluated, mother and I would go home with several tiny envelopes full of assorted pills.

During the Glendale years, my mother had a miscarriage that my sister Vickie was the first to realize, when she spotted an ambulance headed in the opposite direction as we walked home from school on Central Avenue. Vickie somehow recognized our mother through the ambulance window as it whizzed by. I don't know how she spotted her, but she did. We ran all the way home, only to find that yes, our mother had been taken to the hospital. She lost that pregnancy but she came back home a few days later, safe and well. So that story doesn't have too-terrible of an unhappy ending.

There were not always smooth feelings experienced in the new Clarke household in Glendale. I chose, or my mother chose for me, to remain a Stevens, in the midst of the Clarke family. It must have been jointly decided with input from my father, and I'm glad they made the decision. I have always felt close to my father, to that side of my family as well as to my mother's family. But I didn't really connect so much with the legacy Clarke strain, though my brother Mike and sister Vickie have always been close and beloved. Perhaps it was because of difficult feelings between E.E. and I. She was very protective of Vickie and took great pains to fuss with and comb her hair nicely in the mornings before school. I was pretty much on my own. Also, my stepfather often was the one who got up with us to send us off to school, I suspect because of my mother's delicate health at the time. But he was a bit surly in the kitchen, and either made what he called "mush" (which was in reality, I'm sure, quite tasty oatmeal but the name was such a turnoff to me that I hated it) or very greasy pancakes fried in bacon grease. Instead of being appreciative, I just didn't enjoy the whole experience as much as my sister Vickie did. She on the other hand, probably didn't enjoy her rare visits with me to my grandmother's house as much as I did. Perhaps because, on one of those visits, as part of what I thought of as part of some adventure we were playing at, I locked her into the playhouse that my grandpa Stevens had made by converting their no-longer-in-use wood-shingled chicken house. Vickie, frightened, panicked to such an extent that she kicked the wooden door down from inside, which of course didn't set well with my grandpa. But her anxiety was understandable.

One Sunday morning my mother and Tom had both gone to work for the day on some musical production, and I was to go with Vickie and Mike to their mother's. I was never exactly sure how to act when we went there, so I always watched Mike carefully. If he laughed, then something must have been funny and I laughed. I was nervous about going, but excited, and presumably, had to go because no one would be home at our house as our babysitter was supposed to have the day off.

So, we are all dressed up, and we go running out the front door together and down the driveway, to Maudette's car. Mike and Vickie get to the car first and start to climb in. But when I get there, Maudette stops me. She says, "Sally dear, I didn't say you could come this time."

I feel embarrassed, like I have done something wrong. She doesn't want me to come to her house. I don't want her to win. I try to smile, like I didn't want to go anyway. I say, "Oh, I know . . . I just came out to say goodbye."

The car door closes, and Mike and Vickie wave goodbye as

they drive off.

I stand on the curb waving back, trying very hard not to cry but the tears are coming anyway. Then I walk back into the house alone. Anna, our babysitter will be upset. I wish I had gone to my grandma's for the weekend.

I don't like to say mean things about people that other people loved. But this is a memoir. I have to tell the truth. So it is the truth that there were hurtful moments along the way and that day was one of them.

Another truth: Tom, my stepfather, did have a short temper. I understand, as I myself also seem to be short of patience these days, though mostly with myself. Mine is more like becoming easily frustrated and impatient with my own failings. But I don't throw things at helpless animals. I just remember one day when he backed the car out of one of those slots in the three-car garage, and something was in the way— he must have been in a hurry—but he got out, picked up what turned out to be a heavy basket or crate or something, and threw it at a duck that we had, which of course badly damaged the duck. I also had to witness a time or two in the beginning years of his taking a belt to my stepbrother Mike. I guess in those days that was a more common thing, but it seemed brutal and violent to me. He never dealt with Vickie or me that way, and I don't think he subsequently dealt with my younger brothers in that way. But that behavior was not uncommon back in the forties.

I think Tom may have had underlying resentment toward Mike, because Tom's first wife, "Twit" (Maudette's nickname— I don't know who came up with that, but it was the only name I remember her ever actually being called by) was pregnant when she and Tom married, and many, many years later she told Mike's wife Gail late one evening as they sipped wine, that Tom was actually not Mike's father, but rather, one of the very well-known film actors at the time was. Gail dismissed the words as some sort of over-wine-remembered fantasy and didn't mention it to Mike till years later. Little "Mickey" was sent to a military school at a very early age, before he knew even how to tie his shoes. He talked later about having lived in fear of facing that challenge every morning. Someday I hope Mickey will write his own memoir. He's a dear, brave man.

Also I remember one day at the Glendale house, when at about eight or nine I was talking on the phone to my friend from school who lived up the road from us. E.E. told me to hang up the phone but we weren't through talking yet and that seemed rude to me so I didn't do it right away. She slapped me in the face. Later that day my grandpa Stevens came to pick me up and take me to my grandparents' house for the weekend. As we went out the front door, E.E. leaned over the railing of the stairs from the upstairs hallway and called down to us in a cheerful tone, "Remember Sally dear, when Tom married your mother, we adopted you right into the family!" I guess it was supposed to be some sort of a caring outreach to make up for the slap, but it hurt more than the slap did. I didn't want to be "adopted" into anyone's family. I had my own. And boy, when my grandpa told my grandma about it, she wasn't moved toward warmth and reconciliation either.

My grandma Stevens did all the things that Peter Fonda talks about his mother having done in the early chapters of his memoir and his life. She canned fruit, made jams and preserves in glass jars, and stacked them in the cupboards. She grew a little "victory" vegetable garden, and she had fruit trees in the back yard—peach, plum, and apricot, which provided her with ingredients for those jams. She baked incredible cakes, and her Sunday dinners were served on the English BWM & Co. Trentham antique blue and white china that still to this day, I get to admire through the glass doors of my own dining room sideboard. Their home was by no means elegant, and the dishes may have been handed down to her from family, but by the time they reached my cupboard, they had to be well over a hundred years old.

My weekends at my grandparents' were the times I think of as the nurturing days of my life. My grandmother made most of my clothes, and there was an upright piano in their living room where I would sit and, I'm sure, drive my grandfather crazy, playing as best I could all the sheet music that publishers in those days sent printed copies of to the singers and performers in the business. My dad was on the mailing list for all those lead sheets. I remember the sheet music to "White Christmas" when it first came out, and I remember the verse lyrics: "The sun is shining, the grass is green, the orange and palm trees sway . . ." It seemed like it was a long jump from those words to a "white Christmas" and I didn't quite get the relationship between the verse and the chorus. That was probably because I had never experienced a "White Christmas" myself, just the orange and palm trees swaying. But Irving Berlin definitely knew what he was doing.

There is a medical building now on Riverside Drive where my grandparents' house once stood. In 1954 the Hollywood Freeway, the 101, was completed, and it stretched out beyond Hollywood into Studio City, the San Fernando Valley, and northward. The work had gone on for several years, and in the process the new freeway clipped off the backyard of my grandparents' house and sort of commercialized that stretch of Riverside Drive. But in the earlier years, we would walk my grandpa's little dog Scottie at night with our flashlight along Riverside Drive. Across the street from the house, acres of cornfields stretched along the road, and in the flashlight's beam we would find frogs that had been run over by passing cars and splattered along the road.

My grandma hung her wash on clotheslines out beyond the white picket fence that divided the rose garden area from the chicken coop/laundry line area. I can still remember standing barefoot one day on top of a large oil can so I could help her hang the sheets. Unfortunately, I had failed to notice that the can was covered with red ants. That wasn't such a good afternoon.

In 1950 a restaurant was built across the street from grandma's house, and I would lie in bed at night by my bedroom window and spy on the customers through the restaurant windows with a pair of my grandfather's binoculars, as they gnawed on their ribs and hamburgers. I guess I must have given way to the detective instinct in me.

I realized I had really forgotten about how different the world was in those days, until I read Peter's memoir. I had forgotten about the rations, the victory gardens, the unavailability of butter, and therefore, the necessity of using that oleo margarine that came in the plastic pouch that I hated so, which you had to color by squeezing it and smooshing it around till the little tablet of color worked its way into the awful stuff. And I had forgotten that I was not the only kid whose dad went off to war.

My stepdad Tom had wanted to be a pilot when he was younger and WWII began, but his poor vision kept him from being able to pursue that goal. He began his music training as a classical singer, doing opera roles, and eventually did considerable opera chorus work in Los Angeles. He also sang with a quartet, The Guardsmen, or The Lady Killers as they were labeled in one of the films in which they performed. They spent a great deal of their time on the road, performing in live appearances, so there were long periods of time during our years in the Glendale house when Tom was away and my mom was running the household on her own. I can remember her doing the laundry by hand for all of us, with a scrub-board in the little laundry room attached to the garage before we acquired a washing machine. Eventually my grandma got a new washing machine and passed her old one along to my mom, which was very kind, given that my mom had previously divorced her son and broken his heart. So then my mom had a washer and a wringer at least, which had to have helped. I also remember mother and my brother Mike sitting out on the lawn under the clothesline, hand-squeezing dozens of grapefruit to make grapefruit juice with an old hand-press juicer. I don't know how Vickie and I escaped fruit juice duty, but we probably wouldn't have been strong enough to accomplish much with that hand-press thing.

I also remember a day, very early in the first days of our new "sisters and brother" relationship, when Vickie and Mike discovered I was afraid of spiders, so they gathered up spider webs on the ends of sticks, and chased me all around the yard. I got back at them though. I too had discovered something: while I was afraid of spiders, I was not afraid of dead duck and goose heads, and apparently, they were. And there were quite a few of them left behind there by the previous owners after they harvested their chickens and ducks. I discovered that if I stuck one on the end of my finger and pulled back on the top of its head, their beaks still opened and closed. So I managed to chase Vickie and Mike all around the yard with the dead duck heads silently quacking at them. Sooner or later, we all find our own special gifts.

We lived in that Glendale house from about 1945 to 1950. In those days, on rare occasions, I would go with my mother to the radio broadcasts, and I went with her one year on Easter Sunday to the Catholic Radio Hour. They were doing a special program with many guest stars, and at that time many of the Hollywood actresses and actors were Catholic. But many were invited to participate who were not. Loretta Young was there, along with Jeff Chandler, Jimmy Durante, Muzzy Marcellino, and Ann Blyth. I managed to get their autographs, legendary stars now, all of them, in a little autograph book that I took with me that still lives among my souvenirs and fragments of childhood. It has a worn red cover, and it is so full of autographs of famous folks that it would today probably be extremely valuable, had I not traced over them all repeated times with pencil, carefully trying to learn how to forge the signatures. Alas, I had peculiar motivations in those days.

Don't know whether I thought to absorb their talent from being able to write like them, or absorb their money from their checking accounts. But I wasn't really old enough to know that much about checking accounts.

And that wasn't my only criminal activity. I'm not proud of this, but—one day walking home from school up Central Avenue, my sister Vickie and I wandered through the five-and-dime store we would pass by every day. We did not have any dimes with us, but we noticed how everything was so available, right there along the aisles. I didn't want to take anything for myself, but because my stepfather traveled a great deal performing on the road, I thought he might like a baggage tag. And for my mother's pretty long brown hair, perhaps a lovely hair clip.

When we got home and shared our gifts but unfortunately were not able to produce a sales receipt, my stepfather marched us back to the store and made us return the items to the owner and apologize. We felt embarrassed, guilty, and terrible, and knew we would still have to walk by that store every day, but most likely would never be brave enough again to walk in, even when we did have some dimes in our pocket. That was the end of my criminal career, and I'm embarrassed to tell you about it, even today.

But I have drifted away again . . . let me return for a moment to the Peter Fonda memoir. As I dove deeper into its pages, though there continued to be links on a sort of ethereal level, it was apparent where our lives split off on different paths. The Fonda family vacations were spent in Hawaii, or Rome, or Connecticut in lovely upscale settings, often because Henry Fonda was filming in one of those places, but also because their lifestyle dictated that it was so. My vacations, on the other hand—well, they weren't actually vacations but I did have one trip to Girl Scout camp in the summer between fourth and fifth grades. I got very homesick, but my camp counselor hid comic books under my pillow one day and that set the world back in balance again. I can still remember the black-and-white snapshot of my friend Cheryl and I waving out the window of the rickety yellow bus as it drove off to the camp.

One summer, when I was ten years old, I took the train with my grandmother and grandfather Stevens to Chicago, where my dad was filming those industrial films and late-night Englander Mattress commercials for the ten o'clock news. And from Chicago, my father and I flew to New York for the weekend to visit my mother, who was visiting *her* family in Brooklyn. My grandma Pietsch, her mother, had passed away, and Grandpa Pietsch had moved from Fargo, North Dakota to Brooklyn to live with his daughter and her husband, a Baptist minister. So my father and I flew to New York. I think my father might still have been in love with my mother, but I never was able to confirm that. While in New York we did all the things excited tourists do. We visited the Statue of Liberty, we ate in an automat, we went to the top of the Empire State Building, and then we flew back to Chicago.

During our years in the Glendale house, things sadly did not go financially as my mom and Tom had hoped or expected that they would go. They worked as session singers in the film scoring business before residuals existed for SAG members. So when work was thin, there were no "residuals fairy" envelopes delivered to their mailbox, as there later came to be for all of us in the business after 1960. They struggled to keep things going there, but eventually, the lovely Glendale house on Kenneth Road became too expensive to hold onto. Unable to sustain it or even pay the property taxes, they finally had to sell, and we moved to a more remote neighborhood up in the hills above Burbank and Glendale, to Tujunga.

CHAPTER 8
THE TUJUNGA YEARS

In 1949, mother and Tom bought a house at the end of a narrow, steep dirt road, Marcus Avenue, that led up into the hills of Tujunga, a mountain community on the edge of Glendale and Burbank. Marcus Avenue was much smaller and less elegant than Kenneth Road in Glendale. The house had grown "like Topsy" around a square concrete structure that an artist had built earlier as his studio. The artist was Kirby Sumner, and his family soon became our friends, his daughter my "best childhood friend forever," Margit. That little concrete square had been transformed into the dining room of what was now our new home, and around it grew a kitchen, a sort of long den/family room, two very small bedrooms and a bathroom, and a little entryway and hall from which a stairway led, up to two more tiny bedrooms and one slightly larger one.

This was the next chapter in our family life, and Jon and Lydia, our new brother and sister, were born after the move to Tujunga. Charles was just a toddler at the time, and they were all closer in age than we older three siblings, so they grew up in slightly different settings with slightly different experiences than ours had been in Glendale. By this time I think we felt more like a family, but I think Charles, Jon, and Lydia shared much more closeness together as they grew up, after we older kids had gradually moved off to college. Vickie and I were the big sister babysitters during their youngest years.

The hillside house, being the last on the little dirt road, was quiet, had a beautiful view across the valley to the mountains on the other side of the little town, and really had total privacy. My sister Vickie and I eventually learned to love it, to charter paths and make maps of the mountain trails beyond the house where the fire road led up farther into the mountains and wildflowers. But when we first made the move, I think we were all a bit depressed. This was a dry area, no beautiful rolling green lawns as we had had in Glendale, no towering trees or fruit and avocados from the garden. And, we were soon to learn, no really effective plumbing. We used to have to carry the used dishwater out in buckets and dump it over the fence onto the dirt hillside above the little dirt road. The bathroom situation was not much better. The house was built on granite, which is not the ideal setting for cesspools as there is nothing for them to seep into, and that's what the house was hooked up to. So from time to time, toilets backed up and bathtubs failed to drain; and thus, baths were ill-advised. At one point I took to bathing in my swimsuit with the garden hose outside the back door of the kitchen. Privacy was not a problem, but the temperature of the water could have been more welcoming.

It still is not clear to me, seventy years later, whether it was a situation that just was unsolvable, or if we just didn't have the means to solve it. Or perhaps, whether it was just not a priority in the eyes of our parents. I remember my mother had an obsession with shoes, and occasionally I would go with her to one of the discount shoe stores, from whence she would leave with a stack of shoe boxes filled with high-heeled, stylish pumps. I've wondered over the years whether the cost of one of those shoe expeditions could have done anything toward solving the plumbing problem in a more permanent way. But

I suspect not.

At one point, mom and Tom took over a little laundromat as a hoped-for new source of income in the nearby community of Sun Valley. This was when laundromats were just coming into vogue. My brother Mike worked there sometimes after school, folding other people's laundry and wrapping it up in brown paper. I don't think that venture lasted more than a year or two but I'm sure it helped to cover a few of the bills. Ultimately though, it became more of a burden than a benefit, and they moved on.

About that time, the Los Angeles schools were experiencing a shortage of teachers at the high school level. My mother had graduated with two degrees from North Central College of Music—one in voice, and another in piano. She did not have a teaching credential, so she began taking the necessary courses and doing some assistant teaching, and soon she was a full-time teacher at Mount Gleason Junior High School, the school adjacent to our high school, Verdugo Hills High.

My mother eventually grew to love teaching, to connect deeply with her students and to feel great compassion and a measure of responsibility for those whose needs in life went beyond what their own parents could provide. She tried to help them with food, with counseling, with whatever she could do. When she moved on to North Hollywood High School, which is where she taught until she retired from teaching at the mandatory seventy years of age, she used to come over to my house in Toluca Lake and gather oranges and avocados from my trees, to take to school for the kids she was especially concerned about.

Meanwhile, my stepfather had found work coordinating publicity and other parts of the operation with the Philharmonic, the Greek Theatre, and the Huntington Hartford Theater on Vine Street in Hollywood. The Huntington Hartford was the primary live theater in Los Angeles at the time. Prior to this, he had tried selling Electrolux vacuum cleaners door to door, but did not have the personality or the questionable ethics required to sell things to people who he could see obviously could not afford them. So his sales were not exactly off the chart, but we did become the happy owners of, and I to this day still use, yes, an Electrolux vacuum cleaner.

His work with the Philharmonic, the Greek Theatre during summer months, and the Huntington Hartford kept him busy with long hours often involving evenings. He also remained active with "the Four A's," the group of the four performance unions which included the American Guild of Musical Artists (AGMA), the union he had become most active in because of his work with the LA Opera Guild. I think it was from my stepfather that I really learned the great value of unions, and from whence my own dedication and volunteering commitment grew. My unions SAG and AFTRA, now the merged SAG-AFTRA, have blessed my life for sixty years now.

This activity associated with the Philharmonic and the theaters also allowed my mother and Tom to enjoy tickets to concerts and plays, which was a bonus they would not otherwise have been able to afford. And they took advantage of it. They enjoyed plays at the Huntington Hartford most especially, and went to gatherings at James Doolittle's home, who at that time was the manager/producer at the Huntington Hartford. And Mike, Vickie and I participated in the ushering and renting of seat cushions, thereby enjoying many artists we otherwise never would have gotten to see.

During our high school years before she began teaching full time, my mom did do one engagement in Las Vegas as part of the singing group with a recording artist who used group vocals and performed a kind of Americanized Brazilian music, Les Baxter. And around that time, both mom and Tom joined a touring theater company and traveled with Tyrone Power in the road company of *John Brown's Body*. For this trip, they were on the road traveling for several months, and Mrs. Jordan, a very nice older lady, came to stay with us. She too, of course, was a Christian Scientist.

A little side note: while our parents were traveling, the occasion of my fourteenth birthday came up. One of my activities during these high school years was belonging to the Junior Art Association of Verdugo Hills, and the friends I made there really became my social circle. I decided to have a birthday party at our house, with the approval of Mrs. Jordan and mom and dad, and set about planning for it. We did not do a lot of entertaining, and had no resources to host it extravagantly, so I knew it was going to be a more modest gathering than I might have wished. But we baked a birthday cake, Mrs. Jordan and I, and had potato chips and snacks, and little sandwiches. I couldn't find anything in the house large enough to make a big batch of fruit punch. I looked every-where and finally, in the service porch, I found a white plastic bucket. So I set about mixing up a huge batch of punch, after appropriately washing and making sure the bucket was clean, by fourteen-year-old standards. I mixed a couple of big bottles of lemonade, some orange juice, some Kool-Aid, and whatever else I could find in the kitchen, and set it aside, to wait for ice cubes and plastic glasses. What I didn't mention to Mrs. Jordan was that this bucket had at one time been used to put my little brother's diapers in to soak. But that had been several years ago, and since we were all Christian Scientists, we weren't supposed to believe in germs. The bucket had been carefully washed, and it had been a long time since the bucket had been used for that other purpose. I was sure it would be fine. I cannot swear that no one was harmed as a result of my inappropriate decision, but everyone made it to school on the following Monday so we must assume the best.

The Junior Art Association was an extension of the Verdu-go Hills Art Association, a group of really quite fine artists, musicians, and supporters of the arts who lived in the area. One of the gentlemen in the group, George Stanley, was the man who designed the statue and fountain that still stands at the welcoming entrance to the Hollywood Bowl on Highland Avenue in Hollywood. It is said that he also designed the Oscar statue, but because he was working at one of the studios, the credit went to his superior. Nonetheless, there were some amazing artists in that group, our friend Kirby Sumner being one of them.

Kirby's daughter Margit and I became best friends, and eventually lifelong friends, until she passed away just a few years ago, after a long and heartbreaking battle with advanced Alzheimer's. It was painful to see her go through that experience. But the early brain connections seem to outlive the worst of it, because though she had reached a point where she no longer knew her son or his two children, she always recognized me instantly, and called out "SAH—LLY!" when I arrived for visits. It was Margit, who from about thirteen or fourteen years of age, had to sit next to me on the piano bench of her family's upright piano and listen to the songs I composed obsessively all through high school. Such loving patience she displayed.

I got my first more grown-up job when I was sixteen, a definite upgrade from having earned spending money by babysitting or housecleaning in our little neighborhood. I also had managed to trade those same services for ballet lessons from one of our neighbors, Eleanor Blangsted, who had a ballet studio in Sunland Park nearby. I always managed to find a way to earn money I needed for the things I thought I needed. But at this point in time, I decided it was time to get a real job.

There was a drugstore at the corner of our street on Foothill Boulevard, the main street through town. At Klemer's Drug Store I worked behind the soda fountain and at the cash register when folks stepped up to pay for their aspirin or shampoo. One day Mr. Klemer, who was the owner and the pharmacist, called me into his office. I was nervous. *What did I do wrong? Is he going to fire me?* I knocked on his office door, and he had his white pharmacist coat on, seated at his desk.

"Sally, I subscribe to a service that sends 'customers' out anonymously to evaluate the quality of my employees. I just wanted to tell you that the report of their last visit came in, and you got the highest rating any of my employees ever received."

I breathed a sigh of relief, thanked him, and went back to my work behind the cash register. That gave my self-esteem a much-needed boost!

One day, while on duty at the soda fountain I glanced out through the huge glass windows that fronted the building, facing onto Foothill Boulevard, and caught a glimpse of a little white 1949 MG convertible driving down Foothill, just like the one my father drove. *That's my dad . . . what's he doing here?* I thought. He was supposed to be touring at the time with Holiday on Ice as company road manager. I immediately feared that maybe he had come back into town and not told me. Maybe he had a busy schedule that didn't allow for us to have a visit. I ran out onto the sidewalk just in time to see the little MG way off in the distance, and of course had no idea who was driving it. I was almost afraid to ask my grandmother if he had come into town, because if he was too busy to see me I didn't want to know about it. But that's typical of the gift I mentioned earlier that I have—projecting and sometimes creating the unhappy ending myself.

As I look back on that experience, it was what eventually grew into the self-doubt regarding my relationship with men in general, a projection of how they *really* felt about me, in spite of any loving words they might have said. I knew my father loved me, but he was in my life so little of the time that my imagination took over and thought maybe he didn't really want to spend time with me. I don't think I realized my insecurity in that area until that day when the MG whizzed by, and I thought my father had somehow abandoned me. I managed to project those fears into almost every romantic relationship I've had during my life. Too many of those relationships have ended in tears. Some rightly should never have started. But I think sometimes when we fear or project an unhappy ending, we create it. Most of those tears that came at the end of relationships were for men who really were not "available" for various reasons, but who I admired, idealized, and managed to make important in *my* life, even if I wasn't important in theirs.

Oh yes, there was one other little adventure related to jobs and love life. When I was fifteen, my boyfriend Chic Montgomery—a very adventurous entrepreneur for someone sixteen years of age—had taken the job of selling programs and pictures of the wrestlers at the Olympic Auditorium. He realized if he engaged an assistant, he could sell more of those items, so he talked me into going with him, and on Friday nights I wandered tenuously through the aisles of the Olympic Auditorium, hustling programs, shouting out, "Pictures of the wrestlers here!" to the burly, cigar-smoking, beer-drinking male crowd in attendance.

Chic was my first boyfriend, starting in junior high school. He was one of four children, all of them brilliant, and both of his parents were attorneys. His mother was one of the first woman attorneys in the Los Angeles area. He was a champion gymnastics competitor, and went beyond the organized activities on his own time, like when he did backflips through piles of fertilizer lined up on the high school football field once— there to be spread on the field the next day—in order to win a five-dollar bet that he *wouldn't* do it. He also did some terribly strange, scary stunt from outside the top of the Los Angeles Coliseum wall, but fortunately I didn't witness it, so can't really tell you what it was. And luckily, he survived.

I was happy at Verdugo Hills High School. It was a good public school, I think, except for the football team. In those days Sunland-Tujunga was an area with clean, mountain air, and there was also a tuberculosis clinic in Shadow Hills/Sun

Valley nearby, so there were a lot of asthmatic folks who were drawn to that area. They were serious students, but understandably, not the greatest on the football field. I don't recall that our football team ever made it into the finals.

Margit, Bob Tice, Chic Montgomery, Bob Harrall, Buddy Lovick—these are the names I most clearly remember from my high school years, and our Junior Art Association group, and the people I stayed in touch with into later years. Chic eventually got a scholarship to Harvard, and I went with them the day his parents drove him out to Route 66, where he began his hitch-hiking journey across the country to Boston. We *all* were so much braver in those days. Or maybe we just did what we had to do.

Not long after his arrival there, with my heart sad and lonely, I started getting letters from him on which he would *draw* his own airmail stamps with a red pencil, each one real enough looking that they successfully deceived the US Postal Service. Economy took precedence over all other elements of life. Looking back, that was pure genius. But I wonder if technically, it was a federal offense!

However, inside those envelopes were letters in which he talked about a girlfriend. And there were sleepovers going on with the girlfriend. I think he felt the first throws of adulthood and wanted to share it with me, but shouldn't have. That eventually propelled me out of that relationship and into the "love of my life," at least for the early period of my life, Johnny Richards. Johnny was star quarterback, captain of the football team, president of the Junior Red Cross club, and basically, adored by all. A friend of Chic's wrote to him to share that news, my hookup with Johnny, and when Chic came home for semester break, he did not tell me he was coming. He wanted to surprise me, and win me back. I got on the public bus for school one morning where it stopped on Foothill Boulevard at Marcus Avenue, then continued down Foothill Boulevard to Mt. Gleason where we got off to walk up the hill to school. And there Chic was, already seated on the bus in his Verdugo Hills High letterman sweater, to surprise me. But for me, it was already over.

Johnny Richards graduated from high school a year before I did, but his grades were not good enough for scholarship considerations, and his mother had been a single mom since his birth and had worked as a waitress at Van De Kamp's restaurant to pay their bills. There was little chance of him affording college even if his grades had been good enough to get him in, so he enlisted in the Marines and went off to Camp Pendleton for basic training. Later that summer, when I was working one day at Klemer's Drug Store, Mr. Klemer summoned me and said I had a phone call. I couldn't imagine who would call me at work, except my mother, perhaps.

"Hello?" I said, cautiously.

"Sally . . . it's Johnny. I'm calling from Camp Pendleton. There's something I have to ask you. I, uh . . . well, I know you have another year at Verdugo, but I love you and think we should get married someday. So, would you marry me? And we'll get a piano, no worries . . ."

I was ecstatic at first. I said yes, pretty quickly. But then I panicked and began to muck up the situation with all kinds of concerns, like I could never become a Catholic, which was his faith at the time. Also, I wanted to continue with my goal of working in music, and . . . there were several other demands that escape my memory now. But apparently, they were enough to kill the deal. A few months later, toward the end of my senior year I did receive another invitation to Johnny's wedding but the bride, alas, was not to be me.

And the one I *should* have married and lived happily ever after with, the one I wasn't smart enough yet to realize the value of, was Bob Tice. Bob was the "good guy" in our high school, the one everyone loved. He wasn't a star athlete (I don't even remember if he played any sport—possibly basketball, which I didn't understand or follow) but he had the

sweetest smile, a gentle spirit, and was often our representative when we did "exchange assemblies" at other high
schools. Bob was very tall, probably about 6'3" or so, and in
my later high school years there was a popular hit record of a
song called "Tall Boy" (the artist was Peggy King), and I chose
that song to sing at the assembly performances. Bob would
stand nearby, blushing, as I sang the lyric "Tall boy, tall boy,
standing high above me . . . won't you please smile down on
me, and love me."

Bob, today, would probably have been considered the "Joe
Biden" of our group. He graduated from high school in the
winter of 1955, and joining the Army Reserves, headed off to
training camp. Thinking to surprise me one evening when he
was on leave, he showed up at the front door of our house
without calling first, looking so handsome in his uniform—just
in time to find me leaving on a date with someone else.

We did stay in touch for a number of years after high
school, and after my first marriage ended, we were still
friends, dining together from time to time. But by then we
were too locked into a friendship for it ever to become, for me,
a romance. After having dinner together one evening, as he
was leaving after our goodnight kiss at my front door, he said,
"Someday I'm going to make mad, passionate love to you."
And I replied, so foolishly and wistfully, "Don't you think if
that were going to happen it would have happened by now?"

That was our last dinner date. Not long after, the news
came that he had married the sweet woman he had been
seeing for a while, who became his wife and eventually the
mother of his two boys.

A dear mutual friend of ours contacted me many years
later, to tell me Bob had been diagnosed with esophageal
cancer and had to have his vocal cords removed. He was
unable to speak. The prognosis was not good. We went to visit
him, Margit and I, and Buddy Robinson, the friend who had
reached out with the sad news. Bob was brave, outgoing, and

cheerful, gave us welcoming hugs, and scurried about the kitchen of their home, getting us something to drink. He could only communicate by writing on a pad at this time. At some point during our visit he reached back to talk about our past relationship, and wrote something about him having been "too boring" for it to have worked between us. It brought tears to my eyes. I said, "Never, Bob, never . . . I was too dumb, that was the problem." Somehow the sweet woman sitting nearby, who was his wife, tolerated this communication.

I cried all the way home.

My high school years were an interesting and fun time, and the elements that existed out in the grown-up world were also operating—the "who you know" or "who she's going with" stuff, though we weren't so conscious of them at the time. For instance, I felt like the only reason I was elected as one of the cheerleaders in my junior year was because at that time, I was dating Johnny, the "star quarterback." I didn't identify as one of the popular girls, at least not in my own mind, to the extent that I could have gotten there on my own. But it was a lot of fun, even if I didn't know enough about the game of football to know when I should properly jump up and down and wave the pom-poms. It took a while to get the hang of it.

There were no drugs in my circle of friends, nor smoking— there was the rare social gathering at which someone might have snuck in a bit of alcohol . . . but I don't remember drinking any of it. We were a pretty wholesome crowd. And of course, by the time my senior year came along, with prom and the other festivities, Johnny Richards had gone off to join the Marines, had gotten engaged to someone else, and we were no longer an item. I did have rather a crush on Mike Bergman, another football-playing classmate, and was hoping for an invitation to the prom from him. But the date of the event kept creeping closer and closer, and no invitation was forthcoming. It was very mysterious—none of us knew who Mike was taking to the prom. Finally, I gave up, and my friend Margit and I made other arrangements. We invited our friends Gary Gallien and his older brother Richard as our dates. They both had graduated from Verdugo several years earlier and were very cool-looking guys. As I look back on it now their parents must have made them say yes, because they were way beyond high school proms by that time. But they took us to the prom, and then afterwards we went to a nightclub on Sunset Boulevard in Hollywood. Margit and I had a very memorable prom night thanks to the Gallien brothers. And Mike Bergman showed up, of course, with my gorgeous friend Barbara Michaels, who had known all along who Mike was taking to the prom but loved not revealing it. Barbara always had a sophisticated sense of drama, and of humor.

Then for graduation night, my date to our party was Richard "Buddy" Lovick, another dear, sweet friend who I had known since my childhood years in Glendale, and with whom I'm still friends. Bud and his wife Laura are special people who I'm so grateful to still be in touch with after all these years. He also went with me to Johnny's wedding, and was sensitive and kind about the difficulty of that evening.

Growing up in a big family, having younger brothers and sisters meant there was always some degree of babysitting to do and very little quiet, private time. I think it was during my senior year that I came upon the idea of sending my parents out for a date night one night a week, while I would babysit with my younger siblings, Charles, Jon, and Lydia, and also clean the house. Mike and Vickie had by that time moved on to their next activities. Vickie was living on campus at UCLA and Mike was living with his mother and going to Harbor Junior College. So with mom and Tom out for the evening, I had the house to myself. I could watch whatever I wanted on the black-and-white TV (yes, there was TV in those days—by now we are in 1956). And I could enjoy the solitude, once the younger ones were off to bed. I watched the shows I might not have otherwise seen, and about forty-five minutes before my parents were due back home, I would frantically grab the furniture polish and that Electrolux I told you about earlier and scour the downstairs from one end to the other. The upstairs wasn't part of the deal. Interestingly, I find myself having returned to treasuring that place of tranquility in the later decades of my life. I was divorced in 1993 from my third husband Jack, and have lived alone since then. I am so used to doing exactly what I want, when I want, that perhaps I should have tried it earlier in life. It feels like a pretty good fit.

Footnote: As I was working on these pages and adding details which the reading of Peter Fonda's memoir had inspired me to remember more about in terms of the world of my childhood world, the very sad news came on August 16, 2019, that Peter had passed away. Another sad marker in the passage of time, in the unfolding of years. Thank you, Peter, for your incredible talent, for your uniqueness, and for the courage to tell your story, which helped me in the telling of my own.

CHAPTER 9
FROM A DISTANCE

I'm going to jump ahead now for a moment from those Tujunga years, and share a bit more about my mother, whose life had its shining moments, but also many challenges and heartbreaks along the way. Elizabeth was a magnificent singer and an amazing pianist, and had college degrees in both of those studies. Often at night, we kids would drift off to sleep in our upstairs bedrooms to the sounds of Chopin, Debussy, or Bach coming from the piano below.

But there were other times when I can remember hearing my mother's words at night, through closed bedroom doors, from below, from the dark kitchen at the bottom of the stairs; my mother's words angry ghosts, chasing each other above the slamming of cupboard doors, the clattering of pans. They weren't shouts, they were angry mutterings, whispers, trying to be undetected, but failing.

In my later years, my mother and I took a trip together, our one special trip of my adulthood—of my life, really, as she was so careful when we were growing up together to be inclusive and loving to all six of us. But just a year or two before she died, she and I took a few days and flew up to San Francisco together, had a lovely stay and dined at one of the beautiful hotels on Nob Hill, and then picked up a rental car and drove up into the wine country.

One night during that trip, through the closed bathroom door of our room in the little inn on the coast of Northern California, above the crashing waves, I was to hear once again her whispering, hear the muttering, the familiar, almost forgotten sound. It was a sound I had heard so often in the Tujunga years, but I had set it aside, choosing only to remember the Chopin and Bach floating up the stairs. So many years now had passed, under separate roofs, that of course the sound was strange at first, and then, oh yes. I remembered.

What could be wrong? I asked myself. Was I thoughtless about some detail of my planning? Did I say something at dinner that was hurtful, that was foolish? Did I not consider her? She was happy, she seemed pleased that we had this time together, pleased at the beauty of this place. What could have caused this expression of anger, this frustration?

I would ask her, I had determined. I would be braver than I had been able to be as a child. I would acknowledge that I heard her, that I cared about what was troubling her. I would no longer pretend they weren't there, those angry words thrashing about, pounding the air.

But how to phrase it, how to approach it, that was the challenge.

I remember she came out of the bathroom, and I went in, to get ready for bed. I noticed her freshly laundered lingerie hanging on the rod of the shower curtain, where she had hung it to dry. Maybe the whisperings were just her way of musing, of thinking out loud while she did some simple task. I would ask her. She was my mother. I could ask her and she would tell me.

But the whispers are clearly not musings. I hear them again, coming now from the bedroom, through the bathroom door. They are angry now, they are complaining. They force their way out of her head and into the air, they are adamant, insistent. Had we had some conversation at dinner that upset her, had she not been able to express herself to me? Was she incensed over some political question, had she some dissatisfaction about me, about who I had become? As before, the child inside of me makes the assumption that whatever it was, it was my fault.

When I walk back into our room, she is smiling; she clearly seems to be enjoying this holiday, the two of us, the lovely inn, the little luxuries, so rare in her own life.

I finally ask hesitantly, "Mother, is anything wrong? Are you upset about something?" She seems almost shocked at my question, denying immediately that any problem existed. "Why?" she asks me. "Why do you ask?"

"Because," I reply tenuously, "when you were in the bathroom just a few minutes ago, I heard you talking to yourself, and it sounded like you were angry, or upset."

She smiles, and laughs a little bit, incredulous. "No, I wasn't," she tells me. "I wasn't talking to myself."

Now, it is forty years later. I am in my own house, my grown-up house in Laurel Canyon. Not the one where I lived for so long, the one with the sad ending, but a different house. I have started to make a new home, to make new memories. Maybe that is why I am thinking so much. Recollections of past moments creep back, triggered by the strangest things.

My mother died the year after we took that trip together along the coast. That was the last thing I would have expected on that weekend—that my mother would die soon. That she would become ill with cancer, and that she would die. The faith she had clung to all those years, the teachings of her church which stated that there was no death, there was no evil, there was no matter, that promised us all that these things would not happen. But there it was in her body, which proved to be material after all, a tumor of great proportion, attacking her wellness and her spirit, draining her. There was evil, in the form of this dark thing which would overtake her sooner than we prayed, and in spite of those prayers, ultimately would take her away. There was to be in our experience, in the very literal sense of the word, such a thing as death. It ended things. It parted people who tried to love each other.

And now, my thoughts circle above my head and crash-land back into that evening, above the pounding waves. My mother talked to herself all the years of my childhood, and, I learned on that trip, beyond. Suddenly this day, the possibility struck me. Why had I not thought of it before? My mother really didn't know. Perhaps her selves had split off from each other, like selves do when there is unbearable emotional pain. I have heard of this and believe it to be true. We create a stronger self to cope with our pain, to protect us, to shelter us.

I have the papers from the foundling home, the Children's Home Society in North Dakota. The papers tell the painful story of a little girl, taken to an orphanage when she was four years old and left there. I'm sure there were reasons that had nothing to do with her. It wasn't her fault. But she didn't know that. Then eventually some kind people took her into their home, and later, when she was ten years old, they officially adopted her.

What went on in her mind, and in her heart all those years in between? Was she on trial? Was all of life a test, to see if she qualified to be someone's little girl? To see if she qualified to *be*? She had to doubt herself. And she certainly could never have expressed anger nor hurt.

They might take her back to the foundling home. She would have to be very, very good. Then maybe the new family would keep her.

I try to imagine that little girl, four years old. I picture her lying in the dark, longing for her mother's arms to comfort her. I try to imagine how frightened and lonely and sad she must have been. That would be enough emotional pain to cause you to conjure up another self.

Lizzie was her name, her birth name on her birth certificate. Elizabeth was the name on her adoption papers. Lizzie wasn't good enough.

This is bizarre, this story I have conjured up. I wonder if it is far from the truth. I wonder if Elizabeth left the room, and Lizzie raged, trying to settle the score, trying to address the issues, the injustices. Lizzie must have been pretty sad, and pretty angry about not being good enough.

There were a lot of disappointments over the years that Elizabeth might have needed Lizzie's help with. Life didn't get a lot easier. It looked like it was going to, from time to time, but then it didn't. I looked at those papers from the Children's Home Society of North Dakota not long ago. The tears come easily still. I wish I could put my arms around Lizzie. I wish I could put my arms around Elizabeth. But she only lives now in my heart and in my memory. Sometimes I think about the fact that she lives inside me too, in my genes, in my cells, in my sad and darkest moments. Sometimes still, from a distance, I hear her whisperings as if it were yesterday and they were coming from just there, on the stone path in the darkness beyond the closed door. Or from just down the hall. But there's such a distance now. Farther than the end of the yard, farther than the top of the stair. If only I had understood then, so I could have tried to make it better.

I am still trying hard to understand, so I could make it better, for us both. But you can never fix things from such a distance.

CHAPTER 10
UCLA AND BEYOND

The summer following my high school graduation I needed to work in order to earn some money of my own for college expenses. I was to begin UCLA in the fall and wanted to live on campus. My father had agreed to help me with whatever residence situation I landed in, and UCLA in those days was affordable –the tuition cost in 1957–58 was only eleven dollars a credit. But there were other expenses, and I had always, since I was twelve or thirteen years old, been anxious to find a way to earn whatever money I needed, whether it was by housecleaning in the neighborhood, or babysitting, or eventually that job at Klemer's Drug Store. So a few days after graduating I went out in search of serious employment and found a pleasant low-level job with an insurance company in an office just off Wilshire Boulevard on Catalina Street. It mostly involved filing and answering the phone. The woman who hired me was the person in charge, but there were two gentlemen who were the out-and-about salesmen. It was a small office, and I tried to do a really good job (but of course failed to mention in the job interview that I would have to be leaving in September—I felt guilty later about that).

But even in those days my mind was a wanderer—imaginative and speculative—not about anything in particular, just off-track. And filing was not my finest skill. Sometimes I would hear the salesmen cussing in the other room because they couldn't find something I had, quite unintentionally, misfiled. As I think back on it, at that time it was unusual to have a woman in charge of two men, even though it was a small office, but it was her agency. She understood and forgave kindly when it was time for me to go off to school in the fall, and we remained friends for many years afterward. I visited her in the hospital at the end of her journey, where she succumbed to the cancer that had haunted her for several years.

Things spiced up a bit the summer before I entered UCLA. There was a nightclub, The Horn, in Santa Monica on Wilshire Boulevard. It was owned by Rick Ricardo, a friend of my father's, who also happened at that time to be the on-staff vocal contractor in the music department at 20th Century Fox. (In those days vocal contracting was a management position, someone in the studio hired for the purpose of coordinating vocal sessions.) The Horn had a piano bar and a sort of "open mic" where singers and aspiring performers could try out their material on a live audience. My dad got his friend Rick to agree to let me sing there the summer before I began at UCLA to have the experience of singing in front of an audience, though I was only seventeen, so it was not entirely legal. In fact, it wasn't legal at all. But I was excited about the possibility. I made mental note of the right keys for the few songs I'd memorized to sing, and began the adventure, feeling unsure of myself in that setting, but knowing it would help me eventually to feel more experienced and confident. Much of the time the crowd was busy chatting at the bar and didn't pay all that much attention anyway.

One evening the bongo player noticed how nervous I was, and said sweetly, "You can lean on me, honey . . ." It turned out the bongo player was also a vice cop who just happened to love playing bongos. But he was a very nice fellow, and one evening he invited me out for tea at the end of the evening. It was all very innocent. We went to a drive-in restaurant in Westwood and literally had hot tea. But my dad got a phone call the next morning. Mr. Ricardo decided it was too risky to have an underage young lady hanging out in his saloon who was dumb enough to let herself be seen leaving with the bongo player, especially if he was a cop. So that was my last evening at The Horn.

As it happened, the bongo player was considerably older than me, which I was also too dumb and inexperienced to realize at the time, because he was fibbing about his age. We dated for a while, and became engaged for a short period of time after my eighteenth birthday. My mother was very distressed about the relationship, and I suspect rightly so. But my dad was a lot more savvy. He treated Ronnie with respect, had him over for barbeque and cocktails during one of his visits off the road from the ice show tour, and gave me a chance to learn for myself how inappropriate the relationship was, rather than putting me in a position of insisting on doing something because my parents didn't like it. The engagement was short-lived.

I've always been fascinated too by the coincidence that many years later I would begin what turned into a decades-long relationship with 20th Century Fox TV, as their first-call vocal contractor for many projects, including *The Simpsons,* which I was blessed to work on for thirty years. Mr. Ricardo, by the time I got into the business, had been long-gone from Fox. And the system had expanded within the singer's union world so that by the sixties, the job of vocal contractor had become a category of covered work in the SAG singer's contract, no longer a management employee, or part of the studio staff. The contractor is required to be a member of the union, as well as one of the performing singers in the group. But I'm amazed at the "small world" connections that take place coincidentally beyond our control or even imagining. I'm struck by the incredible coincidence that I ended up doing the job that Rick Ricardo used to do back in the day, and Rick and I never met or spoke except back in his bar, decades earlier.

During the UCLA years, I also found a second job for Saturdays, at a stationery and greeting card shop on Beverly Drive, in Beverly Hills. I continued with that job, working after-class hours at UCLA, and I remember it as a pleasant and interesting experience. I wasn't great at sales because of a degree of shyness, but I tried. One day Doris Day, a famous actress and singer at the time, came into the shop, looking for a greeting card for someone. We had been encouraged to make suggestions to our customers, so I thought I had spotted the perfect card for her, remembering one I had seen earlier in the day. Doris Day's legal name was Kappelhoff. I don't know how I knew that at the time, but I did. And I thought of it as a silly name no one would have known about or assigned to her.

I forced myself to approach her, as we had been encouraged to do with our customers. "Here's a card you might like . . ." I offered in as confident a tone as I could muster. She politely tolerated my offer of assistance and I showed her for consideration the card I had noticed earlier, that said "Happy Birthday from some of the biggest names in Hollywood"—and on the front it listed a bunch of long, European-sounding made-up names that *no one* had ever heard of. Then you opened the card up and inside it said, " And me . . ." And then a place for her signature.

Doris was kind. She read the card. She had a peculiar look on her face, trying to smile. She handed the card back to me and said, "Thank you . . ." And that was the last time I tried giving advice to a potential customer.

Going through sorority rush week between work commitments was challenging. And I knew that because my aunt had been a member of the "Tri Delt" sorority, therefore I was a "legacy," and they had to consider me. I knew too at the time that it was one of the sought-after sororities on the UCLA campus. So each day when I went to pick up the results from the receptions the day before as we visited the various houses during rush week and met the young women who would be giving the yay or nay to us, I would anxiously look through the stack of invitations for the next day, to see if there was one from "Tri Delt." But of course, what I should have been looking for was "Delta Delta Delta." No one had bothered to tell me that. I grew up in Tujunga. How would I know?

So I have no idea whether the Delta Delta Delta ladies ever invited me back to tea, and I eventually joined Delta Zeta, which was not one of the upscale or highly sought-after houses on the campus at the time, but it was the one my sister Vickie had joined, the girls had seemed nice enough, and it was a place to live. I grew to love my sorority sisters there, and as it happens, it turned out to be a great decision. Another one of my lifelong and dearest friends, and former roommate of my sister's, Nancy Keating Wellard, was a sorority sister from Delta Zeta. We have stayed in touch all these years, sharing visits either in her home or mine, sharing emails, and most recently sharing a trip to Bath, UK, for her granddaughter Julia's lovely wedding. Nancy also has had an interesting, rewarding life, partly in Los Angeles working with social charities and then later in Hilton Head, South Carolina, where she was a regional director for the American Cancer Society. She now writes theater and art reviews for her local newspaper there in Bluffton, the *Island Packet*.

The following summer, another temporary employment opportunity presented. A friend of my father's, Mrs. Lanier, had recently become Mrs. Pond, transferring from widowhood to newly-married. She had a lovely home in Studio City next to the one my parents and I lived in years earlier, but my father and she had remained friends, and her new husband Mr. Pond owned an insurance agency of his own. I was hired as an assistant/receptionist/office helper. The woman who managed his office and did most of the work, Mrs. Pomeroy, was a sweet older woman who had been there for many years and obviously knew Mr. Pond pretty well.

When I left work at the end of the day, I had to walk out through the little hallway that led past Mr. Pond's office. And invariably, after a few weeks on the job, he began the process of stopping me at his office door by stepping out in the hall, grabbing me, and kissing me goodbye. And not on the cheek. I was horrified and embarrassed, not to mention very turned off by these advances. It creeped me out, this older man in charge, forcing himself on me. I guess I experienced my first #MeToo moment in Mr. Pond's insurance office in 1958. It made me so uncomfortable I didn't know what to do, and didn't have any experience with such things. I didn't know whether I should mention it to Mrs. Pomeroy or not. But soon she couldn't help noticing what was going on.

So she came up with a plan. Just before I was to head to the back door through the hallway, Mrs. Pomeroy would go into Mr. Pond's office with some "very important paper" she needed him to look at. While she engaged him as she stood there, pointing out some detail and blocking his doorway, I would whiz on down the hall, call "Goodnight, Mr. Pond" as I passed the office, and dash safely out the back door. We ladies had to stick together, especially back in those days. Sometimes it just took more creative thinking than it does these days. Bless you, Mrs. Pomeroy.

Another part-time job appeared during that first semester or two at UCLA, that I managed to see as related to my musical ambitions. There was a coffeehouse near the campus on Veteran Avenue and Santa Monica Boulevard, owned by the brother of "Red" who owned the very famous coffeehouse, the Venice West Café, in Venice, California. At that time, people like Jack Kerouac and Allen Ginsberg hung out at the Venice West Café, and Jim Morrison and other rock artists spent time there reading Camus and Sartre and drinking espresso, sometimes under the influence of LSD. This was the tail end of the beat generation where poetry readings and music was going on in such places, and the dear young man who operated the coffeehouse in West LA and hired me as a waitress was hoping to create the same environment. I, of course, was hoping to sing my songs at his coffeehouse, even though I didn't play guitar and he didn't have a piano yet. So that goal was iffy, and I knew on some level that it might never actually happen. But I told the house mother at the Delta Zeta house that because I was a music major, it would be very helpful for me to be able to "perform at the coffeehouse where I worked," so she gave me permission to stay out past "lock-out," which at that time was ten o'clock on weeknights. It was really at that point just a practical request, so I could work more hours.

I enjoyed my time at the coffeehouse, except for one tiny problem. It was within walking distance of the Veterans' Hospital in West LA, and sometimes one or two of the gentlemen from the residence there would wander in, after having had just a bit too much to drink. Sometimes they would just want to sit and chat, and most all of them were sweet guys, but sometimes they would end up in the restroom leaving behind on the floor most of whatever they'd had to drink earlier in the evening. That was not the fun part of the job, cleaning up the restroom.

My major at UCLA was music and my minor was English/theater arts. I had a passion for all three, though my shyness really kept me from diving into the acting classes with the commitment they required. I loved writing as well from very early in my life, and so hoped somehow to include all three pursuits in my college years.

Because I was the only music major in the sorority house, had done some performing as a singer, and it was known that I aspired to be a professional singer rather than an educator, I was asked to conduct our sorority's choir for the Spring Sing competition. It was intimidating to follow in the shoes of the young woman who had conducted the Delta Zetas to first place in Women's Division the year before, but I gave it my best, and remarkably, we won the Sweepstakes trophy that year. I have a picture of myself on stage at the Hollywood Bowl in an odd outfit that makes me look like one of the seven dwarfs (yes, I conducted at the Hollywood Bowl, just like John Williams . . . well, not *just* like John, but . . .) holding a trophy that was almost bigger than I was.

The following year, the UCLA Spring Sing committee, the group that made decisions about such things, announced that the Women's Division and Men's Division (that would be the sorority houses who chose not to team up with a fraternity and make rehearsing for Spring Sing a social activity) would only be allowed to perform "student songs" in the competition. It seemed that too many first prizes had gone to the Women's or Men's Choirs, and the hipper, more socially sophisticated students were getting pissed off.

This newly adapted restriction was terribly disappointing. We debated whether or not to even bother with the competition. Eventually, determined that I could not spend six weeks rehearsing "Go, Bruins!" with my fellow Delta Zetans, I went to the music library on campus and researched "Student Songs." No one had said where the "students" had to be from. I found a wonderful Scottish folk song, "Skye Boat Song," and a musical setting of "Ae Fond Kiss," a Robert Burns poem, that were, according to the UCLA School of Music Library, defined as "student songs." The ladies of Delta Zeta were willing to take the gamble, so I wrote arrangements for the two songs, we rehearsed and sang them beautifully, and did make it into the semifinals.

And then we were disqualified. Of course it was a disappointment, as we had managed to convince ourselves we would get away with this creative interpretation of the category. But we had known it was risky. Of course, those songs were not what the committee had in mind with their "Student Songs" category. It was still worth the gamble, and at least we didn't have to rehearse "Go, Bruins" in three-part harmony for six weeks. It would have taken a lot of beer to get us through that.

About this time I had also begun to sing in a four-part vocal group put together by a friend and fellow music student, Jack Walker. The group was three guys and myself, and about that time, a producer in New York, Leroy Holmes, had done a recording with a "pickup" group of the same voicing with session singers of "Over the Rainbow." It was a doo-wop version of the song, had gotten a lot of airplay, and was starting to become a hit. The label needed to come up with a group to *be* "The Baysiders," the name credited on the record. Somehow through some connection or other Jack was contacted, and Jack, Jim Mitchell, Jim Patton, and I became The Baysiders. We recorded more sides in the same doo-wop style, to complete the album, and we performed at record hops in the Los Angeles area. I remember going to the El Monte Legion Stadium for one of the hops as quite an adventure, because it was very far east, beyond Pasadena, in a part of town that seemed to me like going to another country. But it was a place where a lot of such events were being held in those days.

By the spring of my junior year at UCLA, I had begun to sing demos for songwriters, mostly at one of the little independent studios, but sometimes at Gold Star Studios, the legendary recording studio on Santa Monica Boulevard and Highland Avenue where so many hits were recorded. A few years later I would be working there with Phil Spector, Sonny & Cher, Herb Alpert, Burt Bacharach, and other artists of the day. Gold Star, alas, is no longer with us. Its commercial property value finally exceeded the value of the legendary iconic studio from which iconic hit records had sprung forth.

Some exciting opportunities in music came up during that junior year on campus. I got hired for the opera chorus of the productions that the Los Angeles Opera Company was producing for public school students to attend. The children arrived on school buses to the Shrine Auditorium from their classrooms all across town, and we performed *Hansel and Gretel*, *Cinderella*, and *The Magic Flute*. I had to join my first union, the American Guild of Musical Artists, which covered classical concert performances and live opera.

My stepfather Tom worked at the time for an artist manager named James Fox, and in my sophomore year, Mr. Fox arranged for me to meet with two young producers, Herb Alpert and Lou Adler, who were partners at the time, just starting out in the business. Eventually, of course, they both went on independently to have remarkably successful careers. Herb had hit records with his Tijuana Brass, and eventually started A&M Records, and Lou went on to produce such artists as the Mamas & the Papas, The Association, and many others.

Mr. Fox arranged an appointment for me to be interviewed at the small office Herb and Lou shared above the little shops on the Sunset Strip at Sunset Plaza Drive. He had been notified that Herb was looking for a young artist to record a new song he had written. Mr. Fox went with me to the meeting and played some demos of things I had recorded. Herb and Lou decided I would be the right person to sing his song, and Herb asked if I had a song of my own for the B side. I couldn't believe this producer was asking to hear one of my own songs. I had been writing by then for several years, so I polished up one of them (which happened to be about Johnny Richards—you remember him) and brought it back the next day. Herb, to my surprise, liked my song better than his, and asked me to write another for the B side, which I did.

We made plans to record the tracks at a little studio at the far end of Sunset Boulevard, and I did the lead vocals. I came up with some background vocal parts, and two of my sorority sisters and I added them. Then Herb had me add some high obligato background vocals. When he played me the string tracks he had added, I was so impressed. I didn't know him as a musician and artist at that time, I only knew him as the young producer who'd been willing to invest in a recording of my songs. I was impressed that he knew how to write arrangements!

Eventually Herb got the two songs, "Silver Ring" and "Maybe," released as a single on Dot Records. I couldn't believe this was happening. It was like a dream come true. I was excited, but I didn't want to be disappointed. I suspect, too, that at the time I didn't fully understand the significance of this opportunity. I just kept hoping the record might get some attention and then we could do more. Beyond that, I had no wild imaginings of becoming a huge star. I had sung obligatos or backup vocals on songs for songwriters who were trying to get a record deal, or to get an important artist to record their song. Here it was, happening to me, still a student at UCLA, and someone actually wanted to record a song I wrote.

James Fox decided we should use the artist name on the record of "Sally and the Sally-Cats." I think he felt we had a better chance commercially that way, based on how the business was at the time. In retrospect, I'm inclined to blame Mr. Fox for the scant success of the recording, based on the choice of our artists/group name alone. I found it just a little embarrassing. (James, if you're looking down from the heavens right now, I'm just kidding. P.S., you told me once that I would be a "late bloomer" and I'm still counting on your psychic abilities to make that come true, but you better hurry.)

Little did I know Herb's talent and musical skills—not to mention his killer-handsome, good looks—would soar him to the top of the music business very quickly. Soon after his first hit with the Tijuana Brass, he and Jerry Moss founded A&M Records in 1962. Its offices and studio were located on North La Brea Avenue near Sunset Boulevard, on the property that had at one time been the Charlie Chaplin Film Studios. So many sessions were recorded there at A&M, with Herb and many other artists all through the sixties, seventies, and eighties. Within its first decade it had become the world's largest independent record company. Years later, in the seventies after a session, I can remember sitting on the outside front steps of the recording studio with Burt Bacharach after a session, listening on a little portable radio with him to the horse races at Santa Anita, where one of Burt's racehorses was whirling around the track.

About the time my record with Herb was released, I also had an opportunity to audition for a short road concert tour that Ray Conniff was to be doing on the West Coast. Ray had, up until that time, been a sideman musician, doing solo trombone and writing arrangements for big bands and other artists, but he had come up with the idea of recording ensemble singer voices doing syllables instead of lyrics, the "bah-dat-dot-dot" of the melodies. His first album had gotten some attention, so he was booking a concert tour to promote the album. I auditioned with the other singers for that first gig in Ray's backyard in the San Fernando Valley. I was nervous, and I wasn't at all sure I could take the job even if I got it because it would mean missing about two weeks of my junior year in the spring semester, which was when the tour was scheduled.

I did end up getting hired for that tour, and though I ended up with a few "incompletes" on my school records, I had to take the plunge. I felt it was an opportunity that would more closely connect me with the business I wanted to be in, and besides, it sounded like such a fun experience.

We rehearsed the material for a couple of days and then set off in the bus, traveling up the West Coast. We played in Seattle, Washington; in Eugene, Oregon, and in several other smaller cities, and eventually finished the tour on Vancouver Island. It was the first time I had seen foreign currency, and really was impressed that I had traveled to another country! I also remember making a snowball along the way at one of the bus stops and putting it in my purse as a souvenir. That seemed like a good idea, at the time . . .

Along the way, the tour was also an opportunity to

promote the Dot record that had, coincidentally, just been released. So the label arranged for a couple of interviews with disc jockeys along the way, and there was a very sweet guy in Seattle, a local DJ I met with, who sent a letter to me later in Los Angeles. He urged me to stay as down to earth as I seemed to be to him in our meeting, and told me the sad tale of another young artist he had met who apparently was pretty full of herself, a quality which he found a bit off-putting and which he felt was to her disadvantage. He cautioned me not to become that way if *my* record should take off. Wish I could remember the name of that sweet DJ.

It was exciting when Herb called to tell me we'd made it on the charts to number ten in Connecticut. But sadly, that was as far as we got. I don't think at the time I really understood what a big deal it was, to have connected with a producer like Herb. We got together one evening in that little office at his suggestion after the record was released to see if we might write some songs together. Here's how sophisticated I was at the time; Herb brought a bottle of vodka, which he offered to share. I brought along a bag of those little individual Mounds candy bars.

The tour with Ray Conniff was the first time I had really sung swing or jazz, and sitting next to Ray on the bus, having him explain to me the difference between the dotted-eighth note feel and the even-eighth note feel, plus other aspects of commercial pop music versus classical music, I realized I would learn more about the business of music by *doing* it than I would likely learn with my studies at UCLA. It was a wonderful experience for a twenty-year-old, traveling with professional, skilled musicians, singing with pros, performing every night to concert halls filled with live audiences. There we were, riding a bus and eating in coffee shop restaurants every night by necessity, but it was definitely a fun experience for me, and I was seeing cities I'd never been in before.

I already knew by this time that I didn't want to teach, so

I was somewhat dismissive of the value of a degree in music. But at that point in time, it was still my intention to return to school in the fall.

That summer, I got my first apartment, a little studio place in a building on Seventh Street in Santa Monica. It was basically one room and bath, but it had a little kitchen space where there was a refrigerator and stove top, and a door to a private balcony porch at the side of the building, from which I could actually see the Pacific Ocean on a clear day. I found another five-day-a-week office job, and it was the first time I really had lived on my own. Even just going grocery shopping at the neighborhood Safeway market seemed like an adventure. Jack Walker, Jim Mitchell, Jim Patton, and I were still together as The Baysiders, and Jack was writing new arrangements for us, hoping to pursue more of our own recording projects. We rehearsed in my little apartment and I, assuming that these very hip boy musicians would want to drink at rehearsal, thought I had to have wine on hand. But knowing *nothing* about wine except the one brand I had seen ads for, Manischewitz, I bought a bottle of it and had it at the ready. I suspect they didn't want to hurt my feelings, and that's why they sipped it.

Jack and I have remained friends all these years, and reconnected just recently to catch up and share memories over lunch. He had continued with his music studies too, after UCLA, and became involved with scoring primarily Christian music projects—for companies, sadly, that always managed to do things nonunion. Jack needed those projects, his work did grow, and he should have been receiving royalties all these years for his writing and his playing. But since they were not done on American Federation of Musicians (AFM) union contract projects, and he was not given credit for the compositions as composer, those royalties sadly never arrived. Some of the most not-good-guys in our business were those Christian folks, the ones selling themselves as the good guys.

In the middle of that UCLA summer, I was asked to consider doing another tour with Ray. This time it was to be a forty-seven one-nighter bus tour, with concerts in cities all over the country. But it started in late September, which meant of course, that I would not be able to attend the fall semester of my senior year. I had lunch with my sweet sorority sister Linda, who had sung with me on the Dot recording, to discuss the dilemma of what to do.

"Oh, Sally, you have to go! You can still graduate, but just a bit later . . ." That helped me feel I wasn't thinking about something totally unreasonable. I knew my parents would not be happy about it, and I finally worked up the courage to tell them that was what I wanted to do, but it took a while. I tried to assure them, and genuinely felt at the time, that I could go back and finish—that it was just a temporary interruption, but an opportunity not to be missed.

But there was another element at work. I had met Dick Castle, one of the other singers on the West Coast tour, and we had dated through the summer. Dick was going to do the fall tour, so it just seemed it was all meant to be. I did return to the sorority house for the rush week before we left, to help with the pledge gatherings that preceded the start of school, but that indeed turned out to be the end of my campus activities.

I knew from the stories shared by the other singers that the Conniff tour would be intense, but I really looked at it as an adventure, because we were in towns all over the country that I knew I would probably never see again. We would ride the bus all day, arrive in that evening, check quickly into our hotel, then head for the concert hall, do a sound test, try to make ourselves presentable, and get on stage for the down-beat. I can still see the faces of the musicians who traveled with us, can remember where they were seated on the bus. Some of them were already part of the recording session community in Hollywood, and others later would eventually become part of it as I did, so we continued to work together over many years.

I remember little roadside diners as we traveled through the South, where in those days you could miraculously get a five-course meal for eighty-five cents. But being in the South at that time was for me, like being on another planet. For the first time in my life, I was seeing a world with Whites Only and Colored above the drinking fountains and washrooms. Our tour began in the fall of 1960, and that was only a few months after the Freedom Riders traveled through the area and civil rights demonstrations had taken place. There were marches and police violence and brutality. It saddened and shocked me to see this existed in any part of our country. I was terribly naïve and had grown up in the small community of Tujunga, California, admittedly a mostly white community. But I had never witnessed racist behavior. There was one little African American girl in my sixth grade class whose mother was in residence at a tuberculosis clinic in the area, and she came over to play at my house several times. And in junior high school I had a crush on handsome Bucky Chung, the only Chinese student in our school. My parents had friends in the music business, all greatly respected African Americans. One couple in particular, Jester Hairston and his wife, were often dinner guests. Jester wrote "Mary's Boy Chile," "Who'll Be a Witness," and many other songs for film projects, and choral arrangements for the Walter Schumann Choir. Jester went on in later years to become a well-known actor, performing major roles into his nineties in several TV sitcoms. (I still have that treasured telegram that Jester and his wife sent me in my senior year at Verdugo Hills High, when we performed *Trial by Jury*, the Gilbert & Sullivan operetta, and I played the lead role of the jilted bride.) I had never experienced or participated in racial discrimination, and I could never have imagined such cruel and wrong things existed in my country.

On that tour with Ray, despite the dreadful cultural things

in the South that introduced us to racism, I also saw the natural beauty of the Atlantic Ocean for the first time, I walked the beaches of Miami, and I experienced the charm of New England when we played Boston and the East Coast summer tent theater circuit. Then we headed back home across the middle of the country, with concert performances along the way.

Dick and I had gotten pretty serious, and we decided to get married on the last lap of that long one-nighter bus tour, in a little church in El Paso, Texas. I shopped for my wedding outfit, a satin-embossed white skirt and jacket and dressy high heels, in one of the chain department stores in Dallas as we passed through on our way west. Ray and Ann, his wife at the time, presented Dick and me on stage that night with a beautiful set of sterling silver flatware, and Ray thanked us for lifting the spirits of the group on that weary last lap of the tour.

When we got back home, we settled into the tiny one-room cottage that was part of a duplex I had rented just before we left on the tour. It was on a side street just east of Wilshire Boulevard. The property belonged to Lawrence Welk, and the lot was to eventually be used to build a large commercial building facing on to Wilshire Boulevard, so the cottage was soon to be torn down. The rental situation was temporary but therefore very reasonably-priced at thirty-five dollars a month. It made a nice, affordable home for us. We slept on a fold-out couch and had a kitty that jumped down on our faces every morning from the back of the couch to let us know it was time for breakfast. In the kitchen there was a very old stove that stood on four high legs, left over from the dark ages, with no oven temperature controls, just basically an "on" and "off." But somehow, I was able to bake magnificent things in that oven. I've since sadly lost touch with the art of baking.

We stayed in that little duplex cottage for a few months and then moved to an apartment building that was a bit more spacious, on Yale Street in Santa Monica. That is where we lived when Susie was born, and where we made our home for the next couple of years. The night she was born, we had gone to my dad's house in Van Nuys earlier in the afternoon, had enjoyed dinner with my aunt Flossie who lived there with my dad and his third wife, Dee, and were watching TV all together in the living room. I had been having contractions that began the night before, while I was scrubbing the kitchen floor in our little apartment. I wanted to get everything ready for bringing our baby home. But having been a Christian Scientist all my life, it was to be my first experience in a hospital, and I was terrified, pretty much, of the whole process.

So I put it off as long as I could, until there was no more denying what was going on. Around eight or so in the evening, my waters broke, and Dick rushed me to the little hospital in Burbank where my doctor practiced. Susie was born just before midnight, so I only had to experience about three hours there preceding her birth. Everything went smoothly, although it was a breech birth which these days would have been handled differently, and Susie weighed almost ten pounds!

CHAPTER 11
THE LAS VEGAS ADVENTURES

Dick had ambitions to be a recording artist and had started down that path with Lawrence Welk. That was always what I'd wanted to do too, but there really wasn't an opportunity to pursue it at that point for either of us, nor did we really know how. Welk had produced four songs with Dick as solo artist, but his association with Welk had not blossomed. He also had worked in Welk's office prior to our meeting each other.

Though we had met a few other session singers through our Conniff connections and were starting to get a little session work, it made more sense to take the job as production singers that was offered to us for two guaranteed months' work at the Sahara Hotel in Las Vegas. So we became the Randy Van Horne Singers with our two friends Wayne Dunstan and Toni, Randy's ex-wife, when Susie was ten weeks old, and performed as part of the fifteen-minute production number, something most of the hotel showrooms had in those days to open the evening for the headliners. We found an apartment in a neighborhood off the strip, and a very nice woman who came highly recommended to babysit Susie every evening. The engagement was extended and we ended up working there for fourteen weeks.

Recently while digging through some boxes of old letters, photographs, and memorabilia that had been in the Tujunga house after my mother and Tom both had died and we needed to empty and sell the house, I came across a letter that I had written to my mother, from our apartment in Las Vegas. It expressed so clearly how the world was in those years, especially for women, in the early sixties.

The letter began:

Dearest Mom and all, even though it is your turn to write, I thought I'd like to send you a hello note. Kind of me, eh what? Susie is sleeping on the couch, Dick went to practice at the Sahara Hotel piano, and I've been reading. I've also composed a long list of things I'm sick of and there's no one here who will listen to my list except you so I will share it with you now.

I'm sick of the bitchy, snotty girl who Toni and I share our 2 X 4 ft dressing room with, who does nothing but praise herself audibly and brings her damn, smelly, cow-sized dog to work with her to keep us company in our closet-sized dressing room, in which we must house ourselves and three monstrous hoop-skirted, floor-length costumes. I'm sick of Las Vegas; of group-singing rehearsals; of Jerry Vale and Eddie Fisher records to which Dick sings along with loudly in order to vocalize; of paint-by-number pictures, of Western TV shows, of cooking dinner every night for Dick, me, and friend Wayne Dunstan who is a bachelor and hence cannot fend for himself; of not being able to say so if I don't like something; of not being able to talk about trying to do something myself (about singing, etc.). And I'm mostly mad because I catch myself feeling this way. Please forgive me for my "sick-of-it-itis," and don't take me too seriously, but I'll go out of my mind if I can't blow off some steam.

I was really enthusiastic and excited last week at the anticipation of writing a screen adaptation of Mistress of Mellyn, which I felt would make a really excellent movie. Then I heard that someone at Paramount Studios apparently shared my enthusiasm because they were releasing the film version shortly. So now I don't know what the X -- to do. I'll never be a famous dancer if I don't go to my lessons, will I? I'll never be one even if I do go, though. I've just recently developed a theory which I may base some sort of writing on—that men, generally speaking, are egotistical and self-evolving. That's only this week's thought for the day.

I bought a box of great fresh mushrooms yesterday for 29 cents. I was mad though, because the lady didn't put my potatoes in the grocery bag, so we had to have Swiss steak and Minute Rice. Tonight is pay day (night) so we will go grocery shopping. Could you, in your next letter which I expect any day now, tell me how to cook a turkey? (Really!!) as we'll be here for Thanksgiving and I hate to serve hamburger. I don't know how to cook a Turkey and forgot to bring my cookbook. Don't forget about the turkey please. Susie-Q is just fine and getting cuter and bigger and more fun every day. I hope you are able to decipher my writing. Please write again soon. Bye for now, Sal.

When we came back to LA at the end of our Las Vegas booking Dick proceeded to file for unemployment for both of us, and that became a rather complicated situation. Our California claim was denied because our employers technically were out of state, in Nevada. So we had to refile in Nevada.

The response from Nevada state offices was that we were not employees, but independent contractors. We appealed that decision, and by the time the hearings in Las Vegas came up, I was once again working at the Sahara, as a solo production singer, partnered with another male singer. As things unfolded, the producers of the opening production number tried to persuade Dick and me to abandon the appeal, but Dick was convinced we should proceed. I began wondering if that was why they had hired me to come back.

One morning as we waited to hear the outcome of our case, we opened the local newspaper to find, on the front page, a photograph of a man's hand sticking up out of the desert sand, holding a dealt hand of playing cards. The rest of the man was buried *beneath* the sand. He had been done away with by the mob—who were, of course, basically our employers—the ones against whom we had filed for unemployment. They owned most of the hotels on the strip in those days, and had caught the guy who was buried in the desert dealing off the bottom of the deck against the house. This was how they took care of their problems.

We found the article somewhat discomforting and were happy when the time came to pack up and head for home. Along the way, the judge who was to hear our case came to see one of my performances at the Sahara. Our argument had been that we were unquestionably employees, that we had been told what material to sing, had been provided costumes, had been directed as to makeup and choreography, worked at their direction, etc. Those arguments didn't fly, and in the end, we lost the appeal. But the judge seemed to enjoy the show. We learned later that although we did not win our claim, because of our case and the issue coming up, all the hotels on the strip had to start paying their talent—the showgirls, dancers, people in those opening production numbers—as employees, with the accompanying benefits. We realized we got out of town just in time to avoid also landing under the desert sand.

It all worked out though, because when we returned to LA the phone began to ring more often and we both began gradually to do more session work, backing artists and doing more recording and TV.

We also auditioned a few months later for Ralph Carmichael, who was Nat King Cole's arranger/musical director and was putting together a concert tour for Nat. The tour was to begin in Colorado Springs, return to Los Angeles for an engagement at the Greek Theatre, and then head to the East Coast for the summer tent theater circuit. It was an exciting project to be a part of, though it would take me away from

Susie, then only about a year old, for weeks. I wasn't sure whether I could handle that. But it was almost two months of steady employment for us both. We decided we couldn't turn it down. This, as it turned out, was the second to last concert tour Nat did before he was to die from lung cancer several years later. We knew that he had been diagnosed at the time, but thought his treatment had been successful.

It was a remarkable opportunity for us—not just as a job, but to have the experience of working with this legendary performer. We were hired and took off for the road again, leaving Susie in the care of my mother for the first Colorado Springs booking. In Colorado Springs, too, I was to meet Dick's family for the first time. His parents lived in Wyoming and drove to Colorado Springs to be with us for a few days there.

That first out-of-town booking was only about ten days, but when we returned home for the Greek Theatre engagement, I had so missed my little baby girl that I just couldn't bear the thought of leaving again. We picked her up from my mom's and returned to our apartment in Santa Monica. I knew I had only a short time with her and then we would be off on the road again. I so wanted to bail on the rest of the engagement, and tried to work up the courage, much against Dick's objection, to talk to Ralph Carmichael about finding someone to replace me. But eventually I realized he was right, in that this would not bode well for either of us in terms of future work or commitments in town, and it was something I just could not do. We were hired for the whole tour and production, part of a twelve-person "choir" of singer/dancers, and it would not have been possible or fair to ask that I be replaced. Dick and I had become friends during rehearsals with Wayne Dunstan, another one of the singers, and Wayne had been in the business much longer than we had, working also as an instrumentalist and arranger. He knew very clearly what the impact of trying to do something like that would be. So after the Greek Theatre engagement was over, I tearfully left Susie behind again with my mother, and we boarded the cross-country train for the New England portion of the tour.

CHAPTER 12
THE NAT KING COLE TOUR, 1962

About one and a half minutes after kissing his eight-month-pregnant wife Marilyn goodbye on the boarding platform of Union Station and climbing aboard the waiting Santa Fe Starlight, our friend and fellow traveler Wayne Dunstan disappeared furtively and without remorse into one of the bedroom compartments four cars forward, with his saxophone case tucked under one arm and Lulu, a shapely, sloe-eyed, LA blues singer tucked under the other. Each of them had arrived at the station with a glazed look in their eyes, and a casual impersonal attitude they hoped would belie the powerful attraction that had been simmering all during the weeks of rehearsal. It was an attraction over which, apparently, they had in the final analysis, no control whatsoever.

It had taken a little of the devil weed to provide them with the necessary courage for the inevitable rendezvous. After all, the situation presented certain complexities, what with their respective families standing on the platform waving tearful goodbyes.

Wayne and Lulu pretty much stayed in that bedroom compartment, emerging only occasionally for a drink in the lounge or a quick sandwich in the dining car, until the train pulled into the station at Colorado Springs. It apparently took them that long to release the sexual tensions that had been building up for three weeks while Nat King Cole's touring company of racially mixed singers and dancers rehearsed in an over-heated, windowless rehearsal hall on the back lot of the old Goldwyn Studios on Formosa Street in Hollywood.

Wayne would watch Lulu move on cue like a cat on stage, into position for her solo, her smooth-fitting sleeveless cotton sheath sliding suggestively from side to side across the generous rounding of her undulating ass and thighs as they progressed seductively toward center stage. She would glance at Wayne as she passed, smiling her close-mouthed, heavy-lidded smile, smoky as her mellow voice, and rich with promise.

At the end of the rehearsal day we would meet, the four of us, at the Formosa Café, a bar and restaurant at the corner of Formosa Avenue and Santa Monica Boulevard that recently was rescued from demolition and declared a historical landmark, as well it should be. It reeked of the oriental mystery that had been Hollywood in the thirties and forties, and you could still feel the presence of the ghosts of starlets who had visited its dimly lit confines after long days on the set, hoping to be discovered by some powerful and benevolent studio executive. Its proximity to the Goldwyn Studios made it a popular hangout in the early days, and though it now seemed a little down at the heels; the food was cheap and good, the drinks were generous, and more importantly, it was the kind of place where if you were of a mind to, you could count on a certain anonymity, should you be there with someone you *shouldn't* be there with. That was part of the mystery that the Formosa Café still reeked of in 1961. You could just feel it in the air, and absorb it from the old black-and-white framed photographs of actors and actresses from another era.

None of us in the troop were particularly surprised at the pairing of Wayne and Lulu. And you could hardly blame either one of them. Wayne was tall and lean, dark and sexy himself, a mysterious vagabond of the road, a jazz man who had played with Stan Kenton, who had ghostwritten charts against impossible deadlines, who had consumed too much scotch, smoked too many Chesterfields and would have been better off in the long run if he'd just stuck to the devil weed he used for recreational and consciousness-altering purposes. In other words, to the world of women among whom he moved, he was irresistible.

Lulu had the unfortunate lot of being born a Black woman in an America still struggling through the racially bigoted culture of the early sixties. Then the mother of a nineteen-year-old daughter, she was still very glamorous—enough so to be singing for her supper, way talented enough to get noticed, sexy enough to get pursued by sexy gentlemen, but sadly, perhaps *not* unique enough to ever become a star, despite her dearest wishes and all the soulful performances on and off stage that she could deliver. She was just one of many singers in the business, a little luckier than some, but not quite as lucky as she needed to be.

Nothing about road life was real or had very steadfast rules. Wayne had tried to establish himself in town, looking for session work, had gotten married to his sweet wife Marilyn, and had a child on the way, not all necessarily in that order. Eventually he switched from Chesterfields to Kools, but he was still to die of lung cancer some years later.

I was twenty-two years old and a new young mother myself, grateful that I had not had to entirely set my dreams of working as a singer aside, but somehow had worked it out so that I could earn a living in the music business but not feel I had entirely abandoned my little baby girl. Dick and I met Wayne on this, our first "big" road gig, and subsequently had been invited to his apartment and met his wife Marilyn over dinner. We admired her valiant but nonetheless failed effort at executing a recipe from the pages of the big *Good House-keeping*'s red and white-checkered cookbook, a staple in the kitchen of every young bride in the fifties and sixties. We'd played at being grownups. We'd talked about babies, about rents, about recipes, about what we'd do to find the next gig once this one was over, and about the fantasy of getting into recording work, which we knew could change the universe for all of us.

We sat at their dinner table talking about who we knew, each of us, that might lead to more work in town. Wayne and Dick, of course, did most of the talking. Marilyn and I escaped every so often to the kitchen to remove the empty dishes and discuss recipes and the new baby on the way.

Wayne felt encouraged about Ralph Carmichael's work in town, as Ralph had moved from primarily the Christian music world into more the commercial recording artist world, so maybe there would be some sessions with Nat when the road trip was over, he optimistically suggested. We were still in touch too with Jay Meyer, who had contracted the Ray Conniff tours, and maybe more activities with Ray would open up. None of us knew the other busy contractors at the time, but we knew who they were; Bill Lee, Johnny Mann, Thurl Ravenscroft. We just had to figure out a way to connect with them.

Our dreams at the time were focused on making a living, on paying the rent. Dick was able to more actively pursue his own dream of becoming a successful solo artist, doing songwriter demos and hoping the right person would hear them, but I knew that the songwriter/artist career was off the table for me, at least for the time being. I was on a new path, that of being a mom, and still being a part of the music business as a professional session singer, even though that role felt sometimes like just being part of the scenery.

I liked Wayne's wife very much, but it never occurred to me then to question his behavior, or to hurt her by telling what I knew. It was, after all, the sixties. He was my husband's friend, and I was just a dumb "chick singer" still terrified of this new and confusing world within which I barely felt I had a right to exist, let alone to make waves in, over issues that didn't seem to bother any of the other people around me.

So, our train pulled out of Union Station, and the journey began in more ways than one. That summer was filled with events that would shape my life, and as it turned out, the lives of a whole nation. Jack Kennedy was newly in the White House, and the world as a whole still seemed innocent. Wars had always previously been fought in defense of clear principles of right and wrong, or so we believed. Americans had not yet been cast out of Eden by the events that were to follow; the assassinations, the bitter racial strife, the Vietnam debacle, and the growing pains of the sixties and seventies.

On a personal level, touring with Nat King Cole, one of the biggest stars in the industry at the time, was a big step up from the forty-seven one-nighter band bus tour that had begun my professional road-touring career. And I had thought at the time that *that* was the greatest thing that could happen to me. I had won the chance to work with professionals I knew and admired; I was starting to feel linked to the industry. The band tour had been rigorous, but it had sprung me from the last weeks of my junior spring semester at UCLA, had rescued me forever from the French class finals and lecture halls of which I had prematurely tired, and had exposed me to faraway cities like Milwaukee, Boston, and other exciting points south. It had also brought Dick into my life, and I guess at twenty years of age a glimpse of the world and a chance to perform and get paid for it was more important than creature comforts.

But Nat's tour was a bit more upscale, because he was an icon, a well-respected star, and there we were on stage with him. And a crowded bus was no longer the mode of transportation from city to city. We were now comfortably traveling on the cross-country Starlight Express, dining with linen tablecloths and napkins. Los Angeles was disappearing in the darkness behind me. Only this time I was watching railroad tracks ribboning back into the night instead of a highway, and a lot had changed. Now I was a wife and a mother, leaving my little girl behind with her grandma for six weeks, while I went off with Dick, hoping we would earn enough money to sustain us over the following few months, if we planned carefully. I was trying as hard as I could to fit into a grown-up world, with a husband I knew at best only rather superficially. And in Colorado Springs, I was to meet my new in-laws for the first time.

I have vivid memories of sitting in the club car on that journey by rail, sewing by hand a herringbone wool tweed sheath dress like the one I had seen Marilyn Monroe wear in the movie *Niagara Falls*. All around me, people were drifting deeper into their convivial stupors, smiling at each other across the smoke-filled air that hung over their melting ice cubes. I didn't drink, because I hadn't yet learned how. And I didn't smoke because though now married with a family of my own, I was still fearful of my devout Christian Scientist mother's wrath, should she somehow discover that I did.

I remember the smell of the Colorado mountains, of the muggy summer rain, of the apartment we thought was so fine, where we stayed during our ten-day engagement in Colorado Springs. Its burgundy Formica counter tops and automatic coffee maker were vastly upscale from the tiny one-room cottage we had once called home. Mother Plenger, Dick's mother (his legal name was Elmer Plenger) arrived almost at the same moment we did, with a brown paper bag of groceries under each arm, bespectacled and matronly looking, and unrelentingly chatty and cheerful. Poppa Elmer followed, smiling the long-suffering smile, which I soon learned he had forced himself to adopt because for the last thirty years of his life he had lived with a woman who pulled tricks like pocketing waitress's tips from coffee shop booths on her way out of restaurants and thought it was cute, who was constantly, and in every situation shamelessly, amused at her own cleverness, and who never, ever stopped talking. To these facts he had finally become reconciled. What was there to do but smile?

Alvira Plenger, a native of Wyoming and now a teacher

and shaper of our nation's children, shared with a giggle that she had passed her college exams and earned her teaching credential by having her husband take all the tests in her correspondence courses.

On one spring evening early in our courtship during the very first short ten-day West Coast Conniff tour, as we walked back to our hotel after the concert, Dick sat me down on a bench in the park overlooking the California State Capitol Building in Sacramento and sang "Be My Love" to me at the top of his lungs in the moonlight, unabashedly. If he'd been kidding, I could have handled it, but I quickly realized it was seriously meant to impress. I tried to convince myself that it was petty to feel embarrassment and that a lot of girls would have been flattered and appropriately awed, living out a scene from some MGM musical. But I cringed a bit, hoping no one else was out strolling through the park and saw the performance.

Sadly, Dick and I eventually got another chance to learn of the racial discrimination still going on in our nation, that our fellow singers in Nat's racially mixed singer/dancer troupe faced on that tour. One of our friends shared with us while we were in New England that the subtle message they were being given when they were unwelcome in a restaurant or bar was to find in their cocktail glass an ice cube with a fly in it. And this was New England in 1962.

CHAPTER 13

THE NORTHRIDGE YEARS

A year or so after completing the concert tour with Nat King Cole, Dick and Susie and I moved from the apartment where we lived on Yale Street to our first little house in Northridge, a modest but sweet neighborhood in the north San Fernando Valley. My dad cashed out a life insurance policy in order to provide us with the down payment, deciding that the proceeds would be of more help to me at that time in life than later down the road.

I was twenty years old when Dick and I married, and he was twenty-six. Years earlier he had graduated with a teaching degree from college and completed a tour of military duty in Europe. I was only just beginning my life as an adult. We had come from very different backgrounds, and the differences in who we were became more apparent as the years of our marriage unfolded. He was a truly good person, but I still remember looking at other couples when we were out in the world and thinking of our marriage; that if this is what marriage is supposed to be then, okay, I'd stick with it, but if it is supposed to be more, if it is supposed to be more like how those other people act, how they look at each other—then I feared I had made a mistake. I don't think I knew what it meant to truly love someone yet. I also didn't know how *not* to respond to something I wasn't yet sure of. I was, and probably still am somewhat, at this advanced age, a people pleaser. So if Dick loved me, I should love him back. I'm not even sure that either of us understood deeply what the kind of love was that inspires a marriage and keeps it together.

About the time we moved to Northridge, we both started to become more established in the business, but our careers developed at slightly different paces. Dick was a very talented singer, and still, as he had early in his career, he aspired to become like Vic Damone or Andy Williams, a successful solo recording artist. He would practice two or three hours a day in our one-bedroom apartment in Santa Monica when we first were married, at the top of his second tenor lungs, singing along to Al Martino records. Al, admittedly, was not one of my favorite artists, and I tried to be as patient and supportive as I knew how to be, but it drove me a little crazy. In the session singer world, Dick's talent was also excellent—fine musicianship, excellent sight-reader. But there were so many others as well, competing in our business, and the opportunity to be hired as soloist was rare. So though he was a fine singer, there were so many in the community whose *only* ambition was to be a busy session singer, and the competition was stiff even for group session work.

In order to understand what "success" means as I talk about it here—in our world, or the world that eventually became my world—the goal was to succeed within that world. It didn't mean you had to become a famous artist or songwriter, it just meant you would get to work with those who were, and as often as possible. It meant you got to do TV and radio commercials, which paid very well if they ran "prime time." It meant you got to work on film scores, on television scores, on awards shows. It meant you rose to the top of a highly competitive community comprised of some of the best musicians and singers in the world. In those days even more than now, you had to be an excellent sight-reader of music scores, you had to be adaptable to various sounds and styles, and you had to understand the professional aspects of the business to reach that success. And if you were lucky, success would last a couple of decades. You would basically earn a good living as a singer. Not every session singer wants to be a solo artist. In fact, most don't. They want to work in the industry they love doing what they love, and be part of a community, which is what choral and ensemble singing feels like.

Also, it seems like every success in our business greatly relies upon luck. You have to have the right ingredients, but if you don't also have the good fortune to be in the right place at the right time, the prize skips over you to the next guy. I had inherited my mom's soprano high notes, and as it happened, had a few chances early on to sub for one of the busiest sopranos in town at that time, Loulie Jean Norman, who was winding down her career but still sang beautifully. So on those occasions I had a chance to show what I could do, which was a light, high soprano tone without vibrato, and just a little shimmer at the end of a phrase if I was singing the top note in a choir. It was a sound kind of in vogue at the time, and I guess one that people responded to, because I began to get more calls through 1963 and 1964.

I also at that time auditioned for the Johnny Mann Singers who were about to begin work on the first season of the *Danny Kaye* variety TV show, and I was hired to be part of the group. That was the good news, that things were beginning to happen work-wise, and we could pay our bills. But it was the bad news for Susie who, as she has told me all these years later, understandably felt "invisible," because I eventually had to be gone so much of the time. My little girl really got shortchanged in terms of time with her mother.

By the second season of *The Danny Kaye Show*, Dick and I had separated, and my neighbor across the street, Sylvia, who was the mother of Susie's little friend Julie Marvin, agreed to start taking care of her during my work hours. It helped their family a bit financially, it allowed Susie to have the companionship of other children, and it was a huge help to me. But I would often be gone the whole day, or an afternoon into the evening, and I would come home, go across the street, and carry Susie home in her pajamas late at night, then have to head out fairly early again the next morning.

Susie and I were able to do some of the things I told myself were precious to childhood, like the pony rides, and meeting my mother and my younger brothers and sister for Saturday morning picnics in Griffith Park. There were birthday parties in the backyard where Susie and her little friends enjoyed the birthday clown performances. We had kitties, and a little dog, and at one point a rabbit that ran freely about the rooms of our house. But that really never made up for the imbalance on the side of mother-daughter time.

Dick did truly have a beautiful voice, and during the first couple of years of our marriage, we used to go down on Saturday nights to the Aragon Ballroom by the Santa Monica Pier where he would be invited by Lawrence Welk to come up on the bandstand and sing a song or two.

This too often, however, was after we'd stood by the bandstand for a couple of hours waiting for Lawrence to notice his presence. I always had the feeling Welk *had* noticed, but also had his own agenda for how the evening should go and didn't mind keeping us standing there.

Early in our relationship when Dick was really more connected with Lawrence Welk, Mr. Welk took his office staff to lunch one day at a little coffee shop in the area, and I was invited to go along. At one point, Welk speared a chunk of pineapple that had come with whatever he had ordered, held it up to the group, dangling from his fork, waved it over the table, and asked "Does anyvun vant dis peez uf biy-na -bull?" (That's how he talked.) He was really a down-home kind of guy, reluctant to waste even a piece of pineapple.

Dick did several solo appearances on the Welk TV variety show, and on one occasion Lawrence introduced him by saying "And now, Dick Castle, from Greybull, Wyoming, will come out and sing for us. Elmer (that was his real name) tell dee audience where you-a from and wha-d you a-goin' do-a sing-uh."

I know it was very disappointing for Dick not to have become successful as a recording artist. And though we both did make it into the session singing world, I was maybe a bit luckier or at the right place at the right time, and it seemed to go a little better for me. Dick did a lot of live performing along the way, some touring as the re-established vocal group, the Lancers, that sang with the Guy Lombardo orchestra. He had a natural, pleasant way with audiences, and though things didn't blossom into the career he had originally hoped for, I believe he really enjoyed the performance aspect of that long career. Even into his later years, he enjoyed gatherings at his house where friends shared their music, singing and performing together for each other.

Dick and his eventual partner-in-love, Rayme, were together in his little house in Studio City for many years, and it was a heartbreaking loss for him when she passed away in her early fifties. In the later years we were always able to be friends, to share holiday gatherings at our daughter Susie's home, to enjoy the grandchildren together. And when I began to do some vocal contracting, I always included Dick in the choral film scoring sessions when it was appropriate to do so, if he was in town.

I know ours was a painful divorce for him, when that time finally came for us. But I had tried as hard as I could. I had heard that the first five years were the most important and formative years for a child, so I figured I would at least commit to that, for the sake of our little girl. As we journeyed through those years, I realized I had not really known this man with whom I shared little in common except for music, and as I looked around at other couples who seemed to have much more in common and looked happier, more connected to each other, I eventually realized I could not stay in that marriage.

CHAPTER 14

THE 1965 DATEBOOK AND EARLY SESSIONS

Shortly after I began writing these memoir pages, I dug out of the archives a few old datebooks that had survived the years— a couple from the sixties, from the seventies, and into the eighties among other memorabilia buried in the garage. I was hoping their pages might remind me of specific projects or names of artists I'd worked with. But their pages took me instead to quite another place, a much more emotional and personal view of those years. My terrible habit of holding on to stuff, although it has resulted over the years in a garage loaded to the rafters, is kind of a blessing, because memories tend to fade a bit over four or five decades, and I was delighted to rediscover them. I had used those datebooks as a kind of journal, too.

The earliest one was from 1965, a year of many changes, professionally and personally. And the years preceding that were my introduction into not only the music business, but also into the journey that began the ups and downs of my adult life. They included notations about the difficult times around the divorce, the failed attempts at marriage counseling, the guilt I felt about ending the marriage, and the transition from married mom to single mom. Additionally, they include the transition into the community I was to be part of for the next fifty years.

In 1963 I began working on the *Danny Kaye* TV variety show in its 1963–64 first season. I continued with the show for three years. I was that time also beginning to become more established in freelance session singing work in Los Angeles, and the pages of the datebook reflect that growing activity. The recording sessions were becoming more frequent, along with the *Danny Kaye* TV schedule, *The Red Skelton Show*, and several *Ed Sullivan Show* broadcasts, which I had been surprised to see. I hadn't remembered they'd ever taped the show in California. The *Hollywood Palace* TV show was also an occasional occurrence for both Dick and me, usually just a one- or two-day work call. And along the way were numerous artists' record sessions and the growing presence of more commercials, radio jingles, etc.

All the TV variety shows involved usually two or three days of activity. There would be a music rehearsal with the singers, perhaps a wardrobe fitting, then an onstage blocking or choreography, often a pre-record, and then the day of the show—a dress rehearsal, also taped just to have editing available if needed, and finally the show itself, with audiences filling the seats.

I was not contracting at all in those early days, and didn't really want to. I did add contracting in the early eighties after twenty or so years of working only as a singer for other contractors, and a soloist for various composers. But my record-keeping in that 1965 datebook consisted basically of writing down the name of the studio and the time of the session, plus the name of the contractor for whom I was working. Occasionally I included the name of the artist if it was a record session, though I didn't always know who the artist was until I got to the session—or if it was a commercial, the name of the product. Going through this 1965 datebook, I ran across sessions for Doris Day, Billy Vaughn, Vic Damone, Johnny Prophet, Ed Ames, Robert Goulet, Andy Williams, Neal Hefti, Bill Henderson, and Stan Freberg. Those were some of the artists recording in that more structured recording business of the day when major labels had artists under contract, handled their careers, produced their albums, and hired freelance union musicians and singers to work on them. We all worked together in a large studio, partitioned off; the artist in the solo vocal booth, the singers in a separate vocal booth or on risers, and the orchestra set up by instrumental sections. Sadly, those days have all but disappeared. So much is done now separate track by sections, overdub by overdub. Rarely does everything come together in one room, at one time, even for film scores.

At that point in my journey in the business, I assumed my job was to just show up on time, read the sheet music the arranger put in front of me, sing in tune, fill out my W-4 and go home. I was not supposed to bring attention to myself, nor distract from the contractor in charge. As a result, the details of so many of those early sessions have fled from my mind. I do remember that even quietly observing from across the room, I found Andy Williams to be charming, Robert Goulet to be handsome, Stan Freberg to be funny but also a little self-absorbed, and Doris Day to be delightful.

Some years later, after Andy William's divorce from his wife Claudine Longet, Andy invited me to dinner one evening. We dined at Dan Tana's, the legendary restaurant in West Hollywood that's actually still in business in that same building, recently having celebrated its fiftieth anniversary. By this time I had worked on Andy's sessions many times over the years from 1965 forward, so felt like I knew him a bit more, and though it was somewhat intimidating to be dining next to such a celebrity, we had a lovely evening. We sat in one of the big leather booths along the side wall, and I enjoyed seeing the waiters fussing over him, taking care of him so attentively. Andy was obviously a regular visitor at Dan Tana's. It was the first time I'd gotten a tiny taste of the "celebrity" world, and despite my shyness, I eventually found myself chatting comfortably with him, as the waiters whisked back and forth refilling our wine glasses. I was a bit surprised when, back at my house on Yoakum Drive later that evening, Andy took a marijuana joint out of his pocket and asked if I'd like to share a smoke. I did, of course. But who knew Andy Williams did that!

Some of the notations in that early datebook reflected only the name of the contractor who had called me, but those contractors were often associated with certain artists—for example, Jack Halloran, a very busy vocal contractor who usually used a group of eight singers, did a lot of sessions with backup vocals for Frank Sinatra, Dean Martin, and some of the other Reprise artists. We once did a session for Ray Charles at Ray's little studio in south LA. People in the business those days used to refer to this Ray Charles as "the blind one," not the "deaf one"—the "deaf one" being the *other* Ray Charles, an excellent choral arranger and singer based in New York, but who was known within the industry for his singers sometimes sounding a tiny bit flat.

The song we did on Ray Charles's session that afternoon was a hymn, and I suspect not quite authentically enough gospel-sounding for Ray on our first couple of run-throughs. His helper guided him over to where the singers were standing around our microphone, and Ray commented with a smile, "Okay, but sounds like y'all are doin' a kind of Presbyterian soul, you know?" Eventually we got it, moved a little deeper into the sound he was looking for, and Ray was patient, gracious, and pleased.

Jay Meyer, another vocal contractor, did most of the early Ray Conniff sessions, and a Christmas TV special done around this time. Sara Jane Tallman, who was married to Andy's musical director Dave Grusin, worked on the *Andy Williams* TV show and also contracted a lot of Andy's sessions. And Jimmy Joyce and his Jimmy Joyce Singers worked a year or two later on the *Smothers Brothers* TV variety show, but also did many other recording and TV projects with various combinations of voices, and was contractor for the *Hollywood Palace* TV show. So the sessions for those contractors listed in my early datebooks involved those artists with whom they were most associated at the time.

There were some evening rehearsals at Jimmy Joyce's home, and I remembered one in particular, in an earlier year, 1963, when we gathered to prepare for an album that we were to record of Alfred Burt's beautiful Christmas carols. The lyrics were written by his father, Bates Burt, an Episcopalian minister, and traditionally were sent to friends as Christmas cards. Eventually Alfred composed the music for his father's lyrics, and those songs—"Some Children See Him," "Caroling, Caroling," and others . . . are still among the most beautiful songs in existence. Many have become well-known traditional carols over the years. Jimmy Joyce was a very conscientious vocal contractor, and he wasn't at all shy about scheduling rehearsals prior to his sessions, in order to ensure that his singers did the very best job possible with their performances. For the Alfred Burt carols project, we sat on folding chairs in his living room and ran through all the arrangements, carefully making notes of our cutoffs, etc. Jimmy's youngest son David, who eventually joined the singer community and has worked on sessions and taught jazz vocals at several colleges here in town for decades now, was on *that* rehearsal evening still crawling around on the floor between our chairs. Bob and Jon Joyce, David's older brothers, also became treasured colleagues of mine over the years, I just got a little head start on them!

There were a couple of more established contractors who booked the choirs for film score work, and there were calls in the datebook for a couple of those people, Bill Lee and Thurl Ravenscroft. Thurl was famous for his very low bass voice, and later in his career, for voicing "Tony the Tiger" in the commercials for Kellogg's Frosted Flakes cereal. And Bill Lee, in addition to contracting singers, did the singing for many of the lead actors who starred in major musical live-action and animated features, but were not "singers" in their own right. He most famously sang for Christopher Plummer in the film *The Sound of Music*.

On the variety television shows, each broadcast usually involved a three-day schedule, and the singers were often the same from week to week, so we became our own little community. For *The Danny Kaye Show* those schedules included a three- or four-hour rehearsal the first day with the singers that involved singing as part of the table read where the cast reads through the scripts, the choral director, and then a wardrobe fitting.

We were always there for the table read so the producers could get a general sense of how everything would fit together, even the music. All of the writers—and there was always quite a team, maybe eight, ten, or more—sat at the side of the room in their folding chairs watching as the lines were read by the cast. We soon learned it was easy to tell which of the writers had written which joke, because that writer was the one laughing the loudest. This was how they hoped to guarantee that their joke stayed in the script!

Then usually the next day or evening, there would be a music rehearsal with the orchestra and a pre-recording with Danny, if he was performing a musical number, or with the guest star, if there was to be a special musical number. Then there would be a run-through the day of the taping, and later, the taping of the show itself. This pretty much was the schedule for Danny's show and also for *The Red Skelton Show,* which I worked on a number of times. Alan Copeland was the choral arranger for Red Skelton's show, and I sometimes filled in if one of his regulars was unavailable, or I was added if the group was expanded. His regular team included Jackie Ward, Vangie Carmichael, and Sue Allen Brown, three of the best singers in the business in those days, and Diana Lee, Bill Lee's daughter, also was a Red Skelton regular. I was highly flattered if called in to substitute for one of them. But with Danny's show I was a weekly part of the vocal group and sometimes participated in on-camera sketches, etc. It was really a wonderful training ground for the business, and I made friendships among that community that lasted for decades.

For the premier season of Danny's show, Johnny Mann, the very busy and successful choral arranger and singer at the time, was hired as choral director and vocal contractor. But I suspect Johnny's personality was a bit too strong, too much of a distraction for Danny to deal with when we did on-camera work. So Johnny was eventually replaced by Earl Brown, also a very wonderful arranger/composer and singer, but someone who sucked less energy out of the room than Johnny did, and had no aspirations to become a star himself, as I suspect Johnny might have. Earl Brown and Billy Barnes created much of the special material that Danny performed on the shows, and Billy on his own was an incredible songwriter. "Have I Stayed Too Long At The Fair?" and "Something Cool" were two of Billy's better-known songs from the *Billy Barnes Revues*, live stage shows that ran at the Las Palmas Theatre in Hollywood during the fifties. Both of those songs had been hit records by artists of the period.

Variety television was a wonderful opportunity for some of the younger singers in those days too, because commercial production was making its way westward from New York, and the busier, more established session singers didn't want to tie themselves up for two or three days in a row and miss a chance to do a national Plymouth spot or a United Airlines commercial where they'd get the big bucks. Occasionally one of the really busy session singers would join us, and I remember watching in awe one day as one of the busiest lady singers in town sat during a lunch break on rehearsal day, filling out her bank deposit slip, listing check after check after check from the pile of paychecks she had brought along that day. I was in awe, trying not to be noticed as I sat nearby. She wasn't trying to impress any of us, she was just making good use of the lunch break time.

On a more personal note, 1965 was also the year that Susie's father and I were divorced, and there were notes about the things that occurred between us at that time. There was no romance in our lives, no soul kind of connection. We were going through the motions of being a responsible married couple, trying to make our way in the business we were both a part of. But this marriage had happened too early in my life. I just didn't really know what it meant to truly love someone yet.

As we both became established in the business, our careers seemed to develop at slightly different paces. Dick was a very talented singer, but even though Lawrence Welk had produced four songs that were released with Dick as an artist, things didn't break for him as he had hoped, in that direction. In the session singer world, his talent was not that unusual, and though he was a solid, good musician and a fine singer, there were others in the community whose only ambition was to be a busy session singer, so the competition was stiff even for the group session work.

Also, it seems like every success in our business greatly relies upon luck. You have to have all the other ingredients, but if you don't have luck, the prize skips over you to the next guy. I had been fortunate to inherit my mom's high soprano notes, and as it happened, had a few chances early on to sub for one of the busiest sopranos in town, Loulie Jean Norman, who was winding down her career in the sixties, but still sang beautifully. So on those occasions I had a chance to show what I could do, which was a high, light soprano tone without vibrato, and a little shimmer when it was the top note in a choral sound. I guess it was a sound that people responded to, because I began to get more calls through 1964 and 1965 for choral work.

Dick and I grew more distant from one another, and notations in that datebook reminded me that we began a brief attempt at marriage counseling in the summer of 1965. I remember clearly one of those sessions, which we would do together, and then would also follow up with individual sessions. The counselor, who was a young man and probably not the most experienced counselor on the planet but part of the group that was covered by our union's insurance plan, commented to me one day that Dick was a hail-fellow-well-met kind of guy, who wanted to put forth a pleasing personality, not necessarily his real personality or an expression of depth, or of genuinely what he felt. And as for myself, one day I was sitting opposite the counselor and he reached out his hands toward me. I didn't know what I was supposed to do, so I took his hands in my hands. He then pointed out that this was what I did in life. I responded as I thought I was expected to respond, not necessarily how I wanted to respond. Which was probably how Dick and I got involved in the first place. It was very revealing of my pattern of responding to other people, instinctively, but not acknowledging my own feelings.

Eventually, I knew that the counseling was not going to improve things, and somewhere later in the datebook was a note I made that indicated some kind of problem: "called lawyer re: Dick followed me." In August, a note about an Ernie Freeman session at Goldstar Records where "Dick caused a scene"; in September there was a notation about a court date "Order to Show Cause"; and on December 15, a hearing in Divorce Court. As I have managed to do throughout life with most of the negative experiences, I've managed to pretty much forget the details of that difficult period of time.

Meanwhile, in the summer of 1965 when Susie was four years old, she and I made our first trip back to upstate New York where my father and his fourth wife Dotty had a charming old Victorian inn, the Osborn House, up in the Catskills. It had belonged to Dotty's family and she and my dad had now taken over and were operating the inn in the little town of Windham, New York. There was a stream that ran alongside the property, a big swimming pool where the children played during the summer months, a huge barn that still looked like it would accommodate cows if needed, a garden, the main inn structure, and additional buildings with more guest rooms, a golf course up the road, and across the street, the Bar and Grill, where at night my dad would sing with the little band that played for dancing. In the winter months, there was a busy ski lift in the area, and a few years later Dad and Dotty began to keep the Osborn House open in the winter months for the skiers as well as for their summer guests.

This was the first of many summer trips Susie and I took there, and I treasured those times, because even if it was only a week, it was an uninterrupted week where Susie and I could have three meals together every day, and she would have family around her. My father and Dotty had two little boys, Susie's two "little brothers" John and Bruce Stevens, though they were actually her uncles. Their first son, my brother John Stevens, was actually born on my twenty-fifth birthday. And Dotty's son Murray, from her first marriage, was about ten years old at the time of our first visit. Again, in that 1965 datebook were notations during our visit; "Susie and I saw home movies"; "Susie fell and bumped her chin"; "Hawaiian night at the grill—Susie hula-danced"; "Went to the Game Farm Zoo"; "walked with Susie to the golf course."

And on that first trip to New York, we had to connect from flight to flight through Kennedy Airport in New York, up to Albany. We made the connection late in the day. I was not an experienced traveler yet and journeying on my own, with a little child, I was fearful we would miss our flight. I held Susie by the hand and we ran from section to section of that huge airport, me in tears, crossing roadways I know we never should have been crossing, franticly trying to find our way from one terminal to the other.

At the end of that first visit—visits that would become a tradition over the next ten years or so—it was back home to our little house in Northridge. In the process of the divorce, Dick had at first insisted that he owned half the house, and that I had to buy it back from him. We had basically lived in it for about a year and a half, prior to separating. But I insisted we also pay my dad back the loan he'd given us for the down payment, and that kind of ended the conversation. The down payment had been $2,000 and the house payments were $97 a month. In those days, $2,000 was a lot of money, more than Dick could come up with to pay my father back. I know that our divorce was painful for him. Although in the beginning, the marriage had not been what he wanted, by the time we had been together for almost five years, I think he was content and settled, and I know the *divorce* was by then absolutely not what he wanted. But I know that for me, it was something that had to happen. When it first came up in conversation, I was trying to treat it as if it was something both of us were agreeable to. I made a little budget, showing how I could manage with only a small amount of child support, child support which as it turned out, would disappear a year or two after the divorce. The budget included the usual essentials of life, but also Susie's Saturday morning pony rides.

Dick moved out of our bedroom and was sleeping on the couch. One night I woke up, went out into the living room in the middle of the night, and found him crying. "What's the matter?" I asked, concerned, thinking perhaps he didn't feel well.

"What do you think?" he asked. And I knew, finally of course, that I had to admit to myself how painful the divorce was for him.

There were some later, conflictive, unpleasant moments before things smoothed out. We had a mutual friend, Carol Lombard, one of the singers who had been on the first Ray

Conniff tour, and Carol had started to do more vocal contracting about that time. She was hiring me on some of the record sessions as a backup singer, and we became good friends. Since we both loved the beach, as did Susie, and the only cost was the parking if we took our picnic lunch, in the summer months Susie and I would often meet Carol at Santa Monica for a day on the sand. One day I received a postcard in the mail from Dick, addressed to "Susie Castle" (who, fortunately, couldn't read yet). It said something about mommy and "Uncle Carol," implying a quite different kind of relationship than our gossipy girl-hangs had been. I guess he had a hard time accepting the fact that the marriage could simply have been over, so needed to imply a lesbian relationship to justify my wanting a divorce in order to preserve his pride.

Dick eventually moved on, to the very loving relationship of twenty or so years with his later-in-life partner, Rayme, who he met shortly after we divorced. He did a lot of live performing and touring, but also continued to do some session work, and when I started to do vocal contracting in the eighties, I included him when I could in many of the film choir sessions that I worked on. I was grateful that later in our lives when we became the grandparents of Susie's two little girls, we could all gather at Susie's home for holidays and feel again like a family. By that time I had wandered into, and out of, two more marriages. I think I've learned as life has unfolded that my problem with marriages was not getting out of them, but getting into the wrong marriages in the first place. It had to do, I think, with my inability to say no, not just in the moment, but as relationships developed in a direction that in my heart, I suspected was not what I wanted. In not wanting to hurt someone's feelings, I ended up breaking their heart. I had romantic dreams, too, of the perfect person—and I shaped whoever the person of the moment was *into* that image. Then of course, later, had to face the fact that on some level I hadn't been brave enough to really think things through.

When we lived in Northridge, Susie's little playmate Julie Marvin and her family lived across the street from us, and the Marvin household eventually became Susie's home away from home during my working hours. It was a blessing for us all, especially after the divorce. Sylvia was able to earn a little extra income for their family of three boys and Julie, and Susie was able to spend time with her best friend in a happy family setting. They'd played together since they were toddlers. In those days Helms Bakery used to have big yellow trucks that did home delivery and sales of fresh baked goods, and the two little girls would stand on opposite sides of the street in their bathrobes waving at each other, waiting for the Helms man to come along and blow his whistle, so their mommies could run out and buy them doughnuts.

I was so grateful for the arrangement with Sylvia, and I would wrap Susie up in her blanket at the end of the evenings after the *Danny Kaye* rehearsals and carry her back home across the street, if the rehearsal or work call was an evening one. There was also another very nice older woman who came to our house to babysit if scheduling required that, but I think Susie preferred being at Julie's.

There are other notations in that little 1965 datebook of "parents meeting" at the Montessori school that Susie was attending for preschool, and "Halloween party at Susie's school," "Lydia sleeps overnight," "Dinner w/mom and Tom" —it seemed like more family events with my family began to show up than there had been on those pages earlier in the year. I remember feeling self-conscious at the school events, being there as a single mom, and especially during the pre-school days, I just felt outside the circle. But the activities grew, with family and in life, and friendships deepened.

The session activities also began to grow. Susie and I continued to live in the little house on Stagg Street in Northridge, and I was still working on *The Danny Kaye Show*. In my heart, I had never given up the secret wish that I might be "discovered" somehow, that I might be an artist, or at least be asked to do more solo vocals. And one day in 1966, my phone rang, and Ginny Mancini, Hank's wife, was on the other end of the call. She was also a busy singer, and we had met while working on *Danny Kaye* and *Red Skelton*. We continued to work together on several other projects.

Ginny was booking the singers for what was to be the Mancini "family" Christmas album. She called to hire me for the session, but also to ask me if I would be comfortable singing a solo on one of the songs. I wasn't sure exactly what that would involve, but I said of course. And I was nervous, but excited.

We recorded the album at RCA Studios, which is another one of the wonderful studios that no longer exists in Hollywood, but once stood on Sunset Boulevard just west of Vine Street. And the solo I was to sing was just the bridge of one of the songs, "The Christmas Song" (chestnuts roasting on an open fire, etc.). We did a couple of songs, and then it was time for me to do the solo, as we began to record "The Christmas Song."

We did it all in one continuous take, the group vocals and the solo. I was just placed close to the mic and stepped closer in for the solo, which was the bridge of the song. The concept, I think, was that this would imply one of the Mancini twin daughters had sung a solo on one of the songs in the "family" album, so they wanted someone with a younger sound, not one of the more established, older singers. We recorded the number, I did my solo along the way, and then we took a break.

As we started to go out into the lobby for coffee, the producer approached Hank and said, "Come in and hear this!" And one of the older singers, who I greatly respected, had come over to me after the last "take" and complimented what I had done, which was a little improvisation in the melody that just felt right, but I hadn't really consciously planned it at the time. When I went into the booth to listen to the playback, I got the sense that it was not appropriate to draw a lot of attention to myself, nor did the people in the booth feel comfortable doing so. The project was Hank's, and we were just part of the picture. But I was so thrilled, because it seemed I had done a good job. I have a copy of that Christmas album, and from time to time it's still played on the air at Christmas time. It was a very special moment for my twenty-six-year-old self, to sing a solo for Henry Mancini, such a famous and respected composer, surrounded by more established singers who'd already been around with him for a couple of decades in the studio.

Two or three years later Hank asked me to sing the demo vocal for a song he was submitting to the Carpenters for Karen Carpenter to sing, "Sometimes." His daughter Felice had written him a sweet note about how much she loved and appreciated him, and it literally became the lyric for the song. We did the demo at Hank's little office in the tall building then on the southeast corner of Sunset and Vine. Hank played the piano, I sang the song, and he sent it off. The Carpenters did record it soon after, but I still treasure the 45rpm disc recording of the demo we did, though it is scratchy and shows its age. It's a gift to have recorded Henry's song with he himself playing the piano.

CHAPTER 15
DINNER AT DANNY'S

Danny Kaye was a brilliant performer, and though he had a reputation for being a very complex guy in his personal *and* professional life, for the most part with us, his choir of sometimes eight or so singers, he seemed to enjoy being part of the ensemble, joking with us, conducting us and being featured, with us singing background for him. We did that often on his show. His brilliant musical arranger, Earl Brown, and Billy Barnes, of the *Billy Barnes Revues*, wrote special material for the show. Billy's *Revues* were very successful live shows that were produced in Hollywood at the Las Palmas Theatre, a small theater just off Hollywood Boulevard. Billy wrote some wonderful songs for those reviews that became hits when recording artists discovered them—"Have I Stayed Too Long at the Fair?," recorded by Patti Page and Barbra Streisand, and "Something Cool," recorded by June Christy. Billy and Earl were a wonderful team as writers, and remained dear friends for many years.

Danny also had two very sweet young women on staff as his personal secretaries. They were both somewhat shy, and Danny seemed to delight in putting them in the spotlight somehow, or embarrassing them, making them blush—not necessarily in an unkind way, though I suspect sometimes they felt it was unkind. To add to his source of material, they both were from places in the South, so he could imitate their southern accents and further embarrass them. The show was taped at CBS Television Center, a big studio complex at the corner of Beverly Boulevard and Fairfax, in Los Angeles, adjacent to the Farmers Market, which was a sprawling complex of little stalls and scattered buildings that offered food, clothing, gadgets, ice cream, and all kinds of things for sale. There was also, and still is to this day, a Du-Par's restaurant on the Farmers Market property. On our lunch breaks we often wandered through the stalls or grabbed lunch at Du-Par's. It held special memories for me because I could remember going there with my mom as a little kid. Du-Par's has since become almost a historic landmark in the Los Angeles area, but the one in Farmer's Market is the only one left.

The weekly routine of the show began with a three-hour vocal rehearsal, usually on Thursday afternoon, and sometimes earlier on that day we'd come in for our wardrobe call, a costume fitting, depending upon what we were involved in that week. Fridays were the on-camera rehearsal days, running through the sketches, polishing the vocal performances, and often on Friday evenings we would rehearse with the orchestra and pre-record songs that needed to be pre-recorded, if they involved choreography or movement on stage. Then Saturday would be the taping of the show, first with a taped dress rehearsal with a live audience, and then the show itself.

It was very important that we look exactly the same on camera at the taped dress rehearsal as we did on the actual taping of the show, because sometimes they would have to cut in part of the performance from the dress rehearsal if there was a problem in the show itself. So we would be in wardrobe and full makeup for both the dress rehearsal and the taped live show. But of course, I was so new to the process I didn't really understand that, and no one had explained it to me. I just thought the dress rehearsal was—a rehearsal. One disastrous day early in the first season before I really knew my way around, I hadn't had time to really do my hair properly for the dress rehearsal, so I pulled it up into a ponytail. Then, between dress and the show itself, I went to "hair and makeup" and they fixed it beautifully, as it should have been. (Looking back on the situation, I'm surprised the people in hair and makeup didn't know enough not to change my hair, but perhaps they were as new to television production as I was.) Obviously, because of the discrepancy in the two tapes, there was no cutting back and forth from the dress rehearsal to show during our on-camera number with Danny. The director was furious, and I definitely heard about it afterwards. I felt so embarrassed, like a total idiot. I was grateful that wasn't the end of my relationship with *The Danny Kaye Show* by my having made it so obvious that I was a beginner in the industry. But I didn't know how long they'd put up with me.

Danny's weekly guests comprised a roster of some of the biggest stars in Hollywood at the time, and it was a gift to see them up close at work. One week during the second season, the French composer Michel Legrand was the guest star on the show. It was very early in Michel's career, in terms of his being well-known in the states, and I remember a couple of the other singers on the show, much more sophisticated and experienced than I, and a bit older, found him a bit geeky; perhaps didn't know all he had done to that point in his career, and kind of made fun of him behind his back. Or maybe it was the thick French accent. But my friend Ian Freebairn-Smith and I, who just happened to know more about him, were totally in awe. As they began to realize his genius, the other singers became just as in awe.

There was, and as a matter of fact, for nearly fifty years remained, a place across the street from the CBS Television Center on Fairfax, a place called the Farmer's Daughter Motel. It had a restaurant/bar, which became our after-hours hang-out following the evening pre-records for the show or late afternoon rehearsals. I remember one wonderful evening after rehearsal during the week in which Michel was the featured guest, when Earl, Michel, Billy, and I went across the street to the Farmer's Daughter, had a couple of drinks, and decided to go piano bar hopping. I often thought about the other customers in some of those bars that night, when Michel Legrand sat in for a song or two, and they probably went through their whole lives never realizing it was an iconic composer they'd been listening to close up in those intimate settings!

Most nights after the evening pre-record, Earl, Billy Barnes, myself, Harvey Korman (who played Danny's foil in most all of the sketches and went on to do the same for Carol Burnett for many seasons to follow), Jackie Powers, my dancer friend who worked on the show, and one or two of the cue-card guys (before there were electronic teleprompters, there would be people on the set holding up huge cardboard cue cards with the performers' lines on them in VERY large print) would all stroll across the street and settle into one of the big round leather booths, where we'd sip our cocktails and talk about the day's events from *our* perspective.

Often too, we'd play this wonderful game where one person would start at the top of a blank page of paper, write two lines, fold the top line over out of sight, and pass it on to the next person. That person would add their two lines to continue the "story" from the one line they could see, folding the first of *their* lines over so it wasn't seen, then pass it on, and so it would go, around the group till we'd filled up the page. In other words, from line to line, no one clearly knew the drift of the story, so just went where it occurred to them to go with their two lines. After it circled the booth, one of the guys would read the stories aloud. You can only imagine, with Harvey Korman and Billy Barnes as part of the group, what those stories turned into! I wish I could remember a few. But they got funnier and funnier as the evening progressed, the stories got off-track, and the second frozen daiquiri kicked in. I always loved writing, and in that setting, to have my writing mingled with Billy Barnes's and Harvey Korman's—well, it just didn't get better than that.

During the week that Michel was Danny's guest, Danny decided to invite Michel, Earl, his two secretaries, and myself up to his house for dinner one evening after rehearsal. I was incredibly excited, as I didn't normally hang out with the star. Danny had a reputation for cooking fine Chinese cuisine, and also at that time, for piloting jet airplanes, something very few people did in those days. He was quite accomplished in many areas of life. I rode with Earl after rehearsal up to Danny's house, which was on one of the winding roads that led off into the hills from Benedict Canyon Drive. Benedict Canyon was one of the lovely, woodsy canyon roads that lifted up into the mountains from the flat, mansion-filled, star-studded flatland streets of Beverly Hills below.

Driving over from CBS, we went up Fairfax Avenue to Sunset Boulevard, then headed west, along Sunset through the residential area, bordered on each side by huge, elegant homes set back from the street behind green rolling lawns and palm trees. We passed the elegant Beverly Hills Hotel, a huge landmark still all after these years, its pink stucco building stretching over several blocks, and then turned right, heading up onto Benedict Canyon Drive.

About half a mile up into the canyon, Danny's street cut off to the right, and we wound further up into the hills. Finally we pulled up into a long circular driveway and stopped in front of the most majestic-looking home I had ever seen. White pillars stood on either side of the front door. A doorman let us in and guided us into the kitchen area where Danny was busy doing the preliminary preparations for our meal; then the doorman somehow disappeared for the rest of the evening. We didn't see much of the house on the way into the kitchen, but it was obviously large, elegant, and intimidating. I was twenty-four and had never been in such a mansion-like setting. Earl was sweet and tried to make me feel less nervous about the evening. Danny was all set to cook, and Michel, Earl, the two secretaries, and I sat on barstools at the bar that partitioned off his chef's work area and watched him chop and stir. He did a magnificent job. But I was surprised at the casual setting of our meal . . . we just stayed there at the bar and ate. In retrospect, that was nice—you could say he treated us like family. But I guess I expected in a house like that, that we would be dining in a formal dining room with elegant settings and crystal wine glasses. I caught a glimpse of the dining room off to the right, with its velvet-cushioned chairs and elegant chandelier hanging above the enormous empty table as we five huddled over the tiny bar. There were photographs facing us from high on the wall behind the bar, of Danny in his pilot's gear, standing proudly beside his jet plane.

We finished our meal, and then Danny ushered us into the living room, elegantly appointed with several comfortable couches, beautiful glass-topped tables, and elegant table lamps bordering the room. Impressive artwork hung on the walls. I still was somewhat intimidated by the surroundings, and certainly by the company. I tried to act like this was just another evening at "my friend Danny Kaye's house." Danny arranged us about the room, and I was seated on a little sofa next to Michel, Danny was sitting with one of his secretaries, and Earl with the other. We sat for a bit, making awkward conversation, and then Danny oddly just got up and very casually, began to walk around the room, turning off the lamps, one by one. I didn't know what to make of it. I sat there in the dark long enough for Michel to share with me that one of his ambitions was to compose music *while* making love. (Don't tell him I told you that. He really is a very lovely gentleman, and it didn't happen *that* evening. Besides, this was very early in Michel's career, and he *was* a young Frenchman. We forgive this kind of thing from young Frenchmen.)

I didn't quite know how to handle this situation with the turning off of the lamps. I didn't want to offend Danny, I didn't want to lose my job, I didn't want to make Earl leave before he wanted to, as I had driven with him. He really was the person I worked directly for and *he* worked for Danny too. I finally just quietly excused myself for a moment, tiptoed out into the hallway where I had noticed a phone earlier, and called a cab.

Earl came out, concerned that I was upset. "Oh, no . . ." I assured him. "It's just getting late and I should get home . . . you know, the babysitter and all . . . I don't want to interrupt your evening!" I didn't want to break up the party, and I hoped Earl would cover for me with Danny. I think it ultimately speaks to Danny's modest attempts at inappropriate behavior that this was the extent of his wildness (at least with us), given his powerful position in the world. Nothing was ever said about the evening, and I can't testify to what went on after I left, but I suspect it was nothing more than a sort of "celebrity spin the bottle," in Danny's mind.

Danny was quite a character. He was one of those people who I think honestly believed there was nothing he couldn't do. He conducted orchestras live in concert to raise money for a children's charity. He piloted those jet planes, he was a gourmet chef, he danced and sang, he made funny faces and entertained millions on screens all over the world. One day a visitor on the set of the show, knowing that Danny proudly considered himself a musician, got to chatting with him about music, musicians, and so forth. At one point the visitor asked Danny for some reason if he played the cello. Danny thought a moment, and then replied perfectly seriously, "I don't know . . . I've never tried." So much for humility.

A couple of years later, Jacques Demy, the director of *The Umbrellas of Cherbourg* (1964) directed another French film, *Les Demoiselles de Rochefort* (1967) for which Michel Legrand wrote the music. They came to Los Angeles to record the English version of the score for *Les Demoiselles*" and Earl helped them cast the character solos and put together the vocal ensemble. I got to work with Michel again at that time, and have wonderful memories of being on the scoring stage at MGM Studios in Culver City, where so many of the iconic films of Hollywood were scored, with Michel and Jacques, doing the English versions of all that music. My good friends Jackie Ward and Sue Allen did the leading roles of the two "Demoiselles" and some of us had other small solos and ensemble parts within the score.

Later, in 1969, Michel came back again to Hollywood, and I was hired to record a solo version of "Ask Yourself Why," the song he wrote for the French film *La Piscine*. The song was eventually recorded by Barbra Streisand for commercial release in the USA, but the version heard in the film is mine. And because it was a foreign film, and we recorded the solo to an already-recorded track in a small studio at Columbia Studios, part of a big complex at Sunset Boulevard and Gower Street in Hollywood, it didn't register at the time that it was for a film. In the early days of my work, I often didn't know the details of what I was working on, who I was working for, etc. I was just there with Michel giving me some directions, and it felt very comfortable. Possibly because that was a foreign film, there was no SAG paperwork.

After the last show of the last *Danny Kaye* season, Bobby Scheerer, the director of the show, had a gathering at his house for the cast and crew. He lived at the end of Yoakum Drive, a little, narrow, winding road that ran off to the east from Benedict Canyon about halfway up between Sunset Boulevard and Mulholland. It was not a pretentious area at all, though it was in what was still considered Beverly Hills "postal," but rather a quiet neighborhood with small, woodsy houses tucked away that had been built randomly over the years on the ivy, oak tree-covered hillsides. I fell in love with that little neighborhood, and a year or so later was able to buy a tiny house there, moving from Northridge in 1966. On one of the visits Susie and I made to look at the property, there was a wild deer roaming up across the hillside behind the house. Susie got so excited when we saw it... "Oh, mommy, look, look...!" She'd never been that close to any kind of wild creature, she'd only seen them at the zoo. When Christmas rolled around that year, all Susie wanted that year for Christmas was a baby deer. I did everything I could think of to make that happen, but of course there were rules against having pet deer in Los Angeles, so all I could do was try to assure her that maybe the one we saw that day lived nearby, and it would come back if we put tempting treats in the backyard.

I thought at the time that the move to Yoakum Drive was a positive one, because it was a "Beverly Hills Postal," and the new public school where Susie would be starting kindergarten was to be Warner Avenue Grammar School in West Los Angeles, at the time considered an excellent public school system. I thought that was a good choice for her schooling. But it turned out to be a difficult move for her because it meant leaving her friend Julie behind, and sadly, there were not many children on that little street. Susie rode on the school bus from the canyon down to Warner Avenue, did eventually make some friends, and joined a Brownie troop, but I know there were many lonely days for her. I felt guilty that I'd taken her away from a neighborhood where her little friend was, and that we'd found ourselves on a street with no kids to play with. We had a lovely older white-haired English woman who babysat, and she was great about playing games with Susie when she was little, but it's not the same as having real playmates. On the drive over to the new house the day we moved in, I taught her in the car, to try to keep her spirits up, a little song I knew as a child, "Make new friends, but keep the old...one is silver, and the other is gold!" She sang along, but not too enthusiastically.

Once she started kindergarten at Warner Avenue school,

she did meet other friends and we could arrange play dates. There was also a little girl she got to know a bit farther up the street, and sometimes they would play after they came home together on the school bus. I was comforted by that new friendship and her family seemed kind.

But one terrible day an afternoon session that I assumed I would be home from before Susie returned from school, went overtime. And it was pouring rain. Racing home, I found Susie sitting on our front porch, drenched in the rain. For some reason, the family up the street wasn't welcoming that day. It broke my heart to find her sitting there, alone, soaking wet, and I beat myself up for not having scheduled a babysitter just in case I were to be late. But it was too late to fix it. It was difficult with the freelance recording session work to plan effectively. Most of the time, it was a guess, and usually I had my bases covered. But not that day.

A few years later we moved to a slightly larger house on Westwanda Drive, another cross-street off of Benedict Canyon, just two blocks farther south toward Sunset. And Susie did find a new best friend who lived two doors away. But those first few years at the Yoakum Drive house were lonely and I'm sure, often sad, because that was the beginning of some very busy working years for me, which took me away for many hours.

CHAPTER 16
LATE SIXTIES RECORDS & JINGLES

During the sixties and seventies, the music business in Hollywood was a different world from what it is now. And in my own experiences, the changes that took place in the years between the pages of the 1965 and 1969 date books were dramatic. By 1969 I was firmly established at the core of the session-singing world, working side by side with the musicians of the "Wrecking Crew", the guys who played on everything, from jingles to hit recording artists to film scores. There was a more structured record business in those days – labels signed artists, labels produced and paid for sessions, and it was a given that they would use union players and singers on union contracts on those dates. On many of those datebook pages the day moved from a 9:00 am session at Universal, to a 1 -5pm session at the Annex, to an 8:00 pm - 11pm or midnight session at Western Recorders, each often for a different contractor and a different project.

In the weeks where that happened more than once or twice, I realized as I looked through these pages how it must have felt to Susie, my then eight-year-old little girl whose mom was missing in action so much of the time. Being a single mom in those days was not easy to manage (I'm sure it isn't easy in today's world either) though I was fortunate even after our move to Benedict Canyon to have found some wonderful care-givers. But schedules sometimes changed last-minute, sessions sometimes ran over-time, and there was no longer the "best friend" across the street to play with, to fill the after-school hours with. It was hard for her, I realize now- much harder than I realized at the time. And when mom gets home at midnight from a session, and must be up at 6:30 to make the school lunch and get the little one off to the school bus on time, she is not always the most patient person in the world. I guess we do the best we can. But so often now, knowing what I do about life, about how important those early years are, I long to be able to do it over, and do it better. In those days too, parenting after a divorce wasn't as much a shared project as it is today. In some ways I suppose that's good – there is, I'm sure, less conflict with decision making, etc. between divorced parents. But there is more shared responsibility. I remember calling Susie's daddy in a panic one morning shortly after we separated, when I had gotten a call to work and had not been able to find a baby-sitter, hoping I could bring Susie to his house for a few hours. His reply basically was, "Gee, I'm sorry, but you wanted this divorce". He was "unavailable" to help out. I have to clarify to be fair, that later in life he was very present for Susie, they worked and sang together, she learned a great deal about the business and about music from him, and they were very close in the later part of their lives. But in the early days, things were not always smooth.

As it was, in those sixties and seventies years in the business, things were so competitive that if you missed even one or two of those session calls, your place was quickly filled, and if the new guy worked out, that could mean the end for you. So those of us who were lucky enough to be on the small team of first call singers, with contractors like Ron Hicklin, Vangie Carmichael, Jackie Ward, John Bahler, Johnny Mann . . . we tried never to miss anything, lest we risk missing it all.

With commercials work there was a paper trail, from the moment we walked into the control booth at Bell Sound

Studios in Hollywood, or Chuck Blore's office, whose studios were on Argyle in Hollywood, there was paperwork to sign, either from an agency or a well-prepared contractor if the session was for a commercial. Scattered through the pages of that 1969 calendar were notations of sessions for Plymouth, Spearmint, Chevy (that one involved Jimmy Webb!) Ford, Admiral TV, and numerous other products. Many of those sessions of course, were done as demos the agencies would present to the clients for approval or consideration, and quite possibly might never hit the airwaves. So we ran from session to session, most of the time making modest paychecks. But good records were kept and agencies behaved responsibly. If a commercial demo *did* hit the air, if it became part of a major campaign, it was a bit like striking gold.

I remember one commercial I worked on for Jack Halloran, probably somewhere around 1966, for something new and strange called "Mastercard". It was this little plastic thing with which you could go into a store and buy things. You didn't' have to write a check or use cash. You could just give them this little plastic card, and voila! (I had one of the Standard Oil little plastic cards, which had by the way been canceled when news of my divorce reached their offices. Never mind that I had been the one paying the bills with the money that primarily I had earned for our household at that time. I was the "wife" so–out you go, little lady, in 1965.)

The singers were all fascinated with this new product, "Mastercard" that you could use any place, as we listened to Jack Halloran explain it to us.

Today, several things have happened that have resulted in dramatic changes in our industry. First, technology --- which has allowed for voice-over commercials and singer tracks to be done from home studios to instrumental tracks sent from a music house or a producer. Those can be done as auditions or as finals – but there is no person or office involved to send along a contract or confirm what the rate should be, or even specify that it must be on a union contract. For some reason, advertisers seem to have become terribly intimidated by the idea of dealing with the union. So they offer "buyouts" – sometimes at figures which exceed the cost they would incur if they *did* do the spot on a union contract. It is a somewhat complicated pay structure, because the fees depend a great deal on what the airplay ends up being, and sometimes that is not known at the time the spot is recorded. Maybe there needs to be a simpler system worked out. And with new media -- what streams currently on internet, etc. – it's almost like the wild west out there. If you *do* manage to get something on a union contract but the overall budget for the project is below a certain figure, you may end up having to negotiate your own rates. It's a new area of work, a new process. Perhaps things will smooth out along the way.There are times though, when I feel so grateful to have been a part of the business when I was, and sad for the young people now struggling to try to make a living with their craft, their talents, their art--when some producers don't seem to be willing to pay for it.

Returning to stories from the "golden age'- back in the day, if we were at TTG Studios on Mc Cadden Street off of Sunset and La Brea, or Evergreen Studios in Burbank, or the Annex in Hollywood, for a record session or to record music for the Ice Follies or Ice Capades --if we worked at Capitol on North Vine St. or Columbia Studios at Sunset and Gower, it was all part of a smoothly operating system. Most traditional artists recording at that time – Andy Williams, Ed Ames, Vicki Carr, Frank Sinatra, Dean Martin, Sammy Davis Jr. – all used backup singers, usually a mixed group of eight singers, four guy and four girl singers. There were also sessions for the Johnny Mann Singers and the Percy Faith Singers, slightly larger ensembles, and composers like Hank Mancini and Michel Legrand used small choirs to perform the works for their album projects.

Then there were also more contemporary rock groups like

Paul Revere & the Raiders, or Gary Puckett & the Union Gap – which were mostly self-contained, but sometimes added some group vocal backup sounds in addition to the singers in the group. I remember on one particular session at Columbia for Gary Puckett & the Union Gap, we had arrived early and the musicians were still recording their instrumental tracks. At this particular session apparently, the producer or the label had insisted on utilizing some of the musicians from the Wrecking Crew to augment the band members. It was obvious that this decision had not been met warmly by at least one of the guys in the band, who had asserted his place as a core member of the group by setting himself up directly behind the guitar player who had been brought in to record his part, and playing along. I never learned how the guys in the control booth handled that, whether he was picked up on mic or not. But I loved seeing that kind of assertiveness on the part of the young musician. It was their band, and dammit, he was going to play on their record just like he had played on all their other records.

Once too, on our way into that same studio, Columbia at Sunset and Gower, we were waiting to enter at a side ramp for an earlier session to finish up, and the band members from Sly and the Family Stone were also nearby, instruments piled up, waiting to go inside. I was in awe of them. To me, they looked on the far side of adventurous—I assumed of course that they regularly did drugs, hung out in shady places, and probably were all armed. (None of which of course, was actually true.) Later I got to know the sister of one of the guys in the band, who was a session singer and the sweetest person in the world. She did a lot of Gospel work in town. I think my reaction to the band, my thinking they looked "dangerous" was because anyone that hip had to live a wild lifestyle and was therefore dangerous. I considered myself *so* un-dangerous, so vanilla and uninteresting by comparison.

I remember another session there at Columbia when we

recorded some background vocals for an Andy Williams project. Andy was not in the studio, but Dick Glasser, the producer of this particular album, was in the booth running the session. "Hot Pants", the very *short* version of shorts, had just become the fashion of the day – were *very* embarrassingly short pants worn as if they were perfectly normal attire by young women as they went about their daily business. So of course, being style-conscious, I had bought a pair – pale blue denim, with a matching jacket. This was also the period of the famous "bra-burning" era, the beginning of the feminist movement. I had not advanced to that level yet, but I did wear my "hot pants" to the Andy Williams session this day. I can't recall the specific comment that came from Dick Glasser in the booth, but a lewd remark was forthcoming over the head-phones, something about my appearance that day, and the "hot pants". Embarrassed, I responded by blurting out, "Oh, Fuck off!" I *never* spoke that way. I don't know what took over in my language control system that day. But it did shut Dick Glasser down for the rest of the session. And my fellow singers didn't quite know what to make of it. I'm pretty sure that was the last time I wore that particular outfit to a session *or* told a producer to fuck off. And very sure it was the last time I spoke to Dick Glasser in that way. He graciously allowed me to be booked on other sessions and the incident was never mentioned.

Looking through the list of top 100 hits of 1968 and 1969 I find a lot of the folks we worked with listed there. In 1968, Herb Alpert recorded "This Guy's In Love With You" by Burt Bacharach and Hal David, and I sang on it and got to contract the background vocals. We did the session at Goldstar, the studio which was legendary for being the source of so many hit records in the early years. Sonny and Cher recorded there, and Phil Spector made almost all his records at Goldstar, occasionally waving a loaded gun around between takes. The session for Herb was the first time I had been in any studio with Burt, and he was there, playing piano on the record. Herb was there too, doing his vocals in the vocal booth. What a great memory to have had all these years. Shortly thereafter, I worked with my friend Jackie Ward who contracted Burt's first West Coast live concert as an artist himself, in San Diego. Burt was using four female singers in those early concerts and The Carpenters were his opening act.

On that same list of hits I noticed Gary Pucket & the Union Gap, Sly & the Family Stone, Simon & Garfunkel, The Beatles, Aretha Franklyn, Gary Lewis & the Playboys (Ron Hicklin voiced some of those records) The Bee Gees, Jose Feliciano, Dionne Warwick, Sergio Mendes... it was a really cool musical time.

In 1969 after a rather long break, Elvis Presley snuck back onto the charts with "Suspicious Minds". I had worked with Elvis the year before, for B.J. Baker, another singer and vocal contractor, on the *Elvis Presley 1968 Comeback Special*, a TV show produced in Hollywood. So I guess the "Comeback Special" worked for him!

Also on the 1969 charts were songs by Three Dog Night, Sly & the Family Stone, The Fifth Dimension, The Archies (singing their hit "Sugar, Sugar" written by my friend Andy Kim, who also had Baby I Love You on the charts that year) Bob Dylan, Jackie De Shannon, Glen Campbell, Harry Nilsson, Tom Jones, Paul Revere & the Raiders, B.J. Thomas, Marvin Gaye...it makes me smile just thinking about all those artists and the songs they recorded that I loved so much. We didn't sing with all those artists, but we did sing with quite a few of them.

One of the sweet memories I have is of Glen Campbell, before he was a star and was just part of the Wrecking Crew. The musicians were usually all set up and ready to go by the time the singers walked into the studio and when I walked in, if Glen was on the session, he would pick up his guitar and sing "Sally was a good old gal"! *Glen Campbell,* for heaven's sake.

In 1960 Frank Sinatra had started his own label, Reprise Records, and the offices for that label were located in the United Recorders building, 6050 Sunset Blvd. in Hollywood. Many of Frank's own sessions were done in United A or B, and typically as he would arrive, my heart and every other woman's heart in the room would quicken its pace. Frank would run through the song standing by the conductor/arranger's podium, and then he would record one or two takes, maybe three at the most, of a song and he would be done. He was so well-prepared, so skillful on the mic, nothing in those days had to be repeated or fixed. No one sings the words like Frank does. I mean literally, rolls through them, pronounces them – embraces the consonants and the shapes like he does.

Frank's hits count had begun to suffer by the mid-sixties, and Jimmy Bowen, a staff producer for Reprise, convinced him to record "Strangers In The Night", a song he really didn't want to record, in 1966. But it became a huge hit, and a number of hits then followed. We worked with Jimmy Bowen a number of times there at United Recorders, for Frank, for Keely Smith, Dean Martin and Sammy Davis Jr. sessions. One evening, when Frank was dating Mia Farrow, she came with him to one of his sessions there at United, along with his entourage of bodyguards and business handlers. Mia was twenty-one and Frank, fifty years old when they were married, and on this night they had just begun to date, or make it known that they were dating. She looked very young, and had just cut her hair very short in declaration of her own self-hood. Often it felt like we were flies on the wall, watching the important stuff going on around us with the famous people with whom we just somehow miraculously found ourselves in the same rooms.

We did many sessions in the back studio at the end of the hall at Western Recorders on Sunset, where Wayne Newton recorded many of his vocals. The Mamas & Papas and The

Association recorded in the smaller side studio off the hall, usually with Bones Howe, the engineer of the decade at the helm.

And across the street, on the other side of Sunset at Gower, in Columbia studios, most of the Percy Faith sessions took place, and also many of Andy Williams' and Jim Neighbor's sessions. It was so interesting to see this character everyone thought of as "Gomer Pyle", the country bumpkin, open his mouth and hear his beautiful operatic voice come sailing forth.

Occasionally one of the very hip groups, like Country Joe & the Fish, or The Association would do some song that required additional voices, or female voices, and I would get to sing on something a little more contemporary than what I considered most of my session work to be. Also when Simon and Garfunkel split up and Art Garfunkel did his first solo album, *Angel Clare*, I was hired to sing the solo obligato on the song "Barbara Allen". We recorded the vocal as an overdub in a small studio in LA after the track had already been done. I really never knew the backstory of that project until recently, when I went to hear Art speak at an event here in LA and looked up more information about the record, only to discover the instrumental track was recorded in Grace Cathedral, NYC. and that my friend Jackie Ward, the wonderful singer with whom I worked so often during the sixties and seventies, had sung the section at the beginning of the record, which was a duet harmony line with Art. All the recording work was fun and challenging, whether it was for a record session or a jingle or a pre-record for one of the television productions, or a film score session on one of the film studio scoring stages.

In 1969 Ron Hicklin hired me to work on the Burt Bacharach score of *Butch Cassidy & the Sundance Kid* on the 20th Century Fox scoring stage. I sang lead in the eight-voice group, and had some solo lines in the score. Burt's score was unusual for its time, and the very popular song "Raindrops Keep Falling on My Head" was written for the film. Shortly after that, Burt asked me if I was available to travel in concert with him, but my father had just had a serious health issue in upstate New York, had been hospitalized, and I just felt I had to be there with him. So I missed that first opportunity to travel with Burt. A couple of years later I worked on the score of *Lost Horizons* and ran into Burt shortly afterward at a Grammy event. I made a point of telling him that if he ever had a vacancy for another singer, I would so love to work for him in concert, and he said something like "Oh, you're too busy now to go on the road!" He was being very kind and flattering. (I think he just wanted me to beg him, so I did!) I traveled for the first time doing one of the solos from *Lost Horizons*, "The World Is a Circle", and the song also involved a children's choir, which my daughter Susie, then age eleven had sung on for the film score recording, so she got to go along as part of the children's choir, performing with the Jimmy Joyce singers. They also needed a chaperone or two, so my younger sister Lydia, who was about eighteen or nineteen, got to go along too as one of the kid wranglers! Then, beginning on the next concert tour, I joined Burt's group as one of the four girl singers, did a little solo work along the way, and thus began the unfolding of the Bacharach Years.

CHAPTER 17

SINATRA, THE SMELL OF GARLIC & THE WRONG TRAIN

As the Ron Hicklin Singers, we found ourselves with more and more activity in the recording business in Hollywood as the sixties unfolded, and we worked side by side almost on a daily basis with the "Wrecking Crew," the recording musicians who were at the core of every record session or jingle recorded in town. They actually *were* some of those "artist" bands, anonymously, doing the sessions but not the live concert appearances. And we singers began to hang out after evening sessions at the places where the community of those very hip musicians, radio DJs, record producers, and artists hung out. One of the most popular and special places was Martoni's Restaurant on Cahuenga Boulevard just north of Sunset. It was a classy (though in a mafia-hangout kind of way) Italian restaurant rumored to have been owned, at least in part, by Frank Sinatra. The entrance was on the sidewalk that ran northward up from Sunset, one block over from the RCA Studios. During those years a great many projects were done at RCA, so Martoni's was the natural place to drift over to following sessions there, but we often would end our evenings at Martoni's no matter where a recording session had just taken place.

In order to get to the dining area of the restaurant, you sort of scooted along through the narrow space behind the barstools at the bar, where on most nights you'd find at least two or three DJs, the currently unemployed ones easiest to spot by the number of empty glasses and overflowing ashtrays in front of them. Low lights, Sinatra playing over the sound system, the scent of garlic unmistakable in the air.

Our little group was usually comprised of Ron himself; sometimes Ian Freebairn-Smith, a singer but also a composer/arranger who had begun to work with record artists and also wrote a lot of commercials in the midsixties; Stan Farber, singer and dear friend who had been part of Ron's original four-guy vocal group, the Eligibles; Al Capps, who had also sung with the Eligibles and was beginning to do arrangements for some of the biggest stars of the era; Jackie Ward, wonderful singer and friend who had begun also to do contracting as well; and Carol Lombard, (the singer, *not* the movie actress who had been married to Clark Gable and died in a plane crash). Carol was one of the first vocal contractors who had hired me to do session work in town after we met on the first Ray Conniff tour. She became a lifelong friend over the decades, and I'm proud to be the godmother of her son Christopher Afarian, though I did a miserable job of it over the years of his youth. I think I got to maybe only one or two of his high school football games. Chris was brilliant on the football and soccer fields. Carol worked on some of the early Elvis Presley films and records, and also worked with a lot of the soul artists of the day with producer/arranger H. B. Barnum.

Sometimes too, the group at Martoni's included Sue Allen Brown, a wonderful singer with some amazing credits through the fifties, sixties, and seventies; Vangie Carmichael, singer and another of the vocal contractors busy at the time; and Jimmy Bryant, singer and also a composer/arranger for various artists, for Ice Capades sessions, for the Lido shows in

Paris, France, and other music projects of the era. In the seventies the Bahler brothers, John and Tom, became part of the group and eventually established their own projects, John moving into jingle producing, and Tom, into songwriting and producing, working closely with artists like Michael Jackson and Quincy Jones. Ron himself eventually established Killer Music, his commercials production business and recording studio, and had tremendous success as a jingle house. But mostly in the early days it was Ron, Stan, Jackie and I, and Ian, with a special guest or two upon occasion, hitting Martoni's after a gig.

Usually we'd run into a few of the musicians from the Wrecking Crew. They too would drift into Martoni's but they more often than not ended up hanging at the bar. We worked almost daily with that amazing crew of musicians who could play anything, any style, read any score instantly . . . that is, except for Glen Campbell, who played with the Wrecking Crew before he came into his own as an artist. He was not a "reader" but he had such a great feel on his instrument, the guitar, that Tommy Tedesco, another amazing sideman, would play Glen his guitar part once through, and Glen would nail it on the first take when the red light came on. Often Glen would come up with new riffs that were even better than what the arranger had written, and that was fine with most of those arrangers.

Our little group of singers usually sat at a corner table at Martoni's, the five or six of us, after finishing the backup vocals behind Andy Williams, or Sinatra or Dean Martin (we're talkin' the late sixties/early seventies here) and pretended we belonged with the high rollers who'd spend the evening in that backroom private space, discussing their next big deal. Actually we'd just observe them, for the most part being quite happy with who we were.

There was a room upstairs, a sort of semi-private meeting space where deals were also concluded or events and celebrations held that were even slightly more private than what the main downstairs area would provide for. A sign hung over the stairway leading up to it that actually read The Up-A-Stairs Lounge. One evening, upstairs in that lounge, Sinatra presented Bill Cosby with three Gold albums. Cosby had recently been signed as an artist to record with Frank's new record label, Reprise. Events like that went on nightly.

We would often run into some of the celebrities of the moment. One evening Mama Cass Elliot was sitting at the bar, most likely waiting for a colleague. And in the little private booth toward the rear of the dining area, which you could see into through a large open area in the partition that separated it off, we might see Sammy Davis Jr. or Frank himself, with a group of pals.

Another interesting couple of guys who often visited Martoni's, and who I had somehow met because of a recording session they did, were the Scotti brothers, Tony and Ben. Tony had a deal as a recording artist, and at that time was also pursuing a career as an actor. He had one of the leads in *Valley of the Dolls*. The Scotti brothers later went on to establish a production company and a record label. My impression of them at the time was that they were connected in many ways and on many levels with the activities of Hollywood (and possibly with the owners of Martoni's). Both had also played professional football, Ben, as an NFL player for the Eagles. As producers, they later created the very successful series *Baywatch*. Ben and I went to dinner a couple of times, and I remember distinctly one night after he picked me up, when we made a stop at one of the hotels along the Sunset Strip because he had to "drop something off." We left the car with the valet parking attendant as it was to be a quick stop, and ran into the bar, where a group of several older, very Italian-seeming gentlemen were having a drink. They greeted each other in their native tongue, and Ben handed off a brown paper bag of . . . something. Then we continued on to dinner. I couldn't shake the feeling that I had just participated in a drug run. Most likely that was a creation of my lively imagination, and someone's dad from out of town had just forgotten his toothbrush.

On one particular night, the current object of my affection and I were to officially celebrate the happy culmination of an overly long relationship, he being a man who for some time had been unable to decide whether he was married or single, just about the time we met. But that question finally became settled in his mind, or so it seemed, and he'd suggested announcing the happy news of our engagement that evening at Martoni's, to the pals who'd been witness to the long, ongoing drama of our precarious relationship. No ring had been purchased, so there were no visible clues, save the constantly adoring look in my eyes whenever we were together.

We'd finished the first round of drinks, anticipation hanging in the air. These friends knew us well, and suspected what the reason was for the gathering that evening.

But the conversation began to drift from one unrelated subject to the next, while another round of drinks was ordered, the clock ticked relentlessly toward closing time, and the man of my dreams grew quieter and quieter.

Finally, as the crowded restaurant began to thin, and other customers paid their checks and bid the bartender goodnight, one by one our friends decided to bid uncomfortable goodnights as well, and left, like passengers realizing they'd gotten on a train that was never going to leave the station.

I realized I'd stayed too long on that same train, and eventually said my own goodbye to that particular relationship, and moved on. I experienced such disappointment that evening, after three or four years of an off-and-on relationship, that it pretty much ended it for me. He apologized for the evening and tried to get things back on track, but it just never was the same. He eventually moved on as well and has been happily remarried over the last thirty years or so. But for a long time after that evening, Sinatra and the smell of garlic made me cry.

Sadly, Martoni's was destroyed in the 1994 earthquake in Los Angeles and never restored. A little recording studio now fills that space, and one of the gentlemen who worked in the restaurant had managed to get together enough resources to leave Martoni's and open Marino Ristorante in 1983, another beautiful Italian restaurant nearby on Melrose Avenue. Marino's still serves its delicious dishes and carries on the tradition of fine Italian cuisine.

CHAPTER 18
THE OCCASIONAL #METOO DAYS

We pass through many interesting stages as we journey through life and through this fascinating business, and sometimes the memories of our earlier experiences pop up years later in the context of what is *then* going on in the world. Thus it was that with the revelations in October 2017 of the sexual harassment charges (and more) against Harvey Weinstein that brought what seemed like hundreds of women out of the darkness with their own tales of such incidents—in Hollywood, in government, in all aspects of life—I found myself thinking back a number of decades ago to my earlier years in the business, wondering if there had been any of those incidents that I had just quietly swept aside. But as I thought back, for me those incidents didn't happen so much with celebrities or show business folks in the crass ways they've been described in the newspapers this week. Those kinds of incidents happened, for the most part, in the course of everyday life—getting grabbed by my medical doctor as I was walking down the hall on my way to check out with his receptionist and having a kiss forced on me. This man was, in my young mind, an authority figure accosting me. I was new not only to being *grabbed* by some doctor, I was new to doctors, as I'd grown up in a Christian Science family. It happened early in my life when I was just making my own decisions in life. I was totally inexperienced and didn't know how to handle that. I don't think I ever said anything to anyone about it. His intern in that office, a very sweet and proper young gentleman, many years later became my primary doctor when someone referred me to him, and he had his own practice. I hadn't recognized his name, but I remembered his face and mentioned the incident to him. He didn't seem terribly surprised, but also was hesitant to comment.

And a bit earlier, when I worked in that insurance office the summer before beginning classes at UCLA in 1957, my boss Mr. Pond did his number of trying to grab me as I passed his office on my way to the parking lot.

In the entertainment business, however, the choices I made were more my own, in terms of what eventually did or didn't become romantic involvements. Yes, they were often with people I worked with or for, because that was my world, my community. Those were the people I met, got to know and care about, and the relationships always began in a respectful way. I dated several people that I worked with, or for. Those relationships always began from a working relationship and lasted years, not just a few hours in a hotel room or an office. So things worked pretty well, in that regard.

There were only a couple of rather uncomfortable moments that I recall happening in a workplace setting. And they weren't hands-on physical confrontations, but just awkward performance situations I found myself in, I guess not unlike an actress who might have to do a nude scene as part of a role, or say some line she felt uncomfortable with. One situation, I suspect, was a setup created purely for the fun and frolic of the guys (I won't call them gentlemen) in the control booth. We were scoring a film in 1967, *The President's Analyst*, with composer Lalo Schifrin. Lalo is originally from Buenos Aires, Argentina, and had begun his career playing and composing jazz, and writing arrangements and compositions for other jazz artists. From there, he began to develop his remarkably successful film scoring career. He is well-known for his body of work during the sixties and seventies—famously for his *Mission: Impossible* TV theme, and for the many film scores he did for the Clint Eastwood films from the sixties through the eighties. I was privileged to work on a number of those Clint Eastwood films with him. At the time, particularly in the sixties, the breathy, soft, kind of intimate sexy female sound seemed to be in high demand, and I was someone known to make that sound. So I did the solo cues for *Dirty Harry, Cool Hand Luke, Coogan's Bluff* . . . and later in 1972, for Michael Small, the score for *Klute* used that same soft female vocal sound, but in a more scary, ominous way.

For *The President's Analyst,* a score I worked on in 1967, Lalo had written some group vocals for three girls and three guys, and Vangie Carmichael, his vocal contractor, had hired the singers. There was one cue written just for one solo girl's voice, and I was asked to stay after we finished the other vocals to perform it. It was an interesting cue, with snippets of other song references, and I also sang a second harmony part with myself. The cue, "Look Up (Joy to the World)," as I listen to it today on YouTube, sounds very simplistic, almost childlike. The whole film was really ahead of its time too, politically I think, as I view the clips today.

While I was singing the cue, for some reason the guys in the booth—I assume the director, maybe a producer too—decided that for one of the love scenes they would like to add some female lovemaking, orgasmic sounds to the music track. So I was asked to stand out on the big empty scoring stage, on mic, in front of all those men behind the glass in the booth, and sound as if I was being made love to. Uh-huh. Not *very* embarrassing. I don't think I was very good at it either, because every once in a while, I caught a glimpse of them giggling through the glass window between the scoring stage and the control booth. I think they were laughing because they could see how embarrassed I was, and that I definitely wasn't a professional at *that* particular profession. Those sounds did make it into the film, so apparently they were actually intended to do so. This was one time I didn't mind not receiving screen credit!

I have a recollection of one other rather uncomfortable solo session in 1984, for the film *Body Double* that had a lot of nude scenes in it. The description on the Rotten Tomatoes website reads: "Brian De Palma invites you to witness a seduction . . . a mystery, a murder. It's *Body Double*, a spine-tingling look at voyeurism and sexuality from the modern master of suspense . . . a gripping adult thriller of eroticism and horror." The composer was an Italian musician, Pino Donaggio, and this was the first time I had worked with him. He wrote some solo vocal cues for the film—very soft, sexy, breathy sounds, a sort of improvisational interpretation of the scenes—for all the provocative nude dance scenes viewed through the window by the voyeur across the way. It seemed to me a much looser approach to "interpretive" vocal cues, but the man was Italian, so maybe they did things differently over there, I thought. And for some reason, I thought it was an Italian film, because, well, *he* was Italian. So I figured I'd never be embarrassed by my performance being seen locally. I remember inviting my brother and sister-in-law to join me for a studio screening of the film I did later receive an invitation to, and suddenly being very embarrassed at the content we were viewing on the big screen. I had focused on the excitement of having done the entire score as the solo vocalist, but now felt like I'd invited them to a porn flick! I don't think my brother Charles minded much, but I'm not too sure how my sister-in-law, Patti, felt. So yeah, even we off-camera performers have to do nude scenes from time to time.

But these situations, a bit embarrassing as they were, never put me personally in harm's way. Oh, there *was* one evening—a producer of some TV show project whose son is now also a producer and adds the "Jr." after his name, so I won't mention it here . . . after a session at a studio in Holly-wood, offered to give me a ride after dark to my car which was parked a few blocks away in a kind of iffy neighborhood. He had been perfectly polite and orderly throughout the session so I assumed he would continue to be so. But I had a hard time getting out of that car, and I remember him, irritated at the lack of cooperation he was encountering, saying something like, "Oh f'Christ sake, come on . . ." as I had to forcefully wrestle my way out of his grasp. But there weren't many of those occasions, or that one wouldn't come so clearly to mind!

There were mostly very respectful gentlemen along the way, and they far outnumbered those who weren't. And as a soloist, except for the little story with *The President's Analyst*, things generally went quite smoothly. *Klute* went very smoothly, but I was nervous as I recorded the solo vocals with the live orchestra, because if I screwed up, everyone in the orchestra—all forty or so players—would have to start the cue over. It was my first really major solo work in an important film working with the live orchestra instead of doing vocals later as overdubs, which added to the nervousness. Another very pleasant solo session was for composer Sid Ramin, a vocal overdub to the already-recorded track of his song "Sugar in the Rain" for the film score of *Stiletto*. I don't think at the time I knew that song was going into a film, and again, I never had a SAG contract for it, though I did get paid for the session. It's very possible that at the time of the recording, Sid didn't even know the song would end up in the film. I assure you we weren't knowingly doing nonunion work at the time, but the contractual stuff, the technicalities of the paperwork, were like Greek to me in those days, just as they are today for the younger new singers in our community until they begin to get more involved with the union and with contracting. By the time I was doing vocal contracting I had learned the details of the process.

Dot Records, Sally Stevens, Artist/Song writer,
produced by Herb Alpert & Lou Adler 1959

Danny Kaye TV Variety
Show, CBS, 1964-65

Danny
Kaye TV
Variety
Show,
CBS,
1964-65

Ray
Conniff
Session,
Singers
& Ray,
1964

Singers, w/ Michael Legrand and Jacques Demy, Recording of English vocals for "Les Demoiselles de Rochefort", MGM Scoring Stage. 1967

"Elvis Presley 1968 Come-Back Special" Singers at Pre-record, Western Recorders

(Left to right) John Bahler, B.J. Baker, Elvis, Sally Stevens, and Bob Tebow recording the *Live A Little, Love A Little* soundtrack at Western Recorders

Sally Stevens, w/ daughter Susie

NARAS (Grammys)
MVP Awards,
Session Musicians
and singer Sally
Stevens, 1972–73

NARAS (Grammys)
MVP Awards,
Session Musicians
and singers Sally
Stevens & Tom
Bahler, 1973–74

NARAS (Grammys)
MVP Awards,
Session Musicians
and singer Sally
Stevens, 1974–75

Burt Bacharach, w/
Singers Gene Merlino,
Tom Bahler, Jimmy Joyce,
Sally Stevens, Carolyn
Dennis, Melissa Mackay,
& Marilyn Jackson, "Lost
Horizons" tour, 1973-74

Left: Burt
Bacharach,
Australia
Tour, 1973

Right: Sally
Stevens,
Headshot,
1978

Above: Sally Stevens, Performance at
The Room Upstairs, Le Café, 1979

Right: Postcard Mailer, Le Café
Performance, 1979-80

Film Shoots, TV Spot for KBIG Radio, L.A.
Below: 1980; Right: 1981

Interview
article, Wall
Street Journal

Sally Stevens Taught Michelle Pfeiffer to Sing Like A Pro

By Joanne Kaufman

Director Steve Kloves took a big gamble on Michelle Pfeiffer's voice. He'd cast the actress, not exactly known for her way with a song, as the singing star of "The Fabulous Baker Boys - and he wanted her to carry the tunes herself. So the call went out for Sally Stevens.

Choir for
Harry Connick
Jr. TV
Christmas
Special, 1993

Concert review

Grammy Jazz Jam

The Jazz Bakery, Culver City
Monday, Jan. 31
By Tony Gieske

She said she spends all her working days or nights in a windowless room where the only light is the faint bulb above the music stand and where the watchword is never sing by yourself and don't sing in front of outsiders.

But Sally Stevens broke the code of the session singer, which is what she is, and came out for the first Grammy Jazz Jam, where she did both of these things. Her voice, which you've heard on many soundtracks, is natural, unadorned and personal, and after softening them up with a touching version of "There Will Never Be Another You," she delicately extracted the broken heart from "Where Do You Start" and left her listeners shattered.

Of course, she had no small ration of assistance from the Grammy jammers, no strangers

themselves to the darkened studio, guys such as Mike Malvoin, the pianist; John Guerin, the drummer; Chuck Berghoffer, the bassist; and Mitch Holder, the guitarist. All were either named to the NARAS Most Valuable Player list or are, like Malvoin, officers of the Recording Academy.

These are the fastest of the fast guys from the studios, as you would be unable to doubt after hearing Lanny Morgan's commanding high velocity alto saxophone solo on "After You've Gone." Or Pete Christlieb's road-hugging tenor saxophone work on the Jerome Kern harmonic swerver "Nobody Else But Me." Or the diffidently spectacular utterance of Steve Huffsteter's trumpet improvisation on a high-speed "Alone Together."

If these guys had a flaw, it was a certain unwillingness to restrain their hard-won and richly reward-

See **GRAMMY** *on page 16*

ywoodreporter.com   Wednesday, February 2, 2000

Hollywood Reporter Review / Sally Stevens Grammy Jazz Performance, 2000

Left: Performance w/ "Chick Singers" evening, Redondo Beach, CA, 2010

Below: John Williams w/ Sally Stevens & Children's Choir / Sony Scoring Stage, Trailer for Harry Potter film

Sally Stevens w/ Clint Eastwood,
Society of Composers & Lyricists
Christmas Event, 2012

Sally Stevens professional
shot, 2017

Singers,
EMMY Awards
Broadcast, 2017

From left to right:
Eric Bradley,
Teri Koide, Sandy
Hall Brooks, Sally
Stevens, Dorian
Holley, Amick
Byram

Screenshot from
SIMPSONS 30th
Season Event,
Universal Theme
Park, CA

Autographed Vocal Chart
from Harry Connick Jr.
Christmas Special
Recording

Autographed Vocal Chart
from Arranger/Composer
Pat Williams – Amy Grant
1st Christmas CD, 1983

Autographed Vocal Chart from James Horner,
scoring session "Mighty Joe Young", 1998

CHAPTER 19

THE SEVENTIES

Throughout the late sixties and early seventies I was especially blessed, in terms of my connection to the business and my recording activities. In those datebooks I found among my garage memorabilia, the pages are filled with, in most cases, some kind of session every day. I was working on the *Sonny & Cher* TV show; I was doing commercials with Ron for various jingle producers (Pepsi, Toyota, Datsun, Busch Beer, etc.). I was doing commercials work for Chuck Blore Agency; there were many recording sessions at Columbia Recording Studios, at A&M Studios, at Capitol Records, United Studios, Lost on Larrabee Studio, and film scoring on the Paramount Stage M, which sadly is no longer in existence. We did record sessions with artists Vickie Carr, Ray Charles, Neil Diamond, Bobby Vinton, Snuff Garrett, Alan Copeland, and Ray Conniff, and that's just a walk through the January and February pages. We worked on the music for the Ice Capades and for films along the way, but in those days, as I was still not contracting but just showing up for work, I often had only the name of the contractor and the time and place of the session. Rarely was there a note of the artist, or the project name. It was like opening a door and finding a surprise party on the other side. I just wish I'd written down the details that were missing, at least after the fact. It's hard to remember them after all these years.

The contractors in those days were primarily Ron Hicklin, but also Vangie Carmichael, Jackie Ward, and John Bahler. Bill Lee and Bill Cole were still quite actively contracting, and Johnny Mann was very busy with the Johnny Mann Singers, which I sometimes got to be a part of. Things were starting to expand a bit in terms of which singers were getting more calls to contract.

Throughout the 1972 book, the pages were filled on the majority of days with more than one project or session. I was pretty much at the center of the work activity, but the painful part was because of that, I was missing in action about ninety percent of the time, in terms of being a present and loving mom to my little girl. By the seventies, Susie and I had moved to the house on Westwanda Drive, and she had found her new best friend one house up the street, so it was not quite as lonely as the Yoakum house had been, but still, I missed so much time with her, so much of her life. Because I was our only source of financial support, I justified my busy schedule at the time, and also because the business was so very competitive; if you didn't show up, they still might find someone they liked better than you. I always worried that somehow, I would spin off the radar and it would be all over for me. As I look back, I can see on those pages how the work grew, but how the time away from my little girl also grew, and I wasn't as conscious at the time of the effect it was having on her. By the time it really hit me, through her sharing the disappointment and resentment she felt still, years later, it was too late to fix it.

In the early seventies too, once I left behind Sinatra, the smell of garlic, and the wrong train behind at Martoni's, I began to date a handsome, very sweet, kind of "Peter Pan"-type guy I met through my friend, musician/composer Mike Melvoin. Mike's wife Connie Ives had a younger brother David, who was pursuing a freelance photographer career at the time and lived with them. He was kind of like the uncle who came to dinner and just settled in. He slept in the upper bunk in their son Jonathan's room and was so the opposite of the gentleman I had been seeing for the last four years on and off that I couldn't help responding to his warmth and availability. We went together for two years, David moving into the Yoakum house with Susie and me, and we sort of became a family.

In 1972, David and I decided to get married, a somewhat impulsive decision motivated primarily by the fact that David and Connie's mother, Edie Ives, was coming out for a visit from New Hampshire, and we thought, *Oh, what a good time for a wedding.*

We made plans to be married at a little church up in Solvang, a charming, touristy kind of town just up the coast and inland from Santa Barbara. It was a sweet wedding—some of my singer friends sang from the choir loft, I wore a long white gown, which I had not been able to do in my first wedding, and Susie was my adorable maid of honor, at eleven years of age. We hosted a reception and dinner at a wonderful old inn, Mattei's Tavern in nearby Los Olivos. It had been built in 1886, had survived since its days as a stagecoach stop on the route north, and offered genuine "old West" charm and great dining. It was a beautiful gathering, and after the reception and the gift-opening, David and I drove on up the coast to the Madonna Inn for our first honeymoon night. We continued the next day up to Carmel, to a little guest house by the ocean we had rented for a few more days.

Back home as a couple, our life didn't change appreciably. We spent many evenings at the Melvoin's in Mike's basement studio where he and his jazz buddies would play for our enjoyment, and of course, their own. It was a very social household, and the socializing tools of the day—marijuana and that white powdery stuff—were quite often in use. They would always make sure the kids were safely quartered in their play area first, or settled down for the night. I tried the white powdery stuff only once, while David and I rode someplace in the back seat of the car with friends of Mike's. Its effect on me was that I became so paranoid at that moment, fearful we would be pulled over by a police officer any minute and hauled off to jail, that it was the first and last time I experienced it. It was not my cup of tea, nor David's. But it was prevalent in the day. I remember one birthday gathering we had for Mike's birthday, at a restaurant called Lost on Larrabee across the street from Larrabee Sound Studios. We sat at a big table of ten or twelve people, in a part of the dining room that was raised just one step up, but it felt like being on a stage. And there in full public view, the powder was passed and snorted. That, indeed, was rather uncomfortable. But that's how the town was in those days—some parts of it anyway.

The intense work schedule continued through 1972 and into the next several years. Still, on the pages of the datebook there are mostly only times and places, and the name of the contractor who had hired me. There was a lot of work for Disney Theme Park and the music for its live events, along with the recording and film scoring sessions.

In August of that year, David and I, with Susie and her childhood friend Julie Marvin, took a trip east to Windham, New York, to visit my dad and Dotty, and then went on to visit David's mother Edie in New Hampshire, David's home state. As we drove through New England, we visited the Gettysburg battleground, and the poet Emily Dickinson's home in Amherst, Massachusetts. Part of the purpose of the travels was that David was making a film, a travelogue of our journey and of the history of his town of birth. Within the film he had conceived of a little dream sequence, for which Mike Melvoin and I wrote a song that we recorded as the film's main title, "Country Summer." I appeared on camera in an old-fashioned gown, an imaginary New England ghost-like creature, visiting from the past.

By that time, in 1973, Susie was busy with piano lessons and ballet lessons, and had already begun a few years earlier to do kid sessions for music projects that involved children's voices. Often Ron Hicklin would call us both, and Susie and I would work together in the studio. I had also, when she was in sixth grade, transferred her to Highland Hall, a private Waldorf school out in the valley that Mike and Connie's children also attended. I would drive her over the hill in the morning, and they'd all ride the school bus together from the Melvoin house.

About this time a singer-songwriter friend, Renée Armand, who was traveling at the time with John Denver as his backup singer, connected me with a songwriter she had been working with. She thought we would work well together. His name was Kerry Chater, and he had been part of Gary Puckett & the Union Gap, but the band had broken up and he got signed as a writer and an artist himself, with A&M Records.

I remembered Kerry vividly from the session we had done with Gary Puckett & The Union Gap at Columbia records a few years earlier. The producer, like everyone else at that time, wanted to use the guys from the Wrecking Crew as the instrumental section for the tracks, but Kerry, offended and determined he should play on his own record (he was in the band at the time) sat in on the session with his instrument, right there behind the Wrecking Crew bass guitar player, and insisted on playing along. I admired his courage and determination. I'm not sure how the engineer or the producer felt.

The writing collaboration with Kerry grew over the next year or so. Also, our neighbor up the street, the parents of Susie's new best friend, were Tom Snow, a songwriter and artist, and his wife Marybelle. Tom wrote a beautiful musical setting for a poem I had written about my sister and our childhood together, called "Child of Mem'ries." He never even changed one word, just set it all to music so beautifully.

There was a wonderful, very successful, and busy sound

engineer and record producer active at that time, Bones Howe, who I had gotten to know through working on sessions with him for Ron Hicklin. One day I got brave and asked if I could meet with him to play some of my own songs. We did meet, and he was very kind and complimentary, though obviously not looking for another artist to produce. But he tried to be encouraging and said, "Did it ever occur to you that you could write about eight more songs like these and you'd have an album?"

It had, of course, occurred to me in a dream fantasy sort of way, but I never believed in myself to the extent that I actually got the courage and focus to do it. Ironically, just a few months ago, in 2020, I came across that box full of faded old lead sheets, lyrics pencil-scribbled above the notes . . . the songs I told you about earlier that I had written during the seventies but never tried to finish or polish. There were some lovely melodies and some pretty good lyrics, but I just never believed in myself enough to focus on becoming anyone other than a session singer. And being busy at session singing, I never felt a particular need for changing directions. I think being surrounded so much of the time with world-class talent, I was hesitant to try to put myself out in a way that indicated I aspired to join them. And again, ironically, there has always been a sense in the freelance music business that session singers are more like technicians than artists—that they don't necessarily have an identity or individuality or whatever it takes to really become an artist. We sing in tune, we do so many different styles that it is believed we never find our own style. I got the feeling that attitude was held by the people I worked for at that time, and always assumed I would come up as maybe a good singer, an okay songwriter, but not good enough for someone to be interested in producing as an artist. I was so blessed with the amount of work I had been doing that session singing did become my focus, and a realistic goal became just staying at the top of that list, doing sessions and film scores and doing concerts with Burt. The work with Burt allowed me to taste moments of "being an artist" on stage in solo performances with him, but my name didn't have to fill the seats. I was part of Burt's artistry.

There was one of my own songs that I had written words and music for, and played for Burt, "Love Is A Mirror," that he seemed to really like, and speculated about producing. And at the end of our tour of South America on the last night, he surprised me by asking me to perform it for the audience. The venue was like a coliseum, a very big crowd. I was surprised and in one way delighted, to think he would take a risk like that, having me perform my own song. And in another way, of course I was terrified. But I did sing it, sitting at the piano playing my own accompaniment, and the audience was very kind and responsive. That's a very special memory.

A few of the songs I'd written during those years I included later, in 2011, when I recorded an album of nine of my own songs plus four other songs I loved by other songwriters. I did the project just for myself, paid for all the musicians and the studio, and had some great weeks working with two wonderful engineers, Bill Schnee and Dan Garcia. Bill Cantos, who did most of the arrangements, played keyboard and the other musicians were James Harrah, Michael Shapiro, and Hussain Jiffry. One of the songs included, "My Heart Remembers," was a song I'd written the lyric for with Ian Freebairn-Smith. Ian had produced that track, and Mike Lang had played keyboards. Ian's daughter Vanessa Freebairn-Smith's string quartet also played on that song.

I had no plans of trying to find a label to release it, as one rarely starts a successful recording artist career at close to seventy years old. But it was fun, it fed my soul, and I had a few hundred CDs produced, with graphics and artwork. My album, *Things I Should Have Told You*, doesn't seem to be available any longer on iTunes or Amazon, though it was for a while. But I have a big box of them here in my den—just send me your address and I'll mail you one!

Also in 1973, I worked on a TV special with Danny Kaye. It was fun to be a part of his world again, a decade later. By this time I had been touring with Burt for three or four years. There was a booking at Harrah's, Lake Tahoe, in the spring of that year, and in May we toured Australia. David came along on the Australia trip as we'd just gotten married, and we shared the adventure of visiting Sidney, Melbourne, Adelaide, and Brisbane. The new Opera House in Sidney was under construction but not completed yet, so we missed being able to perform in that famous hall. We traveled by train out to the "bush" country, we visited a wildlife sanctuary where David took a picture of Burt holding a baby koala bear that I still have tucked away. (The picture, not the koala bear.) The tour was about two weeks long, and I remember calling Susie from a park in Melbourne in the afternoon on Mother's Day, feeling homesick and missing her. We had hired a sweet young woman from Japan, Sachi, to stay with Susie while we were gone. Sachi came to work for us for a while before we left, so that she could learn the operation of the household and we all could get acquainted.

Susie continued at Highland Hall, and there were ongoing activities at the school that I noted throughout that 1973 datebook. Burt also performed at the Greek Theatre for a week that summer, and then we headed to Allentown, Pennsylvania for more concert engagements, and a stopover visit in Windham. I worked a few times on the *Carol Burnett* TV variety show at CBS and on a Johnny Carson TV show produced in Hollywood. The record sessions and commercials continued with Ron Hicklin, and there was a project with Don Costa for Frank Sinatra. The opportunity for writing continued to expand a bit, and later in the year Susie, David, and I went to New Hampshire for Thanksgiving with his mother.

In 1971 Dominic Frontiere, a wonderful busy composer who I'd worked for as a singer on several projects, was kind enough to listen to some songs and lyrics I had written. He was working on an independent production about to score, *On Any Sunday*. It was technically a documentary produced and directed by Bruce Brown about motorcycling. But it also featured Steve McQueen, the actor who was extremely popular in those days, and it eventually did get quite a lot of attention. Dominic gave me a chance to try writing the main title lyric, and the producer liked it and decided to use it.

I'd only experienced riding on a motorcycle twice in my life—once in college, when I was engaged briefly to the vice cop, and once with my dear brother Charles, who took me for a ride so I could get more familiar with, and inspired by, motorcycling. Apparently, I interpreted the experience in ways that bikers identified with, and I must have found a way to express the joy of it, because as recently as the spring of 2020, I had an outreach from someone writing an article for a motorcycling magazine who had hunted me down and wanted to know more about the music for the film. He shared that the film and the music were rather iconic within the motorcycling community. In those days, I was given credit for the lyrics but not for the singing. I had sung a solo for the main title and several other cues throughout the film.

A couple of years later Dominic and I also wrote three songs for the Elizabeth Taylor/Richard Burton film *Hammersmith Is Out*. Dominic was really the first composer who gave me an opportunity to write lyrics for films, and I will always be so grateful to him for that experience and an entryway into more writing. Years later, after he and his new family had moved to Santa Fe, New Mexico, we wrote some songs for a satirical show a producer friend of Dominic's was involved with, called *Viagra Falls*.

In 1976, composer and jazz artist Don Ellis and I began our first writing project together, a song for the film *Ruby*, which Don was about to score. He had, not too long before we met, been the recipient of a heart transplant, and was in a more delicate physical state than he was used to being in, but had a positive attitude and was doing well. Sadly, things took a turn and Don passed away just two years after we had gotten to work together. When we first met to write together, he had enjoyed learning about the coincidence that we had another connection. I was "Jon Clarke's sister"; my dear brother Jon had played in Don's band a decade or so earlier, when Jon was so young they had to sneak him into the Las Vegas lounge to perform. But he played so well Don insisted on hiring him.

Many of those seventies years were sweet for David and me and our life together in so many ways. But it was a challenging relationship. I was the financial provider all during the years that we were together. We set up a photography studio in a rented space, an old brick building that was sort of a historical landmark in Venice and had at one time been the Venice Fire Station. We hoped it would allow David to focus on his photography and try to establish himself on a more professionally independent business level. And because he was such a handsome dude, of course, with broad shoulders and a slim waist, his shirts needed to be custom-made, so there was a little shop in Beverly Hills that took care of that for us. But along the way I began to feel, or at least to fear at the time, that if David and I were to stay together, I would always have two children, Susie and David. The photography work never really blossomed into a business and my concert bookings out of town with Burt, I'm sure, drew me more away from our life. Eventually David and I also divorced. I've hurt too many people along the way, I realized too late in life.

David has had an interesting journey though, and several lovely ladies joined him over the years as partners. He relocated back to New Hampshire at one point, worked there for several years in a friend's hotel business, and spent some time in the Midwest working on a cattle ranch and being an actual cowboy. And then as he told me some years later, he "went out drinking with buddies, singing Viking songs, and ended up in

Copenhagen." There, he worked in live theater as a production assistant, and eventually married a Danish woman, a native of Denmark. He really did settle finally into a field of work that he loved and was a part of the theater community there until he retired in 2020. We stayed in touch through the years, and now we email almost daily. Interestingly, he is as connected to the politics of America from there as I am here, and we have rounds of shared rants. But it is lovely to feel still connected to this sweet man, after all these years.

CHAPTER 20
INTO THE EIGHTIES

Looking back over the decades, I have to recognize and express gratitude for the overall journey, but there were perilous times along the way when I really thought my career would be all over by age forty-five. The freelance business is unpredictable; new people are discovered daily, and I think partly because of my travel with Burt, Ron Hicklin had begun using several very good, and much younger, female singers. Ours is, indeed, a youth-oriented business, and I think surrounding himself with younger singers also helped Ron to seem more current and "with it." Ron had by this time established his own jingle production company Killer Music, and though he was still involved in contracting for film composers, his focus shifted more toward his work in the commercials production part of the business.

My personal life took an interesting turn about this time, and unexpectedly along the way, my professional life also expanded in the way I had tried to avoid all during the previous years. In the eighties, through a couple of fortunate opportunities and my willingness to give it a try, I began to do some work as a vocal contractor. That work continued to grow and gifted me with some of the most wonderful experiences, working more closely with some of the amazing composers in our town. I know it also extended my career at a deeper level for three or four more decades.

Session work had begun to slow for me in the late seventies/early eighties. I was still working, but I think because I had taken the opportunity to travel with Burt, my absence truly had opened some doors for other talented lead singers in town, and I was starting to feel like I was being gently pushed out of position. I had not done any contracting up to that point, but only worked as a freelance singer, so my fate was very much in the hands of those who did.

In addition, there was a problem that developed in the late seventies with a nonunion jingle house in San Diego, Tuesday Productions. Tuesday offered both union and nonunion production services, and in those days advertisers could choose to produce their commercials either union or nonunion if they themselves were not signatory to a union agreement. Tuesday Productions was pulling so much jingle business away from the LA area that the singers' committee and several very active singers felt they had to take some kind of action to protect their union work. They decided to, through AFTRA, notify union singers by letter that they should not be going down to work for the company. Things got so intense that in 1978 Tuesday Productions filed an antitrust lawsuit against AFTRA for interfering with their right to conduct business, After a period of deliberation a judge in the San Diego area ruled in Tuesday Production's favor in 1982, a decision which resulted in putting AFTRA into Chapter 11 bankruptcy and keeping it there for a number of years.

But prior to that suit being filed, Ron Hicklin had his own solution to the problem of our work being pulled down to San Diego. The two young Los Angeles singers doing most of the group work for the jingle producers at Tuesday Productions were Edie Lehmann and Debbie Hall, very gifted young singers who were just getting started in the business, and were already excellent musicians and great singers, definitely deserving of becoming a part of the Los Angeles singer community. Ron Hicklin reached out to them and said he thought they were really terrific, but if they continued to do nonunion work, of course he couldn't hire them. By this time he had established his company and was doing a huge amount of "union" jingles for major advertisers. So the two girls severed their ties with Tuesday Productions, which also reduced, for a time at least, the quality of vocals produced by Tuesday Productions, and Edie and Debbie began doing all of Ron's work. This meant that I was doing pretty much none of it. I hadn't realized at first how dramatically this was affecting me. Edie and Debbie, by the way, are dear friends of mine to this day, have continued working very successfully in the business all these years. They're committed and loyal members of SAG-AFTRA. Edie has become one of the busier contractors in town herself, and we've worked together often on many projects both as fellow singers, or when one of us was the contractor of the choir and the other was hired to sing. Most all of us, in our earliest days, started with smaller nonunion projects as those were the only early work opportunities, and they became the training ground that let us move forward until we were able to step into union work and away from the nonunion gigs.

In those days, anyone who worked in the union commercials area of music was beyond lucky. Television prime-time shows were still the focus of the audience attention, and if you lucked into a national spot for one of the major products/ advertisers, those residuals checks kept drifting into the mailbox. A special commercial done for the Super Bowl half-time show literally made thousands of dollars in one airing. The commercials contract is complicated and just recently the union has made some adjustments to it in order to try to fight back against all the non-union "buyouts" with which the young singers are being tempted. So much of the commercials work went out of the union in recent years. But back in the late sixties, when commercial production drifted westward from New York and Chicago, where it had been primarily, all through the sixties and into the seventies, it was the primary focus of a handful of fortunate session singers in LA.

By the time I began to feel the change in my activities, I wasn't doing much commercials work, but other areas of work were diminishing, and I wasn't sure what to do next. I had always expected, or feared, that based on the youth-oriented nature of our business, my career would fade out in my forties. Now, as those years approached, it really felt like it was happening way too soon. I had never put myself forth in the business as a vocal contractor. I had never reached out nor would I have felt comfortable doing so, to any of the composers I had worked with, to suggest myself for their contracting work. But I was feeling the change within the industry as far as my own singing work was concerned.

One day while I was out doing errands, in one of the stores I came across a huge canvas tote bag about 2 1/2 feet by 2 1/2 feet, and on the front of it was painted a big colorful rainbow, with little stick figures marching in a row beneath it. There was some text under the drawing that said, "When they're running you out of town, get in front of the crowd and make it look like a parade!"

I felt like it somehow was a message from the universe. I bought that tote bag and carried it everyplace. I took it as a sign that somehow, things would change—that things weren't quite over yet. It didn't change anything immediately, but when things did change, I totally credited that tote bag.

I had been doing some weekend singing gigs on my own with a five-piece band that included my brother Jon Clarke on woodwinds, my friend Mark Stevens on drums, Kevin Bassinson as keyboard player/arranger, Jim Hughart on bass, and Tim Weston on guitar, in The Room Upstairs at Le Café. I had had some opportunities to write lyrics for a couple of film projects. I had just done the solo vocal in *The Secret of NIMH* for Jerry Goldsmith. I was actually doing some wonderful projects, but the pace of work with Ron had definitely changed, and I was feeling it.

It was at that time that I also met the man who was eventually to become my third husband, Jack Eskew. Jack was an orchestrator/arranger/composer who had worked in the business during most of the same years I had been working in it, but our paths had not crossed all that much. He had worked with the *Sonny & Cher* TV show and on many other projects in our business, and more recently had taken the position of Musical Director for Disney Theme Parks. That job took him out of the freelance musician world in that he was no longer available to do charts for other composers or producers, but it gave him a weekly paycheck, and many new projects to work on for Disney, as their theme parks were expanding at the time. Epcot Center at Disney World, Florida was preparing to open, and those projects kept him busy and challenged for several years. Coincidentally, Jack and I had both taken the same class instruction in Christian Science in 1979, but we hadn't really known each other at that time professionally or personally.

My taking the class had been the result of an interesting journey. While working with Burt in Las Vegas in the spring of 1978, I began experiencing terribly severe abdominal pains, but no doctor there could diagnose the problem. I was in so much pain that I actually couldn't make the last show of our engagement- the only time in my life that has happened, that I missed a show. When I came back home to Toluca Lake, I saw my own doctor, but he wasn't sure whether it was a tumor or a tubal pregnancy so he sent me home with pain meds. I was living in the Toluca Lake house at the time, with the sweet man I had been going with by then for about four years, Kerry Chater. Our writing collaboration had, along the way, morphed into a deeper, romantic relationship.

At one point, the extreme pain from whatever was going on physically became so great that I just said to Kerry, "Call my dad, call my mom, and call an ambulance—I can't make it to the car!"

I ended up in a little hospital in Burbank having an emergency total hysterectomy. The pain, it turned out, had been caused by a tumor the size of a grapefruit and the accompanying peritonitis that had developed throughout my abdomen. I certainly hadn't realized how serious it was. The tumor was not malignant, which was, of course, a blessing.

At the time I had also had a job as soloist in a Christian Science church in Studio City. It was the religion in which I had been raised, but I had drifted away from it over the years, though occasionally I still had taken a soloist position at one of the churches in the area. I called the woman who coordinated the music to tell her I would be unable to sing that Sunday, and she urged me to call a dear lady, Frances Figgins, a Christian Science practitioner and part of that church's community, for some spiritual help. I did call Mrs. Figgins.

Frances Figgins was unusual in that normally, a Christian Science practitioner will not treat someone under medical care or while they are an inpatient. But Frances stayed with me through the hospital stay, the tests and diagnosis, and then just asked me to let her know the time the surgery was to be scheduled. She would "do her work" for me, and then at the scheduled time of surgery, she would turn me over to the care of God, and know that God, or Divine Mind, would be guiding the doctors' hands and wisdom.

The surgery went well, I recovered, and it made me want to know more deeply about the religion I had grown up with. I also wanted to somehow show my gratitude for Mrs. Figgins's kindness, so I signed up for the class instruction that she was scheduled to teach later that year. And coincidentally, Jack was also in that same class.

Kerry and I ended our relationship a year or so after the hospital episode, around 1980. It had been difficult to balance our lives, our work, my Susie and his two little boys from his previous marriage, etc. It was a very emotional time, because I think we both still cared very much for each other. My travels with Burt kept me from being able to travel to Boston when Kerry had a solo album released as an artist on A&M Records and his band had an important booking there. Burt's concert tour was scheduled for the same time, and I couldn't bring myself to break my agreement to do the tour. I know Kerry was disappointed and I felt terrible for a long time about missing that concert. There was a hit record at the time by artist Dave Loggins, "Please Come to Boston," and Kerry would sing it to me around the house in the weeks preceding the concert, but alas. I just couldn't make it work, going to Boston. And looking back on those days, I feel bad that I didn't try harder. I felt committed to Burt's schedule, and I certainly didn't want to lose that professional ongoing relationship.

The fact that I had been very fortunate in the freelance music business and was doing better financially than Kerry at the time also created complications. Norm Greenbaum, my business manager, had come with us to look at the Toluca Lake house when it was on the market and I was considering it. He told me he thought the house was wonderful, but also that he felt it would be the end of Kerry's and my relationship, and I of course dismissed the warning. I thought he was being melodramatic. But ironically, I think the financial imbalance did have a lot to do with the relationship eventually not working. In hindsight, I'm impressed with Norm's insightfulness. He knew about a lot more than just financial spreadsheets.

A few years later I happened to work for Jack Eskew on a session for one of the Disney events that Ron Hicklin contracted. He and I reminisced briefly about our past class experience with Mrs. Figgins, and were surprised when we realized we had both been in that class, but our paths had never crossed in the business world we had shared for so many years.

On an impulse one day, after another of the Disney sessions in the spring of 1982, I asked Jack if he would like to go to a dinner party with me that I'd been invited to by a legendary actor from radio days, Frank Nelson, a colleague of mine on the AFTRA Board of Directors. Neither Jack nor I were seeing anyone at the time, and Jack seemed to me to be a "regular" guy, the kind of guy who I imagined washed his own car on Saturday mornings—the kind of guy maybe I could, and should, settle down with. He did go to the dinner party with me, and we started seeing each other. The relationship developed rather quickly, partly because we both believed that our common background of Christian Science was kind of the "good housekeeping seal of approval." We had our first date a couple of weeks before Easter, and then after we had several more dates, Jack came with me on set the day I was to shoot a new on-camera commercial for one of the KBIG television spots I had been doing as the spokesperson for the radio station.

I had been their on-camera spokesperson for a couple of years, and I thought it was sweet when Jack asked to be there at the shoot. Things were becoming pretty serious between us, and on the shoot, Chuck Blore, the producer, knowing Jack and I were dating, utilized Jack's presence by having him stand for a couple of shots next to the lens of the camera, so I could look dreamily into his eyes as I walked toward the lens, talking about how "wonderful" KBIG radio station was. I tried to be considerate of Jack throughout the day, asking if he needed anything, etc. but he always replied he was fine, happy to just be there watching the process.

Those shoots were always fun days for me, as I had really done very little on-camera work over the years, and it was kind of nice being fussed over and taking center stage for a few make-believe hours. I had sung the radio station's IDs for several years prior to the on-camera campaign, and the gentleman from the station who was in charge of marketing came up with the idea that they should have a personality on camera who people would begin to recognize and identify with the station. And he suggested to the station that it should be me. That period of time was definitely the only time in my career anyone ever recognized me out in public, because of those KBIG spots that ran so often on television in the LA area.

So at the end of our shooting day, I felt happy and uplifted, ready to celebrate a bit, and suggested to Jack maybe we could stop for a glass of wine and a bit of dinner on the way home. But Jack's mood suddenly seemed to have darkened, and he replied no, that he was tired, that he had been my "poodle" all day and he just wanted to go home. We went back to my house, where he collapsed on my living room sofa and I ended up sitting on the floor next to him, apologizing for the long, difficult day he had had. I've thought in later years that perhaps this evening's behavior should have been a little "alert" signal.

Just about that time too, I had been invited to be part of a delegation from the entertainment industry that was to travel to East Germany, so I knew I would be out of the country for about three weeks. Coincidentally, about that same time, Jack had to go to Florida to Disney World for the opening of a Disney parade for which he had produced the music. So it occurred to us that I could fly to Florida with him, he could meet my dad and Dotty, who were by then retired and living in West Palm Beach, and then I would fly up to New York and join the group flying to Germany from JFK International Airport.

When I came back from East Germany (quite an adventure, which I'll tell you about in another chapter) it was almost the end of May. My dad and Dotty had loved Jack from their first meeting, and we continued to see each other, deciding this relationship was meant to be. We planned our marriage for July 7, even though we had been dating for only three months and I'd been out of the country for part of that time.

We did decide to postpone a reception till the end of the

summer when we could better plan for it, and we had a small private wedding at First Christian Church in Studio City, with Rev. Bob Boch, since they don't perform weddings in the Christian Science church. (There are no clergy, only a First and Second Reader of the material prepared by the Mother Church for the Sunday services.) My close childhood friend Margit Motta and her husband Bill stood up for us, then joined us for a wedding luncheon at Jimmy's, the "celebrity" restaurant in Beverly Hills where the stars dined during the seventies and eighties. Then they waved us off at LAX on our flight to Hawaii.

In retrospect, it's easy to see that this marriage happened as my first marriage had, before we knew each other well enough to understand the challenges we might face and were sure we could both handle them.

There were many such moments like the awkward evening following the KBIG shoot, that occurred later in the marriage and I never clearly understood the complicated person Jack was. Even when we tried three marriage counselors, he walked angrily out of each of their offices. I'm still not clear on what the dynamics were that caused the bumps in the road, but they seemed so often to come out of the blue. I am sure too, that if I had been more willing or more skilled at working with whatever those dynamics were, and tried harder, we might have made things work. I think because this was the third marriage for each of us, it felt important to stick with it, and we did to try to make it work. We were together through our tenth anniversary but separated about six months later.

We had some wonderful times together, and we had some very challenging times. Jack had also been married twice previously, both marriages to the same lady. They had tried to put back together a marriage that had fallen apart and ended in divorce, but the rescue efforts didn't work. He and Judy, his ex-wife, had a son and a daughter, and Jack also had a step-daughter, the child from Judy's first marriage. But the relationship with his stepdaughter had gotten off-track because of some unfortunate accusations during their second divorce and child custody battle. When we were married, I had only known about and met his youngest two children, Jackson and Holly. One day an invitation arrived in the mail to a high school graduation. It had a picture of a pretty young lady on it, named Jacqueline Eskew. I asked Jack who that person was, and the story slowly unfolded.

Jacqui, the name by which I eventually got to know her, had been interviewed by the judge during the divorce and custody hearing when Jack and Judy went to court. Jack later thought that Jacqui might have been fearful she would end up babysitting all the time for the two younger children, and that caused her to answer as she did. But Jack blamed her for his losing custody of the children; after they had all lived with him for two years while their mother ran off with her ski instructor. Jacqui, when asked by the judge who she would prefer to live with, said she would prefer to be with her mother. Jack later learned she had been coached to say that. But the other two children followed suit, and Jack felt like Jacqui had betrayed him.

Up till that time the two had been very close all through Jacqui's life. Jack had taught her to play tennis, the sport he loved, and they had enjoyed the game together. She had gone to the studio with him many times on his recording projects. But he had cut off communication with her after the divorce settlement. He did finally reach out to her, after we received the graduation notice, and in the next year or so she too became part of our family.

Jack's own life had been complicated, filled with much sadness and drama along the way, and I mistakenly thought I could fix a lot of it, at least the part that involved his children. But his earlier life had shaped him.

His father died when Jack was only twelve years old, and his mother soon remarried. His new stepfather struggled with alcoholism, and managed to stop drinking but couldn't stay with that abstinence. When Jack was in his early twenties, in a moment of frustration over having learned that his stepfather had started drinking again, he had gone out in anger and purchased a bottle of liquor, handed it over, and told his stepfather if that was what he wanted to do, to go for it.

Tragically, and ironically, later that evening his stepfather committed suicide, and Jack was the person who discovered the body. He had never imagined that his impulsive, angry action would lead to such a tragic end.

So there had been some painful losses already in his life, and when he lost custody of the children after having had them with him for almost two years it added to the pain and frustration. He was reluctant to risk disappointment again. I worked hard to try to get the children back into Jack's life, into our lives, only to see him disappointed several times when their new stepfather-of-the-week would call at the last minute to cancel their visit. It happened the first time on the first Christmas after Jack and I were married.

The next year we did work it out so they could be with us, and I tried to make it special and memorable. Jack was upset with me over some aspect of planning the holidays, the children's visits or some issue going on at the time that I can't remember now. I guess to express his anger, he didn't get me anything for Christmas that year. It was only the second Christmas of our being together as a couple, it was a conscious decision on his part, and it seemed to be making a statement that was hurtful. The following Christmas though, after my Great Dane, Dejah, died, the last of two Great Danes I had had for about ten years before meeting Jack, he surprised me with the gift of an adorable pedigreed Great Dane puppy for Christmas. We named her "Kathryn-The-Great-Dane." I was surprised and delighted with the puppy, and I called to tell my friend Carol Lombard, "Guess what Jack got me for Christmas?!" Her sullen reply was, "A present?" She had been pretty upset with him the year before.

Jack was basically a fine, honorable, and very talented man. After the initial difficulty of our separation and the property settlement stuff that had to happen following the divorce, we settled into a sweet friendship and would meet at the legendary Musso & Frank's restaurant in Hollywood for lunch every so often to catch up on each other's lives, children, politics, whatever was going on in the world. Musso & Frank's is the oldest restaurant in Hollywood, established in 1919. And the maître d' had wonderful stories to tell of the famous people who had sat in the booth by the front door—people like Charlie Chaplin and others who had shaped the beginnings of the film business. I think we both liked the myth, the history, and possibly the permanence of the place, like it had been there forever, and *would* be there forever, just as *we* would be there forever, chatting over lunch as if nothing had ever gone wrong.

CHAPTER 21
BEHIND THE IRON CURTAIN AND BACK AGAIN

In 1982, the trip to East Berlin that happened at the beginning of my relationship with Jack was quite a fascinating adventure. It was revealing of another culture, a different set of values and rules to live by. And it's timely to share because at this moment in history, July of 2020, we here in America find ourselves immersed in an era that for me is similar, in that it has morphed into a somewhat different culture from the one I've known all these years. It feels lately here in America a bit like Alice going down the rabbit hole, and finding something she never would have imagined finding, not even through the looking glass.

We have in these times moved into a sort of numbing frame of mind. Well, I speak of course only for myself, and a few close friends with whom I share political conversations, following the presidential election of 2016. Apparently, there were enough people persuaded, for slightly different reasons and from various different economic bases, to vote for the guy who vowed to "drain the swamp."

But new critters have appeared consistently in that swamp since his election, the likes of which we've never seen before in this country. Most of his appointed cabinet members and others who he deemed worthy of appointing to head various areas of our government have been removed either by public pressure or willing presidential decree, and replaced with "temporary" personnel who, therefore, conveniently don't need congressional approval and can be hired or fired at the discretion of the president.

And words spill daily from the president's tweets and his very lips, the likes of which we've never heard before from any resident of the White House. Things in the news where we read his words, directed at four members of Congress, specifically the House of Representatives, duly elected representatives from their communities, and all four citizens of the United States of America. Three of the four are citizens by birth, and the fourth, by her own citizenship following the immigration of her parents to this land. In his words, if they didn't like America, they could leave and go back to the "dreadful countries they came from." All four, just FYI coincidentally, are women of color.

Following the few days of controversy around these remarks, the president held a rally in North Carolina, and spewed more rhetoric to the crowd, which inspired his followers to begin chanting, "Send them back!" a chant which has now apparently replaced the "Lock her up!" chants from the presidential rallies, referencing Hillary Clinton.

I didn't mean to get so off on the rails here with politics, but that's very much what my fascinating adventure back in 1982 was about, and it's impactful to me to see how the accusation of "fake news" inspired by the current president from the beginning of his campaign and rapidly spreading among his followers, is so similar to the things I learned about the country of East Germany as it existed then, in my visit in 1982 with a delegation of colleagues from Los Angeles.

There is little difference in the results, as I read the notes in my fifty-or-so-page handwritten journal, between the government officially taking over the dissemination of news, controlling it, and telling its citizens only what it wants them to know and believe, and what the president of our own country has been doing by simply undermining the value and credibility of serious journalism. The free press is one of the things this country was promised when its founders set things up. It has been at the core of our democracy. And it has served the people of this country by revealing many things we ourselves never could have discovered on our own. But so many news sources have sprung up in recent years that are admittedly biased, on both sides of politics, that it's become difficult, and somewhat politically incorrect these days, to be a defender of news. "Alternative facts" were introduced to us during these last four years, and they've snuggled up to various sources of "news."

I've forced myself to tune in to Fox News channel for a short period of time each day, as I take a break from MSNBC and CNN, to see what the other guys are talking about. And I basically rely on Public Broadcast television news and National Public Radio, sources that have clung by their fingernails to reporting the actual news and are trying desperately not to color it with opinion, unless the opinion is clearly labeled "Opinion/Editorial comments."

Note: As of this edit, on January 5, 2021, the forty-fifth president has just lost an election and continues to challenge those results. After eighty or so court cases filed by his attorneys, after three recounts and declarations of valid, honest, and accurate election results by Republican leaders in various swing states in question, and after the Supreme Court with three judges who he himself appointed has refused to hear his charges of fraudulent elections, the man is still on a rampage to keep his White House address, and claims President-elect Joseph Biden is not the president. I rest my case. And tonight we await the results of Georgia's two senatorial runoff elections, the results of which will determine whether or not anything will be allowed for discussion in the Senate under President Biden's presidency, as Mitch Mc McConnell continues to remove subjects from the table.

Back to East Germany. (Oh, I know, you thought we were there already.)

In 1982, I had just been elected to the National Board of Directors of the Screen Actors Guild. And when my dear friend and singer colleague Jackie Ward found she was unable to take part in a trip she had been invited to take with a delegation of people from our industry to visit East Germany, she suggested I might be a good person to take her place.

The delegation was comprised of actors, writers, and directors, and was organized and coordinated by John Randolph, a legendary character actor who also served on the SAG Board at that time. I assumed that the trip was sponsored by SAG, but later, when seated on the plane on our way to East Germany, I learned that it actually was sponsored by the League of Friendship—which meant basically that the Communist Party in East Germany was sponsoring our trip. John had led several delegations on these visits, and his daughter at that time had actually defected to East Germany. At that time, the East German government had begun a program of bringing delegations of workers from all different kinds of occupations, to visit and hopefully to consider migrating there. They had lost so many citizens, prior to the wall being built and the border closed, and they were trying to infuse their population with some new energy.

John Randolph had been an activist during the civil rights demonstrations of the sixties in the South and wherever such demonstrations had taken place. He was a dear, courageous, and loving man, a loyal patriot (I really believe), who honestly was just pursuing any means he thought would contribute to promoting peace in the world. So, what better activity than to hop over to a communist country and find out how they do stuff? In the process, of course, we were able to share how *we* do it. Which may or may not have affected anyone's thinking there. And even if it did, they were certainly not free to say so.

It turned out that most of the trip, in fact, was highly

propagandized by our host country. We were a delegation of about ten people, among whom was actor James Whitmore and his wife; actor Bernie Casey; screenwriter Manny Fried; two dear ladies who were musical theater performers primarily; another woman director/producer, and a younger woman whose parents were involved with theater and had also been blacklisted during the McCarthy era, along with John Randolph. (With apologies, the names over the last three and a half decades have faded for those I did not know well.) Bernie and I remained friends until he sadly passed away in 2017, and we would meet occasionally for dinner at a restaurant we loved that was kind of halfway between our neighborhoods, "Ca Brea," on La Brea Boulevard in Hollywood. I continued to be in touch with John Randolph too, during the years immediately following our adventure in East Germany as I continued to serve on the SAG Board; but the others of our group, sadly, I eventually lost contact with.

My journey on this trip was undertaken just literally weeks after Jack and I had started to date and our marriage took place only weeks after my return. It began when we flew to Florida, which is where Jack was musical director of a new area of the park about to open, Epcot Center, and Jack met my parents. The opening pages of my journal from the trip read:

What a glorious, happy celebration dinner we had last night—Jack and I, Dad and Dotty and Dotty's son Murray, at the Princess Lilly, the paddleboat restaurant at Lake Buena Vista. Daddy was beside himself with happiness and at one time or another we were all in tears. Such a happy evening to get acquainted and celebrate Jack and I finding each other!

(It does kind of sound like someone who had a tendency to highly romanticize their life, right?)

This period of time, by the way, was when my then-husband Jack started referring to me as "Natasha the Red." My political views, to him as a conservative Republican, seemed to fit the label. During the first year or two of our marriage,

Jack let his hair grow long and talked like a Democrat but eventually he returned to his earlier political views and haircut. My father and Jack were concerned about my making this trip, but I felt no hesitancy about it. And at the time, Jack and I were overjoyed at having found each other.

The nitty-gritty journey began with the connecting flight from Copenhagen into East Berlin on Interflug Airlines, an airline based in East Germany. As I noted in my journal, it seemed odd that the plane even offered first class seating as well as our section, given that this nation did not admit to believing in "class" but rather "the people, the workers."

And when we arrived in Berlin, it was like transitioning from technicolor to black and white. The plane was literally grey inside and out, and we passed into the check-in area of the country through ominous grey steel doors, from which the baggage area and airport lobby were not visible. The implication was that if you didn't respond correctly to the security questions, you could spend a long time in that secure area, and never even see your baggage again. Or your country of origin. Armed guards in the terminal, no photographs allowed. Pat, one of the ladies in our delegation, came close to having her camera confiscated when she tried to take pictures of the guards.

Traveling on with our group from the airport by bus to our hotel, my initial reaction to being in the country was positive. In the journal I wrote:

Very moved for some reason, at the newness of this experience and the sameness of all people—apartment dwellers, children with dogs, old buildings, beautiful little gardens.

But then it changed a bit, as the journal continues:

Once inside the city for the most part, things seem to be quite dreary—not much foot traffic, not much activity. In the hotel, my room is rather like a monk's cell—small, simple, but quite adequate. Deep tub for bath—rusty water, though . . . orange. Bath powder scented and orange colored too! Water not meant to drink! Plumbing fixtures, pipes, etc. are all plastic. Most everything above lobby level is plastic. We Americans are indeed spoiled beyond our own comprehension.

This was my first trip to Europe, by the way. So I had nothing of Europe to compare America with, except this rather stark country of East Germany.

We spent the first two or three days of our visit seated around conference tables sipping orange soda and being taught the history of the recreated East Germany, the evolution from free nation to one under the rule of Communist Russia—which was part of the terms of the peace agreement following WWII. And we were taught about how it had been newly created. It was fascinating to hear the reasons for changes that were made. Or at least, the reasons that we were told. Fearful of continuing any fascist ideology within this new state, all those who had been teachers and educators prior to the establishment of the new government were fired, and replaced by teachers who had formerly been plumbers, or electricians or whatever, and were in a matter of weeks trained for their new teaching positions. Therefore, without a particularly strong knowledge of the subjects they were to teach, they followed the new history textbooks, and the history of the country itself was eventually changed. The children who grew up there between 1945 and the time of our visit, 1982, before the wall came down, got a very different story in their history lessons.

During my travels in East Berlin, I discovered I was indeed a loyalist, in terms of democracy . . . and capitalism, at least as it was in those days. And perhaps I was *not* "Natasha the Red" to the core. It seemed that everyone in our delegation except for Bernie and I had some reason to resent America just a bit. They all, or someone dear to each of them, had gone through the McCarthy era, and their careers had been negatively affected by that experience and by the blacklisting within our industry. They were sympathetic to the underdog, which in this case seemed to be the people and the government of East

Germany. The discussions around the table were targeted toward influencing us in that direction, and the conversations between some of my companions in the delegation were very much about praising our current surroundings there in East Germany, at many levels. Perhaps they were just trying to be complimentary and express gratitude to our hosts, but one evening when I was at a reception following the performance we had attended of the opera *Mahogany*, based on a Bertolt Brecht play, I was overwhelmingly surrounded by what was beginning to feel like a negative view of the folks back home. I just let go of the frustration I had been feeling as I listened to the fawning over this great communist country. John Randolph was in my face, praising some part of the evening and our experiences in general, and I burst forth with, "John, I love you, but I am an American—and a capitalist—I love my country despite all of its incongruities, its inequities, and inconsistencies, and it has been very difficult for me to have a steady stream of anti-West, anti-capitalist-imperialist bad-rapping. Sure, it is the way they see it here . . ." and later I noted in my journal notes: *"I just lost my cool a bit. John was so sweet and I hope I didn't upset him."*

I actually left the reception with one of the gentlemen from the cast of the opera we had just seen performed, a young operatic singer from America who, as many did, had taken advantage of being able to perform leading roles in European opera productions, and had been there in East Berlin for some time. I knew it wasn't totally appropriate to leave; I didn't even know if I *could*, and I was pretty convinced that we would be followed, though I never saw any evidence of that. We walked to a nearby hotel operated by one of the Western hotel chains from outside the country of East Germany, had a drink at the bar, and he shared a few things he had learned as a free-floating visitor during his stay. The children at the Young People's Palace, a very up-to-date, attractive structure that we'd visited and had been told held workshops for little children in various fields of the arts as after-school activities—those little children were also, I was told that evening at the bar by the opera singer, taught how to throw hand grenades. Even at the time there in East Berlin, my notes indicate that I took that information with a grain of salt: *"Wish I could know whether this is true."* But the Young People's Palace was very sparsely populated with well-behaved children on the day we visited; the classes seemed to be going on, but I also suspect they were created to impress us and other visitors by demonstrating the advantages offered to the artistic children of East Germany in this communist way of doing things. In my journal, I noted that the name of this American singer with whom I had this conversation was Elliot Paley, but my handwriting is so illegible that I might not be reading the name correctly today. I couldn't find any opera singer by that name on my recent google search so my apologies, dear Elliot, if I got it wrong.

After the initial days around the conference table, we had many meetings with actors, directors, and writers from the Film Actors Union and TV Actors Union, from the Berlin School of Drama, and other organizations, and learned details about how they navigated their careers, what their unions did for them, etc. It was shocking to learn that people in their country did not choose their professions. Their professions, in most cases, were chosen *for* them. If they had different dreams, those fell to the side. And the state subsidized the arts, but therefore also greatly influenced and controlled the material the arts presented. Most of the productions we saw were very politically manipulated, and quite honestly even the actors and directors we met there found it difficult to defend the quality of some of that material. It often was lacking in humor, or in real entertainment value, but was more intended to influence the audience's political thinking and civic attitudes.

More excerpts from the notes on the lectures, in my

journal:

No private business in art production, in the country. All proceeds go into the state budget (which also they say is owned by the people) . . . state collects funds and redistributes it to fields of culture. The state does not have "the right, but has the obligation to make this distribution." No newly elected government could stop financing culture. It is "constitutionally ordained." The organizations we visited are not "unions" but "associations." The Association of Writers, Association of Musicians, Association of Theater Artists, Visual Art, Film and TV. They all have "general assemblies" elected by secret ballot, and those are the decision-making bodies.

As the trip unfolded, things became a bit less formal and structured. We got to know our interpreters, and one interpreter in particular, Jurgen, and his fiancé, became our friends. He shared with us his longing to visit the West, but also his acceptance that this was not possible, presently. Someday, he said, he would have coffee with us in America. We also spoke with several brilliant ballet dancers who very much wanted to travel to the West, but no performances were planned outside of their country. It was assumed that if they left, they would choose not to come back. It *was* permissible to leave East Germany, but only if you were over the age of sixty-five and being supported by the government as a pensioner, as your leaving would relieve them of that obligation. Sixty-five years of age would have been a little too late for dancers to resume their ballet careers in the West.

I found myself writing a poem about Jurgen, which of course I did not share until I reached home. But it's there in my journal, and I substituted "Frederick" for Jurgen's name, lest it ever be discovered by a fellow East German. It was a poem with a sad ending.

I pray, by the way, that the poem never came true, and that Jurgen and his fiancé made a smooth exit, once the dreaded wall came crashing down. But it expressed honestly the way I felt at the time of our visit. I shared his acceptance, but also his hopelessness, and felt heartbroken for him.

The scribblings in my journal were written so rapidly that much of it is difficult to read now. But I found it fascinating to look back on. In one of the early conference table chats, it was explained to us that:

In 1946, the GDR (German Democratic Republic) did not yet exist. There was a vote to deal with the factories of "war mongers" and to nationalize them, to turn them over to the people. They no longer could be private property. We were told that the American administration canceled paragraphs applicable to this from the Potsdam Agreement, vis-à-vis the American sector of Germany. Berlin had been 70% destroyed during the war. "Feudal lords" escaped to West Germany and the working class had to take over, unite and organize. In 1946 the Socialist Unity Party united with the Communist Party. And on October 7, 1949, the GDR was founded. Up until 1973, most of the world had diplomatic blocks against the GDR, considering it a "Soviet Colony." There was a fear that they might be reinstated into the Federal Republic by police action turning a socialist country into a capitalistic country. Therefore, East Germany had to close its borders and build a frontier wall. There were acts of terror, of sabotage committed by the West upon East Berlin. For East Germany, they claimed Hitler's defeat as "liberation." For West Germany, they said it was a "day of defeat."

More from the journal:

In 1960, all farmers merged into cooperative farms, but they still have their own properties within the co-ops, they are not state-owned. They can decide what to produce, how to distribute the wealth. Rents in the GDR are roughly 3-4% of family income. Kindergarten children (this covers age 3-6) pay for their food, and it costs roughly one hour's wage for the week. Sixty to sixty-five out of a hundred children go into pre-nursery school, and the parents have a 26-week paid leave, following the birth of their child. The Socialist Democracy cannot be compared to "free" democracy. The policy is to do everything for the benefit of "the people."

At the time, the GDR has very few natural resources. The main two were lignite, soft coal, which provided 75-80% of heating fuel, and potash, which could be used and also exported. They must import oil, gas, iron ore, and 70% of their trading was done with socialist countries, mostly the Soviet Union, but also other "liberated, developing" countries. The arms race of course must be maintained, as the GDR needs to defend itself.

Out of every hundred families, thirty-seven have cars, and young people prefer motorbikes. They state that a pre-condition to all of their policies is to preserve peace. Two-thirds of the population have never experienced war. No one in the GDR personally gains from arms production. There is no inheritance tax in the GDR.

(Possibly I note now, looking back on these notes, because there was nothing to inherit.)

So as you can see, the early discussions were a bit mind-boggling and rapid-fire, with the dissemination of information. I took notes as best I could, but of course didn't understand half of it at the time.

President Reagan looks at the GDR as terrorists. But the fascists have killed nearly the entire Jewish population of Germany. They describe "terrorism" as state-organized terrorism by Israel against the Arabs, though they said, in Reagan's eyes, it is the other way around. Among other things they shared was that in 1972 their Parliament legalized abortion. Also, that no one can be fired within five years from receiving their pension, unless they commit a serious crime, like robbery or murder. They cannot be declared "incompetent."

In 1945 they did away with the unity between church and government. There were roughly 1.4 million Catholics (opposed to abortion) and 7.9 million Protestants. In 1949 the

*People's Republic of China was founded and it has very good
cooperation with the GDR.*

A question was asked, according to my notes, how far does
communism wish to extend itself within the world? The
answer:

*They expect internal upturning of capitalism. The example
they cited was Cesar Chavez and the 40,000 tomato pickers'
fight for wages in California.*

How interesting to see how the significance of Cesar
Chavez here in California was interpreted by the government
of the then-communist country of East Germany.

A page or two later in the journal were some more personal thoughts:

*Outside the theater tonight—a bird singing, alone and
plaintively . . . it was the first honest, free thing I feel I have
experienced thus far on the trip . . . The children's "Pioneer
Palace" today, really an amazing center for development of
young people's talents—afterschool activities—arts and crafts,
gym, swimming pool, acting . . . seemed to be such a few children participating—must be the cream of the crop! Also,
interesting that their play seemed to be for the purpose of more
propagandizing or "teaching" the children the new philosophy
of their country, of issues of their society. The
"improvisational" play the children performed was about a
worker making a chair poorly. Participation comments afterward from the class were: They thought he was insubordinate;
they thought his "boss" was too patient; they said he should be
fired for his attitude and his poor work.*

It is so interesting to look back on these incidents—to see
how instinctive human nature is, in that the children were so
much more to the point. They didn't jump in and remind each
other that in their country, no one could be fired.

More from the journal:

*Tonight we saw a play—very tedious, as it was all in Ger-
man, and highly propagandizing. I longed to know what the*

lines were that were getting responses from the audience—applause, laughter, etc. The play was about Lenin, but I gleaned it had something to do with modifying the purist attitude of "old" communism into something more workable for the socialist countries of today.

Interesting that today, as we hear our political candidates thrusting the accusations of "socialist" as a scary weapon at their opposition—because of the ideas of just trying to help one another with things like a decent minimum wage, with affordable education, with affordable health care—the people who are frightened by those things and use the word as a weapon have no idea what real socialism is.

The rest of the trip became really one of enjoyment, new experiences, and seeing historic treasures, once the lectures came to an end, and should probably be a whole separate book on its own. We visited Johann Wolfgang von Goethe's birthplace, the family's home in Weimar, which had been turned into a museum. Bernie Casey and I took strolls through the wooded park below the village at dusk, and I watched, for the first time in my life, the magical fireflies darting about. We visited the Green Vault, in Dresden, founded in the eighteenth century—unbelievable, the number of treasures we viewed—in what was called the Jewel Room of the Green Vault. Sadly in November of 2019, thieves somehow broke into the museum and stole huge amounts of the treasures. They did kindly leave behind one of the most valuable of artifacts—the Dresden Green Diamond, a forty-one-carat gem.

Upon my return with this interesting group of new friends, my involvement with the Screen Actors Guild Board of Directors began, and continued for the next eighteen years. During that time Barry Gordon, running for president of SAG, decided he wanted to include a diversity of performer categories in his slate, and I was asked to run as secretary/treasurer. Like my long involvement with the AFTRA Local and National Boards, the committees, etc. this SAG activity became a big part of my life, of my schedule. This work is all voluntary, there is no compensation. But it becomes addictive—at least it did for me, and I suspect for a lot of others. I never cared for the politics of it, but I did find it fulfilling to have a connection where I could speak for my community, express the problems and the needs in our workplace, and try to help in whatever way I could.

CHAPTER 22
THE TRANSITION TO VOCAL CONTRACTOR

I had worked for Ron Hicklin for years on projects for the Disney Theme Parks, before Jack was hired as Musical Director, and for a while after he joined Disney. But along the way, when Ron successfully lured Edie Lehmann and Debbie Hall away from Tuesday Productions, he had begun using them on most all of his projects, and he continued to use them even for the sessions Jack was producing for Disney. Jack liked my singing and didn't understand why I wasn't on the sessions with Ron, so he finally requested that he use me on the vocals, and I did resume working on Disney Theme Park live events again.

After we had been married a year or so, Jack left his position with Disney Theme Parks in order to focus more on freelance orchestrating and arranging, and he resumed working again with Bill Conti on a couple of film projects. Bill also turned over a TV series to Jack to score, after writing the main title theme. Bruce Healey, who was then elevated to Jack's former position for the Disney Theme Parks, eventually asked me to contract the vocal sessions for the Disney park events. It seems that Ron, in Bruce's opinion, was assuming too much the role of "producer" and Bruce felt his authority intruded upon just a bit.

Also, through some lucky twist of fate, I was asked by the

music preparation people at Universal at the time to contract a session for Danny Elfman, when he did his score for *Pee-wee's Big Adventure* in 1985, and again in 1988 for the score of *Beetlejuice*. Both projects involved small vocal groups, just four men and four women. But I established a working relationship with Danny, and when he was hired to write the main title for *The Simpsons* Fox animated TV series, he hired me to sing. That same theme has been airing since the inception of the show, which was, at this writing, thirty-one years ago. My daughter Susie by then was also doing a lot of session work, not just for me, but for other projects and contractors I didn't even know. Her own talent was carrying her forward into the business. Those main title vocals were done by Danny, myself, and Susie. It's one of the most widely heard of all the projects I've worked on, I suspect, and I'm very proud of it, but at the time we had no idea it would ever turn into such a hit. There's that bit of luck, once again, in having been at the right place at the right time, and watching it become such an iconic part of the world of television entertainment.

And that project connected me with the dear lady, Carol Farhat, who has for all these years been the vice president of TV Music, and very much the coordinator for most of their projects. She had formerly been Lionel Newman's personal assistant for some time at Fox, but this was a new area of work for her. There were a lot of details that required knowing about, regarding SAG contracts, singers' rates, etc., and Carol grew to trust that I would know those details, and would do things correctly for Fox. So I was plugged in for many of the projects going forward. I also worked on the first episode and sang the main title for *Family Guy,* the beginning of Seth MacFarlane's hugely successful career with Fox TV shows. The series actually was canceled after the first season, but it ran in syndication and had so many fans reaching out to Fox that they plugged it back in and it has been airing with a huge following since 1999. In the beginning, Seth was very hands-on with the music and our vocal sessions, and it was such a pleasure to work with him. He has since branched out into the theatrical features world, and into live-action TV, with *The Orville*. He's way too busy to attend the vocal sessions, but what a dear, sweet guy he is. And what a talent.

I had done a couple of film score sessions for Bill Conti as a singer and had the opportunity to contract the vocals for one of the Oscars broadcasts in 1987. I continued working with Bill on the Oscars for the next twenty years, and that also expanded my contracting world tremendously. In 1988 I contracted my first Alan Silvestri film score. Alan absolutely became one of my favorite people to work with, and I was blessed to sing on, and contract, many of his projects over the years. The connections to composers grew, and thus, the eighties became the beginning of the contractor activities, and I'm sure that work is what extended my years so very much longer. Being a vocal contractor also, for me and I'm sure for others, deepens one's connection to the project. It gives you an overview and creates a world where you too, must be creative in your efforts to assemble exactly the right voices to bring to life what the composer is trying to convey with his or her music. Too, it often lets you see more of the "inside" of the project and exposes you to a more personal view of how the composer works, how he or she handles the staff, the orchestra and others in the room.

CHAPTER 23
FILM SCORING BEHIND THE SCENES

Being on a scoring stage with live musicians for a film scoring session is a magical experience. The stage goes dark except for the music-stand lights; the scene to be scored is projected onto and fills the huge screen; the skilled technicians are all in their places behind the consoles and dials and levers; there is a moment of silence as the attentive musicians prepare for the downbeat; the composer, so focused, music before him/her, raises the baton in anticipation; the red "Record" light comes on; the clicks count off and the warning streamers move across the screen, telling the conductor that the downbeat is about to happen—and then the music—which in most cases is what breathes life and emotion into the scenes on the screen—fills the room, and suddenly, it all makes sense. It all comes together.

It doesn't always occur that way anymore, sadly, and the sessions don't always take place in Hollywood. The film world is changing. Technology is changing. But I was blessed to experience it during what we now think of here as the "golden years." Three of the major scoring stages in Hollywood are still in operation at the writing of these pages; Sony Studios, formerly the MGM scoring stage in Culver City where Judy Garland sang "Over the Rainbow" and so many other magnificent scores were created; the Newman Stage at 20th Century

Fox Studios, about fifteen minutes north of Sony in Century City, and the Eastwood Stage on the Warner Brothers lot in Burbank, which Clint Eastwood rescued from threatened extinction a decade or so ago. There is still considerable scoring done in those spaces. But partly because of technological advances, and partly in consideration of the bottom line (which seems to be what life is all about in so many areas of the industry these days) a lot of the film scoring has left Hollywood for London's Abbey Road, for Prague, or even Seattle and Nashville, which have become centers of nonunion orchestral and choral scoring. The movie lots for Paramount Studios and Disney Studios are still in place, but their scoring stages have been transformed into other uses. Todd-AO Stage on the CBS Radford Studios lot in Studio City was also once a busy scoring space where many beloved film scores were created, but that's now also been transformed into office spaces. And as of this week, with the announcement that Disney has just bought 21st Century Fox Studios, who knows what will happen to that magnificent legendary lot, with its Newman Scoring Stage and its other production facilities. Hold your breath, and say a little prayer. Currently, brilliant Seth MacFarlane is keeping the scoring stage alive with his live orchestral scorings for *The Orville, Family Guy*, and *American Dad*.

I felt the history of Hollywood filmmaking the first time I walked onto the MGM lot when I was twenty-one and found my way onto the scoring stage to work on *How the West Was Won*. The composer was Alfred Newman, a bit of a legend even in those early days, and Ken Darby was the choral director. I had gone to radio studios when I was a child with my mother when she worked as a session singer in radio, film, and sound recordings. But I'd never been on a studio lot. There is a sacred energy in those places. And I felt it the first time I walked onto the MGM lot as a professional singer myself. *How the West Was Won* was scored in 1961 and in those days, and for several decades to follow, whenever there was choir included in the score, we usually recorded on the scoring stage live with the full orchestra, all the music being performed and recorded simultaneously. That process has changed somewhat over the years, and now more often the choir sings to tracks previously recorded, and even *those* tracks have been layered section by section; rhythm, strings, horns, etc. until the orchestra track is full and complete. At the time of the writing of this chapter, the most recent film scores I contracted the choir for were *Deadpool 2*, for Tyler Bates, and *Finding Dory*, for composer Thomas Newman, Alfred Newman's son. It was incredible to realize that fifty-five years after working for his father Alfred Newman on *How the West Was Won*, I was still around, now working with the next generation of the Newman family, Thomas. I had hoped it wasn't destined to be the last film score I worked on, though it would be a nice way to wrap up almost six decades of film scoring! As it turned out, following those sessions, I've had the chance to sing on several more—most recently, a session for Alan Silvestri, on the score for Steven Spielberg's recent production, *Ready Player One*, on the Eastwood Scoring Stage, Warner Brothers Burbank lot. Alan has been one of my very favorite composers over the years, and to be in the same room again with Steven Spielberg, such a legend, was additional reason to celebrate. On this recent day I was working as a singer for another vocal contractor, Rick Logan, who did a fine job of running the session, conducting the choir, and coordinating with the booth.

Just before the session began, as we were all assembled on the risers on the huge scoring stage ready to begin the first cue, Steven came out from the control booth and stood next to Alan, to speak to the singers for a moment. "This is the first project we've had singers on in some time," he said, "and I just wanted to thank you all for being here and lending your voices." He spoke so graciously, and everyone was as thrilled as I was to be on the scoring stage again with Steven Spielberg.

And just a few months ago I had a call from composer Nathan Barr, composer of the scores of *True Blood, The Americans, Sneaky Pete,* and *Hemlock Grove,* among other TV series projects. He had been hired to score a new series for Amazon Prime, *Carnival Row,* and his wish was to use voices on the Main Title and underscore cues for the project, but the budget was beginning to look daunting. The SAG AFTRA contracts for singers and actors is based on a "per episode" scale fee. That is traditionally how individual episodes have been scored as they are produced over a period of time, usually week to week, during the length of the season run.

But the new "streaming" productions are scored differently. Usually after the entire series has been shot, then the scoring takes place with multiple episodes scored on the same session. Nathan's initial outreach to me was to ask for a budget for a twenty-eight-voice off-camera choir. I sent the budget I thought he needed, which was the episode rate for twenty-eight singers. But what he needed was an affordable budget that would cover vocals in the Main Title (eight episodes only, rather than thirteen which was the usually number, had been produced for the first season) plus some underscore vocals used in various individual episodes.

Thanks to Nathan's kind patience, his willingness to use a much smaller group of singers, (reduced from twenty-eight voices to nine) and much back and forth dialogue with the Union and the SAG-AFTRA Singers Committee, I was able to put together an agreement that the union approved. In addition to the one-episode scale fee, there is the option for a "13-Episode" rate, which is normally just used for the Signature Theme/ Main Titles. But it does allow for "lead-ins and lead-outs" which basically are underscore vocals used more in the olden days to lead in or out of commercial breaks. So we agreed to do the eight episodes for 8/13ths of the 13-episode fee, in one four–hour session. The series is fascinating – perhaps by the time you see these pages you will have watched it. And the music was perfect, supporting the drama, the fantasy world in which the story takes place, and the emotional highs and lows of the unfolding of the story.

I and eight other ladies performed the vocals on the new scoring stage and headquarters Nathan had just built in the San Fernando Valley, Bandrika Studio. He created this incredibly beautiful studio, acoustically designed in great detail, with several goals in mind. He worked with Jay Kaufman, acoustic designer, to rebuild a two-story structure that formerly housed offices with an open floor plan, and Peter Cobbin, one of the senior engineers at Abbey Roads studios in London, has said it is now one of the best sounding rooms in the world to record in.

Nathan also was able to fulfill another dream, and purchased the enormous 1300-pipes Wurlitzer organ, over one-hundred years old and remarkably functional, from the 20th Century Fox scoring stage. The organ had been used originally on the Fox scoring stage in the early days of scoring silent films. It now occupies six rooms and two floors of the Bandrika studios, has every sound imaginable within it, and sits on its own floating structure. Nathan's goal is to "keep alive the practice of recording real musicians in beautiful spaces" and he surely has accomplished this with his Bandrika studio. We ladies were the proud to be the first group of singers to perform vocals in the space. What an honor it was. May it continue to grow in its use and popularity.

During the sixties and seventies, the films we think of as classics were scored by the composers we also now think of as the "classic" composers. In 1962 Henry Mancini won an Oscar for *Breakfast at Tiffany's*; in 1963, Maurice Jarre for *Lawrence of Arabia*; in 1964, John Addison for *Tom Jones*; in 1966, Maurice Jarre again, for *Dr. Zhivago*; in 1967, John Barry for *Born Free*; in 1968, Elmer Bernstein for *Thoroughly Modern Millie*; in 1969, John Barry for *The Lion in Winter*; in 1970, Burt Bacharach for *Butch Cassidy and the Sundance Kid*; in 1971,

Frances Lai for *Love Story*; in 1972, Michel Legrand for *Summer of 42*; in 1974, Marvin Hamlisch for *The Way We Were*; 1975, Nino Rota and Carmine Coppola for *The Godfather Part II*; in 1976, John Williams for *Jaws*; in 1977, Jerry Goldsmith for *The Omen*; 1978, John Williams for *Star Wars*; in 1979, Giorgio Moroder for *Midnight Express*. You see those names repeating on that list—there's a deep connection between the significance of the music in a film and the quality of the film itself. Many are now gone from that distinguished list, but we are blessed to still have John Williams and Burt Bacharach with us, and we lost Michel Legrand only this last year.

Through my nearly sixty years of working in film music, I have wonderful memories of working with many of those composers, either as a singer or as a singer and vocal contractor. Some of the scores were among the Oscar winners, although that was less frequent for singers, as not all orchestral film scores included vocals.

The sixties were really the beginning of my experiences in film scoring and I was blessed to work with some of the very best. *How the West Was Won* fell into that category, winning the Oscar for Best Film. Also *The Sound of Music*, 1965, which wasn't eligible for Best Music or Best Song Oscar as it was originally written for the theatrical stage. I worked on *Dr. Zhivago, Butch Cassidy and the Sundance Kid*, and *The Omen*, all of which did win Oscars for their film scores. Some years later I had the opportunity to work for John Barry on *Out of Africa* and *Dances with Wolves*, and for Jerry Goldsmith on a number of his scores, including *The Omen*, *The Secret of NIMH*, and *Looney Tunes*.

When I began to add vocal contracting to my work in the mideighties, one of the first composers I had the opportunity to contract for was Alan Silvestri, on his scoring in 1987 of *Who Framed Roger Rabbit?* That was also relatively early in Alan's film scoring credits, and eventually there followed a number of other scores with this dear man, who is so talented and so fun to work with. Some of the other scores I sang and contracted vocals on for Alan were *The Abyss, Father of the Bride I* and *Part II, Forrest Gump, Blown Away, What Women Want, The Mexican, Van Helsing, Beowulf,* and *Night at The Museum 3.* What a wonderful time I had.

I also very much enjoyed the opportunities to contract for James Newton Howard, and so appreciated not only his talent as a composer, but his skill for communicating so clearly from the booth what he needed or wanted from the singers. Many composers now prefer to be in the control booth rather than in the room conducting, so they can hear the sound that's coming together and can give input to the sound engineer, etc. The scores I was privileged to sing on and contract for James on were: *The Sixth Sense, Snow Falling on Cedars, Dinosaur, Big Trouble, Unconditional Love, Peter Pan, King Kong, RV, I Am Legend, Charlie Wilson's War, The Last Airbender,* and *Salt.* The vocals on *Peter Pan,* by the way, were especially magical, though all of James Newton Howard's scores have been outstanding.

I treasured my working relationship with James, admired his talent so, and got to know him well enough over the years that when we scored *King Kong* I decided to have some fun. We were working frantically to complete the score—that is, James was working frantically—because his score was replacing the score another composer had done but which had been rejected by the director. The gentleman who had composed the original score was one of the very best, but sometimes the director's concept and the composer's interpretation of that concept just don't jell, and the director really doesn't know that until they experience the two coming together, the action on the screen and the underscore. A practice has evolved over the decades of directors putting together a temp score in some cases, with clips and excerpts from music they feel supports what they were saying on the screen. This is the good news and the bad news . . . it limits the composer's own creativity and I suspect sometimes makes them feel like they are imitating the writing of some other composer. But it also does give a clear sense of what the director wants to hear in the score.

There were several days of recording on the Sony scoring stage for *King Kong*, the vocals scheduled at the end of each of the orchestra sessions whenever scores had vocals included. I happened to have a truly magnificent and very realistic gorilla mask that I had purchased one Halloween to wear with a furry black vest that was by then out of style but worked for Halloween when I took my little granddaughters trick-or-treating. The mask slipped on like a hood and covered my whole head, so the identity of the wearer was impossible to detect. I decided to wear it into the first *King Kong* session, covering the rest of me with my big black trench coat, collar turned up in an intimidating fashion. James was in the control booth, coordinating the session with the director, who was live on a screen by remote from New Zealand so he could hear the new score as it came together. I just walked into the control booth as if I owned the place. No one knew who this strange creature was, but the crew knew something was up. They one by one started giggling, and finally I took the mask off to reveal the female version of King Kong, hidden away. Thank goodness, James Newton Howard graciously seemed to enjoy the joke.

While I was contracting for James, I was on his list at Christmas time as one of the recipients of the best coffee cake in the world, his very thoughtful gift to those who were part of his team. I miss the coffee cake *almost* as much as I miss James!

We lost composer James Horner far too early in his career when he was killed at the age of sixty-one in the fatal crash of the private plane he was piloting in 2015. James left a legacy of outstanding film scores, two of which were also Oscar winners, and others were honored with a nomination. I had worked as a singer for Ron Hicklin on several of James's earlier scores, and on one project, *Sneakers*, a score that featured solo/duo soprano vocal cues, my friend Darlene Kolden-hoven and I were hired by Ron to perform those vocals. It felt quite special to work on that project because the vocal cues were so prominent within the score.

A little later I also had the privilege of contracting vocal groups for James, for *Deep Impact*, *Mighty Joe Young*, and *Beyond Borders*, the latter of which involved African music. I had also recently worked on a film for Hans Zimmer, *The Power of One*, that also used very authentic African music, and James's musician contractor Sandy De Crescent knew of this and recommended me to James.

For Hans Zimmer's score of *The Power of One* we did quite a few vocal sessions, and I was asked to conduct the choir, something I didn't often get to do. Hans and his team seemed so pleased, which made me happy, and I overheard him say to someone that there had been loose talk for a moment of my going along to Africa to conduct more vocals that were to be done there, which would not, of course, have been the most practical idea. And he may just have been kidding. At any rate, the plan was to do some more music in Africa with authentic singers. But I lost out to Lebo Morake, a totally understandable decision on Hans's part. Lebo was from West Africa himself, had worked very closely with Hans and provided the authenticity for the African music we recorded in Los Angeles. He greatly contributed to Hans's score and went on to later also work with Hans on the score for *The Lion King*, the original Disney animated version released in 1994.

Over the years there have been many projects that allowed me to work with a composer as their vocal contractor, something that allows that deeper, more collaborative connection to the project. It's important to understand what that composer is trying to say with the music, what tone the voices should have, what ranges, what "feel," etc. If the concept of the score is a rather traditional and classical style, there are singers who do that best. If it's a lighter sound, a younger sound, it might mean different casting. Most especially, if it is a small group and not a large choral sound, the singers have to be carefully chosen.

I contracted one of the vocal sessions for Marc Shaiman, for his score for *South Park: Bigger, Longer and Uncut*; definitely an "adult" film in terms of its colorful language. Marc called me prior to the session to explain that the words on one of the lyrics were a little over the top, so I might want to consider that and not book anyone who might be offended by having to sing them. It was very considerate of him. I've worked on *Family Guy* for so long that it's not easy for me to be offended by lyrics, and I mean that in the most complimentary way. The lyrics are sometimes over the top, but perfect for the moment. But there are some singers among us who are not comfortable with lyrics like "You Have AIDS" (in a *Family Guy* episode) or "Holy Shit Balls" (the latter from *Deadpool 2* score). I try to respect their feelings. There was one session for *Family Guy* that involved a vocal cue satirically addressing God, one of several cues for the episode. I could see that one dear gentleman was just uncomfortable taking the name of the Lord in vain, or so he felt. I quietly suggested that he could sit this cue out, we would do it with a slightly smaller group.

One requirement of the position of vocal contractor is that he or she must be a performing member of the group, unless it is a man hiring women, or a woman hiring men. It's a good requirement, in my opinion, because it puts a representative of the singers out in the room, on mic, to communicate with the producer, the composer, and the engineer. It focuses and channels the communication, and ideally, the person who puts together the vocal group is someone who has worked with and knows the voices, knows who does what well, knows what the ranges of the various singers are, how their sight-reading skills are, how to balance them from section to section, etc. The contractor needs to be knowledgeable about the SAG contracts, needs to be able to make sure the proper rates are paid and the proper forms are submitted. In the early days of Hollywood, the major production studios had someone on staff who performed the duties of a vocal contractor, but the title of "vocal contractor" eventually became a covered SAG position, and was a required job title on sessions, beginning in the late fifties.

Marc Shaiman was always such fun to work with. Some of the other scores I did with him were *City Slickers*, *City Slickers II*, *The Addams Family*, and *Hocus Pocus*, and the music was generally light in spirit. His humor too, always made the sessions such fun.

We ended up performing a number from *South Park* with Marc as part of an on-camera choir for the 77th Annual Academy Awards broadcast, and it was great fun arranging the auditions for the singers who were to perform on camera. Auditions aren't usually involved with off-camera scoring choirs, but for this on-camera number they wanted singers who could be character "types" visually, but also who would be able to sing the material well.

Early in my contracting years, I worked on several scores as vocal contractor for David Newman, another member of the famous Newman family. David has had a long and very successful career in film scoring, and has more recently also become very involved as the brilliant conductor he is, bringing live film music to stages in concert halls all over the country. And in 2015 and 2016 I had the opportunity to contract for David's brother Thomas Newman, who I'd long been a fan of and had sung for but never contracted until *Bridge of Spies* and *Finding Dory*.

Because of the *Power of One* scoring project and the African music within it, I was also recommended to John Williams by his musician's contractor Sandy De Crescent, to be considered to contract his vocals for Steven Spielberg's film *Amistad*. This was a film that dealt with the traumatic journey of a ship bringing slaves from the coast of West Africa to

America, and an eventual trial in America, which happily ended in the slaves being released from their slavery and allowed to return to their homeland. It was the first of several projects I was privileged to work on with John. He is the most extraordinary man, obviously a brilliant composer, but additionally, so very gracious to his musicians and singers. I remember one cue on the children's choir session for *Amistad* that required a little "step-out" solo from one of the children. On the session there were two little boys I thought he should hear to audition for that solo, and he did so, having each of them sing the cue to the orchestra track recorded earlier in the day. He was so sensitive about the boys' feelings that he had me put them both on the contract and paid as soloists, and just said that they would decide later who should ultimately be the one whose voice was used in the final track. So neither of them had to lose an audition in front of their friends.

There was another cue that John needed to find the right solo voice for—a very powerfully emotional moment in the film when, on the ship's journey from Africa to America, one of the slaves on board, a young pregnant woman, has decided she's had enough of the chains and the world that she was being forced to become a part of. She was on the deck of the ship, sitting on the edge of the railing of the ship, bound in heavy chains. In the scene that one of the solo vocals was to underscore, the focus was on the young woman's face, quietly resolved to what she has decided to do. Waiting till the moment when she can do so while escaping notice, she closes her eyes and leans backward slowly over the edge of the ship, then falls overboard into the ocean, her descent filmed in slow motion as, weighted with the heavy chains, she sinks beneath the waves that crash against the ship.

John's music for the film was to be African in modality, and the language for the lyrics was authentic; the translator was there on the scoring stage for our sessions to help with the pronunciation. But John's music also had the touch of classic quality to it, so the vocalist had to be able to perform in that way. I brought a number of audition demos for him to listen to of singers from our community, but nothing was quite right. At the time I had to be at meetings of the AFTRA Health & Retirement Trustees in New York City and so I decided to arrange auditions at Juilliard, just for the fun of it. There were some excellent singers, eager, sweet young women excited for the opportunity and I took their auditions back to John, but again, nothing was quite right.

Upon my return, a friend in Los Angeles told me that the San Francisco Opera Company had recently hired a new director and there were many talented new young people within the company, so I called the director. He recommended a singer, Pamela Dillard, who happened to be on a concert tour at the time. I reached her by phone in Birmingham, Alabama, and somehow, I knew just speaking with her on the call that this was the right voice. She sent an audition tape, and sure enough, John loved her. He added two more solo vocal cues for her, both very emotional moments, and she had the ethnic quality in her voice that John sought, but also the classical quality that was needed to perform his music.

I recently came across the work file I had kept during the work on the project of *Amistad*, and in the folder, which I had forgotten about, were two pages of single-spaced, typed notes from my first meeting with John. It was fascinating to read those details again. There was much discussion with Steven Spielberg at the time, about whether it might be more appropriate to hire one of the large African American choirs from one of the well-known churches here in Los Angeles. There was a great deal of thought too, as to whether or not there should be an African American choir conductor. Ultimately, their decision was to go with session singers, as the production might be more efficiently done with experienced professional singers hired to shape the sound, and that John himself would be conducting as he was accustomed to doing.

We ultimately did five sessions for the film; two forty-eight-voice choirs with mixed male/female voices, two thirty-voice sessions with women's choir, and one huge fifty-voice children's choir, in which I had mixed a few women to help with reading and guiding the vocal parts. For the children's choir, we had a rehearsal the day before the recording session so we could go over all the music. This normally was not done, but the challenge of the harmonization and the African language made it important to prepare the children in advance for the session on the scoring stage. All the choirs were ethnically mixed and the music, as is much of John's music, had a touch of classical quality, even though it leaned toward traditional African music. So the choir sound was a blend of voices that incorporated both a classical tone and an ethnically authentic, full, and rich feeling and sound.

I must share just a bit more about the special gift of having worked with John Williams and Steven Spielberg, because theirs is a unique collaboration of director and composer, not to mention the fact that they are obviously two of the most incredible, iconic artists in their fields.

They have worked together in this way from the beginning of Steven's career, and it has worked brilliantly. Steven cares deeply about the scores of his films, the importance the music has in supporting the emotions of the scenes, and it shows, when he is there on the scoring stage, totally immersed, watching John and the musicians. I had sung on John's scores as part of the choir on several projects for Jeanine Wagner, who was contractor on some of his earlier scores. It was always evident on the scoring stage how important the music was to Steven.

I suspect that *Amistad* wasn't one of Steven's biggest film box office successes only because of the difficult subject matter. There were some very painful scenes, and when you score a film on the scoring stage, the conductor is working from a huge screen on which the film is projected with streamers, so that the music is coordinated and in sync with the picture. The musicians and singers can also see the screen and the scenes projected. Some of the scenes, the brutal beatings of the slaves, the difficult journey across the ocean in chains, the insensitive and cruel selling of slaves on the auction block—so affected my dear friend Oren Waters, one of the African American gentlemen singing in the choir, to say to me on our break, "This hurts my feelings, Sally!" I understood. On an emotional level, it was a painful experience for all of us to try to sing to those images.

Later I worked with Mr. Williams and Mr. Spielberg on *Munich*, the story of the eleven Israeli athletes and their coach who were murdered at the 1972 Olympics, and the eventual secret plan of the Israeli government, the assigning of Avner Kaufman, to carry out a series of secret assassinations in retaliation, in a worldwide operation that targeted eleven individuals. Along the way, Kaufman begins to doubt the morality of their approaching actions. Surprisingly, Steven received some negative responses about the film at the time of its release from the Israeli government. His hope was to inspire deeper thoughts about peace, about whether the perpetuation of violence ultimately achieves anything. Eventually he was able to overcome that criticism through a focused public relations program that involved the arranging of screenings in Israel, etc., and there eventually became a more positive, balanced reaction to the film.

Munich was obviously another very emotional project, and for certain cues again, the right solo voice had to be found. Of the vocal demos I submitted for John and Steven's consideration, Lisbeth Scott, a lovely LA singer and composer herself, was chosen. The emotion in those vocals will tear your heart out.

By the time we did the session for *Munich*, I had begun to do my series of black-and-white film composer photographs, and asked if I might photograph this session, so I was there on the scoring stage with my camera as well as with the paperwork for Lisbeth when they recorded the vocals. Steven sat on the scoring stage near the vocal booth and the conductor stand where John and Lisbeth were working together to the previously recorded orchestral tracks. There were also several live solo musicians on the session. At the end of each one of Lisbeth's vocal takes, tears were streaming down Steven's face.

At one point during the session I was tiptoeing around the scoring stage with my camera, trying to be unobtrusive but still getting some shots, and I tripped over one of the bases on a sound baffle within the orchestra setup. My camera went flying and then crashed onto the hardwood floor. I was quietly trying to fiddle with it, but it didn't seem to be responding to my advances. Steven said "Here, let me take a look at it . . ." and took it into the control booth. A few minutes later he came out with it, and said, " I think it should be okay now." I thanked him profusely. I will never part with that camera.

In 2015 I was delighted to have one more opportunity to work as vocal contractor for John. He was to score *Star Wars: The Force Awakens*, and largely due to efforts on the part of his musician's contractor, Sandy De Crescent, they were able to keep the orchestra scoring sessions in Los Angeles instead of taking it to London where the previous *Star Wars* films had all been scored. One afternoon my phone rang, and it was John himself.

"Hi baby, this is John Williams. How many low B-flats do you think we could find?" (This man is the most dignified, gracious human being on the planet. When he calls you "baby" it implies kindness and warmth, as innocently as if you were his five-year-old grandchild.) So I got busy on the phone and found twenty-one basses in our singer community who could sing low B-flats, a very low vocal range. The cues were as much for effects as for the musical tones, and they were low, growly, intimidating sounds. Everything worked wonderfully.

John was having back problems at the time and was still

busily engaged in completing the writing of the score, so William Ross, who I'd also worked with on the Oscars several times when he became Musical Director, conducted the choir for John on the Sony scoring stage. A few days later, after the music was mixed to final edit, I was so grateful to receive a call from John. He called to thank me and tell me he was pleased with everything. He is such a dear, gracious man.

And just one more quick story. I wrote a little collection of short personal essays, stories based on some of the articles on my living room mantlepiece. One of them was called "The John Williams Note" about a little handwritten note, carefully framed and placed on my mantlepiece. It is kept visible on my mantlepiece because at this point in the journey, I have a tendency to forget where I place precious notes, so it's just more fun to keep them close at hand and focus in on them every once in a while. The note is written in the writer's script in ink on a small, personalized note card, dated 1-16-18.

Prior to Sandy De Crescent suggesting me to John as contractor for the choir on his score for Amistad, John had used Jeanine Wagner, the daughter of Roger Wagner, the great LA Master Chorale Director in Los Angeles, as contractor for several of his film choirs. I had also worked with Jeanine on a Williams score or two as a singer, and on other projects where we had just sung together, and I was concerned that if I were to replace her as contractor for John, this would be a huge disappointment to her. I mentioned that to John and said I would be happy to just help her, advise with the booking of the singers, if he would prefer not to make that change.

John was so sensitive about that, and explained that he would understand if I just felt uncomfortable replacing her because of our friendship. As the conversations developed, and I reached out to Jeanine to talk with her about it, it turned out that the recording schedule for the film score conflicted with a concert tour that she was already committed to doing with her choir, the Wagner Ensemble, in Japan. So though I was not able to include her to sing in the choir, the timing seemed to be okay for me to accept this wonderful opportunity.

There was a situation that happened several decades earlier, with another wonderful composer I had the privilege of working with, and who actually gave me my first opportunity to write lyrics for film music. That connection recently served as another connection to dear John Williams, and his kindness.

The composer was Dominic Frontiere, and he had won several Emmy and Golden Globe awards, had scored films and numerous TV series shows, and was for a period of time the head of music at Paramount Pictures. I first wrote with Dom in 1971 the lyrics for the main title for *On Any Sunday*, a kind of pseudo-documentary about motorcycling that featured Steve McQueen, and has since become a cult icon among the biking community through the years. It also became somewhat of a tribute to Steve McQueen, who departed the Hollywood scene much too early in his life.

I had worked with Dom as a singer on earlier projects, and continued writing lyrics with him on several others, among which was *Hammersmith Is Out*, a little-known film starring Elizabeth Taylor and Richard Burton, but was not widely shown. (I know this little story is supposed to be about the treasured note from John that sits on my mantle, but bear with me for a bit longer, and soon you will understand why all this other information is coming into play.)

Dominic had married his third wife Georgia Frontiere, formerly Georgia Rosenbloom, widow of Carroll Rosenbloom, owner of the LA Rams, in July of 1980. Surprisingly to many, Georgia had become the owner of the LA Rams when her former husband died, as she had inherited the greatest percentage of ownership of the team. She was the first woman to take control of a league franchise, and early on in her position had upset many by firing Rosenbloom's son, who had been designated as manager of the team, and who most presumed would take over ownership of the team. Carroll Rosenbloom's somewhat mysterious death in 1979 was by drowning in the Atlantic Ocean while swimming near his Florida home.

In 1986, following a long period of investigations and drama, Dominic was charged with having "scalped" some charity tickets to the 1980 Super Bowl. Those of us who knew and loved Dom were convinced that he ended up taking the rap for his then-wife, Georgia, who claimed she had given him the tickets to be "given away." She herself was never charged with any crime. Dominic had refused to testify against her, had pled not guilty to income tax evasion charges against his 1980 taxes, but many felt he had been punished for not cooperating by providing evidence against Georgia. This also to many of us seemed a bit odd, given that he and Georgia had only married in that same year, 1980, following the death of her previous husband and suddenly he was thrust into the involvement with some Super Bowl tickets. (There's also that question about the cause of Carroll Rosenbloom's mysterious drowning, but we won't wander off into that cloud here. Lots of crazy stuff goes on around professional sports, as well as in the Hollywood celebrity world.)

But Hollywood does not necessarily always stand behind its own. When Dom was released, after serving nine months in prison, the result of the conviction of charges against him, most all of Hollywood had turned its back on him. Phone calls were not returned, opportunities were not offered as abundantly. Dom continued to work in music, and do other projects in the ensuing years, but he felt cut off from his Hollywood community.

He eventually married Robin Frontiere, a wonderful, very bright young woman, graduate of Sarah Lawrence, who had been, among other things, a script reader for newly submitted material for then head of the studio, Sheri Lansing. Dominic and Robin established a lovely home outside of Santa Fe, New Mexico. They have four amazingly brilliant children, all of whom Dom was so very proud of, and I was grateful to stay in touch through the years and be able to continue our friend-ship. It was with great sadness that I received the news from Robin in a phone call from her in the fall of 2017 that Dom's earlier diagnosis of lung cancer, which we all thought had been handled and was under control, had advanced severely, and that it was only a matter of weeks. The family was devastated, and I had hoped to make another visit to Santa Fe. I was very touched when soon after that initial call, I heard from Robin that the kids had decided I should be the person to speak at Dominic's memorial service there.

Robin had been fiercely defensive and supportive of Dom, and still held resentments toward the community of his fellow composers and studio executives who had sort of abandoned him, following the unfortunate Rams charity tickets situation. I asked her at one point if it would be all right for me to let a few of his old friends or colleagues in Los Angeles know of his illness, the ones I felt had truly cared about him, so they could get in touch with him. But she asked me not to do so, which I respected, because she felt they had made their decisions about the value of their friendship with him, and she was resistant, understandably, to acknowledge in any way Holly-wood and the painful past experiences.

However, she shared with me that John Williams had been in touch with Dominic through the years, and had recently called, and expressed concern and emotional support. I don't know what projects Dominic and John might have worked on together or what the basis of their friendship was. But it touched me so, to know that John, a man of such renown, and with such a busy schedule himself, had remained in touch with the family and had expressed that kindness to Dom and to his loved ones.

This is when I wrote John Williams a note. I didn't know if he would ever receive it, but I wrote and explained my history with Dominic, the lyric writing and the continuing friendship through the years with his young family. And I told him how moving it had been for me to learn that he had been in contact, stayed in contact . . . that it was not surprising in any way, because I knew what a kind and gracious man he had always been, but that this particular kindness touched me. And I knew how much it had meant to Dom's family.

A few days later, I received the note that now sits on my mantelpiece, from John Williams. I hope it's not inappropriate to share his words here, and I remind you that we were not socially connected or friends in any other way than through our times in the studios and our occasional path-crossing at music events over the years.

In his artistically dashed-off script are the words:

Dearest Sally—

Thank you for the <u>sweetest</u> <u>possible</u> <u>note</u>! You are an <u>Angel</u>—

Embraces—John."

Now, how could I *possibly* put that note anyplace other than where I could see it, and feel it make me smile, every single day? So it lives there, among the other inspirations for the mantelpiece stories.

CHAPTER 24
A PAINFUL LESSON IN THE JOURNEY

Danny Elfman has become over the decades one of the most respected and sought-after composers in the film business. He morphed into film composing after already having had quite a success with his rock group, Oingo Boingo. I sang on Danny's first film score for producer/director Tim Burton, *Pee-wee's Big Adventure*, the beginning of his long partnership with Tim. A few years later I was asked to contract a group of eight singers for Danny's score for *Beetlejuice*. In 1989, I again contracted the choir for Danny's score for *Batman*, another Tim Burton film, and in 1990, on the score for *Edward Scissorhands*.

For *Edward Scissorhands*, Danny used a women's choir of twenty ladies in the score, and additionally for a few cues, a boys' choir. Some of my very most favorite vocal cues of all the film scores I've worked on were those we did for *Edward Scissorhands*. I loved what Danny wrote, and I loved the sound we got on the women's choir; the pure, sweet, straight tones. Later I contracted his vocals and sang for the score of *Batman Returns*.

But then in 1995, an unfortunate situation occurred that very sadly ended my contractor relationship with Danny. It taught me an important lesson as well, and to this day I'm still kicking myself for it and seeking Danny's forgiveness from out there in the universe.

For the film score of *Dolores Claiborne*, I had been asked to contract a group of twelve ladies. Over the three or four weeks preceding the session, I'd prepared numerous budgets and communicated back and forth over the figures with the representative from New Line Cinema, which was the producing film company of record, explaining how the SAG rates worked, what the Health & Retirement contributions would be, etc. This is what usually transpires at the beginning of projects - communications back and forth between contractor and representative from the production company about costs, possible size of choir, scheduling, etc. Clearly, we had been discussing SAG rates and contracts, and since it was New Line Cinema, a very prominent production name in Hollywood, and there were major stars in the film, I had *assumed* we were talking about a SAG signatory film. Never assume.

There was a process in place at SAG at that time called Station 12, a cast clearance procedure where the vocal contractor submits the names of the singers and their social security numbers prior to the session to confirm that they are all current, paid-up members of SAG, so that the producer does not get a five-hundred-dollar fine for hiring non-members. Because I had just worked with all the singers I'd hired for *Dolores Claiborne* on another project a week or so earlier, I knew them to all be current and cleared to work. For some reason, I put off calling the names in for clearance to Station 12 until the morning of the session, treating it as a mere formality. But I nearly had a heart attack when the staff person who took the call at SAG informed me that though the singers were all clear to work, the *production* was in fact *not* a SAG signatory production, and the performers would be in violation of Rule 1 and would be fined the full amount of their earnings if they worked on the project.

I didn't know what to do. Someone at SAG reception connected me with a very helpful staff person who explained that the production could still sign a "post-production-only" agreement, and that would clear the project for the scoring session work scheduled that afternoon and everything would be fine, the project would be cleared for this post-production work we would do. I frantically called Danny's musicians' contractor at the time, Patti Zimmitti, who had booked the musicians for that day. Patti was on the 20th Century Fox scoring stage at the morning session with all the orchestra musicians , recording the tracks that we were to sing to later that afternoon. I explained what had happened, and told her about the post-production signatory agreement and how simple the process would be to correct the situation, that SAG could send the paperwork over, etc.

Patti, understandably, was quite upset, but did reach out and explain the situation to Danny and the producer representative, and told them about the post-production signatory possibility. But the producer from New Line Cinema—the one I'd been speaking with for weeks about SAG rates—said they were not interested in signing. It would have committed the producers of the film to having to pay SAG residuals, and even though the actors were all SAG members, they obviously had not been on SAG contracts when they shot the film, so the studio would have been obligated for the percentage of backend earnings which is normally divided among the SAG cast, but it would have been divided just among the singers. At that time it was roughly four percent of the distributor's gross, divided among the entire cast based on a formula of how many days each performer had worked on the film. It was based on the profits engendered when films went to "backend" use—cassette distribution or TV airings.

I didn't know what to do. Patti, of course, was furious. They were expecting us in a matter of hours. I had to call the other singers and tell them that I had no choice but to cancel the call, to protect them from doing work that would put them in conflict with the rules and invoke a fine, and that, of course, left Danny hanging.

It was absolutely my mistake to have assumed anything about the production, even though the theaters were filled with major New Line SAG films at that time. For some reason, this one was different. It broke my heart, and had I been more experienced at contracting, had I been longer in that part of the game and felt more secure about the relationship with the union, etc. (i.e., if it happened today) I would have shown up anyway and argued my case later.

As it was, somehow Danny managed to pull together a group of ladies who were not bound by the SAG Rules, and the score got completed. I heard later that someone in the offices of Richard Kraft, Danny's agent, helped get some singers to the studio, and was instrumental later in getting my singer colleague, Bobbi Page, to eventually replace me going forward as Danny's vocal contractor for future projects. Bobbi has done a fine job for Danny's projects and very kindly has included me as a singer on some of them. But of course the relationship I had so treasured with Danny as his contractor came to a sad end. I have felt embarrassed and apologetic about it for the last twenty years. Danny didn't object to my being present there as a singer on his future sessions, but it was never the same, of course. I did learn my lesson, and from then on always dotted my i's, crossed my t's, and carefully cleared all singers for work well in advance of the sessions. It's part of our job as contractors to do that and I learned my lesson the hard way on that particular project.

Danny's career has continued to take off in another area as well, in the last decade—he is doing live concert performances of his material from *The Nightmare Before Christmas*, one of the many fascinating projects he did with Tim Burton. He and a cast of singers and character performers have traveled far and wide, performing all around the world, and thankfully, here at the Hollywood Bowl where we can all enjoy the fun. Danny never fails to delight his enthusiastic audiences.

CHAPTER 25

THE BLACK-AND-WHITE WORLD

The year of my sixtieth birthday I treated myself to several adventures I'd long thought about doing. One was a cabaret symposium in New York, which required me getting brave enough to perform live onstage just as myself, not part of someone else's reputation as an artist; one was spending my first of what eventually would become twenty-one summers at the Summer Writing Festival Workshops at the University of Iowa campus in Iowa City, and another was getting involved with some photography workshops. I loved learning more about photography, and originally began working with black-and-white film, later moving to digital. A couple of years after I began the workshops, I was offered several solo fine art photography exhibits of the black-and-white film shots I'd taken while traveling in Europe, and also some local Los Angeles area photography.

In 2002, I had the opportunity to expand that work in photography and blend it with the work I'd done in music for four decades. Through the kindness, once again, of Sandy De Crescent, I was able to begin the series of black-and-white photographs of the composers with whom I had worked over the years, and some with whom I had not yet worked. Sandy approached the first composer I photographed, Jerry Goldsmith, to ask permission for me to come to the session and do some photographs of him, and that project eventually expanded to cover some of the most wonderful and respected composers here in town. The first shoot with Jerry was on the Paramount Scoring Stage M, when he was scoring *Star Trek: Nemesis*. John Williams was the second composer I photographed, for the Spielberg film *Munich* on the Sony stage, when John and Steven recorded Lisbeth Scott performing her solo cues.

When I took the prints from the sessions of *Munich* to show John at his office on the Amblin lot next to Universal Studios, John encouraged me to continue with the composers' photographs, pointing out that no one was chronicling those sessions with photographs at the time. He showed me a framed black-and-white photograph hanging on his wall that Annie Leibovitz had taken recently of himself and Steven Spielberg on the empty scoring stage at Sony for a magazine project, the same stage where I had shot the *Munich* session. Leibovitz's photograph was a scheduled shoot, arranged in advance to look like the stage after a session had ended and the orchestra had gone home. They had set the stage with a few bits of trash scattered about on the floor to indicate the end of a long day. John referenced it as similar to the photographs I had taken during the actual scoring session and had brought to show him, and I was so grateful for his encouragement.

I am also extremely grateful and indebted to Sandy De Crescent for her support and belief in the project. She was very helpful in letting me know what was on schedule so that I could approach the composer and the studio about being allowed to shoot. I only shot orchestral sessions, never the choral sessions, where I was strictly focused on fulfilling my duties as a singer and/or contractor and singer.

It was another whole new experience for me, creeping among the players on the scoring stage, stealing shots between takes as the composers were rehearsing the cues, or lurking quietly in the control booth as they listened to playbacks. And I realized for me, it was actually as meaningful an experience standing in the midst of those extraordinary musicians, as their lush musical sounds surrounded me on the scoring stage, as it was when I was there to sing the notes. Just being in those moments was so special, as you can imagine.

I now have about forty composers covered in the black-and-white film scoring photographs collection, and I've had several fine art photography exhibits of that material, *Film Scoring: Behind the Scenes* in Los Angeles. Some of the photographs were on exhibit at the Association of Motion Picture and Television Producers headquarters, and about fourteen of the pieces were also included in an exhibit at Cité de la Musique, in Paris, France as part of their 2013 exhibit celebrating one hundred years of film scoring.

About ten years ago I established a website that includes the composers' photographs: www.SallyStevensPhotography.com/filmscoring.html. The Composers page includes a photograph and a brief bio of each composer. The website isn't yet complete regarding the other areas of photography, but the composer's page is there if you would like to learn more about some of our wonderful composers.

These days there are so many new young composers, and there is a different musician contractor on the scene now who purchased Sandy De Crescent's business about twelve years ago when she made the decision to retire. He was not as responsive to my continuing the film composers project, so there are many I've not yet had the privilege of photographing. Also, so much of the film scoring world has expanded to include Abbey Road in London, as well as Prague, and even Seattle and Toronto. Those locations allow for nonunion, non-AFM scoring sessions, and much of the work previously done in Hollywood on union contracts is now being done there. It's not as possible to schedule a shoot for a live orchestra session here in town as it once was, but perhaps at some point I'll get back into the game. Standing in the middle of one of those magnificent orchestras full of brilliant musicians playing incredible charts is one of the loveliest experiences in the world. And the privilege of having documented some of the most brilliant composers in our business on film, as they worked from the control booth or the conductor's podium to bring their music to life, is something I am eternally grateful for.

Here are some of the photographs from the Film Composers Black & White Series.

Composer Alan Silvestri
Sally Stevens, Photographer

Composer Alf Clausen scoring the 300th Episode of *The Simpsons*
Sally Stevens, Photographer

Composer Bill Conti
Sally Stevens, Photographer

Composer Burt Bacharach
Sally Stevens, Photographer

Orchestrator & Composer
Damon Intrabartolo

Sally Stevens, Photographer

Composer Hans Zimmer
Sally Stevens, Photographer

Composer James Horner
Sally Stevens, Photographer

Composer James
Newton Howard

Sally Stevens,
Photographer

Composer Jerry Goldsmith
Sally Stevens, Photographer

Composer Marc Shaiman
Sally Stevens, Photographer

Composer John Ottman
Sally Stevens, Photographer

Composer John Powell
Sally Stevens, Photographer

Composer John Williams
Sally Stevens, Photographer

Composer Marco Beltrami
Sally Stevens, Photographer

Composer Michael Giacchino
Sally Stevens, Photographer

Composer Mychael Danna
Sally Stevens, Photographer

Composer Tyler Bates
Sally Stevens, Photographer

Composer Randy Newman
Sally Stevens, Photographer

Composer Terrence
Blanchard & Director
Spike Lee

Sally Stevens,
Photographer

Thomas Newman
Sally Stevens, Photographer

CHAPTER 26
THE TOLUCA LAKE TRAGEDY

The beautiful old Mediterranean home in Toluca Lake that I had been so fortunate to be able to buy in 1977 was a happy home for many years. It was the perfect place for family gatherings, for holiday dinners, for meetings and events. We held weddings in the garden, memorial gatherings, and graduation parties, and it seemed like the ideal spot to spend the rest of my life.

When Jack and I were married in 1982, he had sold his home, and we built a studio in the back of the property for him to work with his music, composing and recording. The building was designed so that it could also be a guest house, if we were to move, or if the space was no longer needed for recording and writing space. When Jack and I separated in 1993, I did decide to rent the space as a guest house, and Sandra Cornwall Mero moved in. She and her husband had just separated, but they were still working together on a project they hoped would be a successful business venture, a little retreat and health facility in the hills north of the San Fernando Valley. Sandra was a lovely young woman from Ireland and was pursuing an acting career, but meanwhile she was working busily with her husband on developing the retreat, and the guest house seemed the perfect temporary solution for her.

In the late eighties and early nineties, Universal Studios Theme Park, adjacent to Universal Studios and located on the mountaintop just across the Toluca Lake Golf Course from my house, was expanding its rides and its City Walk feature, the open area with little shops and restaurants. The Universal Amphitheater had been rather intrusive during the first few years I'd lived in the house, as the sounds from the concerts could be heard in the evenings wafting across the golf course lawns. But eventually, the amphitheater was converted to an enclosed concert venue and the sounds quieted down for a while.

However, as the park grew, the intrusive sounds began escalating again, and in the early nineties, Universal announced its intention to even further expand the park facilities. Our neighborhood residents, myself included, had been making frequent complaint calls up to Universal when the noise got to be too much. When the announcement to expand became public, hearings were required by the city of Los Angeles, and the Toluca Lake Homeowners Association organized efforts to present objections to the expansion before it was officially approved. So we did have a chance to voice our concerns, on the public record.

Additionally at that time, Universal had begun to quietly buy a few private homes that bordered the theme park on the uphill side of its property. The homes in that area were smaller properties and a bit more modest, but even closer to the sounds, and people were selling in order to escape the intrusion of those theme park activities. Meanwhile, an attorney friend had suggested I keep a log of all my calls of complaint up to the Universal Theme Park offices, and the list was growing.

One day I called the office, identified myself, and said, "Once again, I have to let you know that the noise from the rides is so intrusive there's nowhere on my property I can go to escape them!" A day or so later—they were getting to recognize my voice by now—I placed another complaint call to the Vice President of Development's office at Universal, and the young woman who took the message said to me "I think we should arrange for you to speak with my boss." I said I would appreciate that, not really knowing what the implication of taking that call would be. They called back later and arranged a time for her to come to my house so we could meet.

At that meeting, she informed me that Universal might be interested in buying my home. I had heard about the purchasing of lots closer to the park, but I was surprised that they were even considering the homes down below by the golf course, which would be much more expensive properties and the land could never be used in connection with the theme park expansions. To sell them my house was not at all my goal, but by then I had become so exasperated with the out-of-control intrusive sounds that I asked what the next step would be. They told me to get an appraisal, and they also would get one, and then we could talk further.

I could not really imagine selling at that point, but I did get the appraisal and decided to look at some properties to see if I could find a house I might be willing to trade for my present surroundings. Weeks went by, I got two appraisals on my home, and I continued to look at other properties, but I didn't hear from Universal. Eventually, I did find a house I liked very much on a hillside south of the boulevard in Studio City, and I made an offer, which was accepted by the sellers, contingent upon my selling my home.

More weeks went by, and still not hearing from Universal, I struggled with what to do, because the decision-making was out of my hands. Finally, against my better judgment, I reached out to the Vice President of Development's office again, and said I knew that it was not a good business move for me to share the information, but that I'd made an offer on a house, and I really needed to know where they were with it all.

This time, they asked me to come to their office to meet,

and at that meeting they informed me that they were no longer interested in buying the property. The properties on Valley Spring Lane that backed onto Lakeside Golf Course were quite different from the smaller private homes up on the hillside. And I suspect that it would have been very bad publicity, had word leaked out that Universal was buying upscale properties to quiet the noise complaints from the neighborhood.

By this time, things had gotten so disturbing that I was concerned the loud roars from the King Kong ride up at the theme park on the hill would interrupt a memorial gathering we'd planned in my garden for our great-aunt Beryl, who had just passed away. I once more called the office and explained that we had a memorial gathering planned in my garden and would not be able to hear it over the noise. Universal actually, and surprisingly kindly, ended up canceling the four p.m. King Kong performance on the Sunday of our memorial gathering, in order that we might have a reverent and respectful farewell. But by that time, I was just done with the situation. I was also concerned that the property values would start to go down because of the escalating disturbances. (Which ironically, over the years, has never happened. The neighborhood is as beautiful and pricey as ever.)

I informed the owners of the house I had made the offer on that my sale had fallen out, and they released me from my obligation. I found a real estate broker, listed my home for sale, and began again to look at properties. I found eventually the spot that has been my home for the last twenty-three years now, a smaller, but beautiful and peaceful house built in the late forties in the low hills off of Laurel Canyon. Someone also made an offer on the Toluca Lake house, which I accepted, so escrow began on both homes.

As part of the selling process required when a property is sold in California, it was necessary to have a termite inspection. The inspection was done by the small private company that my real estate broker customarily used. The initial inspection is free of charge, but the companies usually come up with some service that needs to be done, so they can have something to bill the seller for. The person who identified himself as manager of the company came to do the inspection and as often happens, they determined that the house had to be tented for termites. I was not willing to do that. I had used a natural process a bit early with orange oil that a different company had done, to treat some problems in the garage area. This company did not do orange oil treatments. They finally settled on, as a compromise, just tenting the office space that was attached to the three-car garage structure. It had originally been the chauffeur's quarters when the property was built in 1928. Jack had used it originally as his writing space before we built the guest house/studio, and I was at that time using it as office space for the writing of a musical I was working on with a composer from New York, Norman L. Berman. It was just a quiet little room attached to the three-car garage at the back of the property, where we could sit uninterrupted for a few hours and focus on our collaboration.

The "manager" wrote up a detailed proposal, assuring me that any and all openings would be securely and safely closed, that all safety measures would be taken, and no harmful toxic chemicals could escape. So I signed the agreement. The tented fumigation was scheduled to take place on Friday, March 7, 1997. I had a recording session that day so I left the front gate unlocked at the end of the driveway and the office space open, in order that they could proceed if I was not at home.

I called Sandra, my tenant in the guest house, to tell her that the fumigation was to take place, that it was limited to the little office space attached to the garage, but cautioned her to be very careful, to avoid even going into the garage, as I knew some of her things were stored there and she might have been planning to do some packing over the weekend. The small area was tented and still secured when I came home from work, and I assumed all was well.

Two days later, on Sunday afternoon, March 9, the couple who had bought my house called to ask if they might come by and take some measurements. When they arrived, they also wanted to look inside the guest house, but because Sandra's car was parked on the driveway by the guest house, I assumed she was at home, and I didn't want them to intrude upon her privacy. I called her number to ask if we might come out but there was no answer, so I went out to knock on the door.

As I approached the entrance to the guest house, through the double glass French doors I could see into the space inside. Sandra was there, lying on the floor of the guest house, her body making jerking movements, appearing to be in the midst of some kind of a seizure. I didn't know what health condition she might be suffering from, but I ran back inside to grab the key, and I shouted at my broker and the buyers to call 9-1-1. Very quickly the paramedics arrived. They were uncertain also as to what she was experiencing, and they carefully moved her into an ambulance and took her to St. Joseph's hospital nearby in Burbank.

As they were preparing to leave, it occurred to me to ask one of the paramedics if the fumigation that had been done two days earlier could have had any effect or be related in any way to her symptoms. He replied no, not unless she had gone into the space, which I was sure she hadn't done, as it was still sealed off. He said even if she had gone into the garage, a large open space on the other side of the wall to the office, it would not have been dangerous.

I drove to the hospital and went inside, hoping to hear that some kind of diagnosis had been made and Sandra was doing better. The doctors asked me about various possible health conditions Sandra might have had, but I just didn't know those details and they weren't able to give me any answers as to what was happening. As I walked through the halls, it occurred to me to call Jack and see if there was any connection between the two spaces that I wasn't aware of. I was almost afraid to call, fearful of what I might hear.

I reached him on my cell phone, standing alone in the dark hospital parking lot, and told him what had happened. Jack informed me that there had been pipes running underneath the pavement of the driveway from the studio into the little office, so that he could run microphone cords through them and set up in the small space to record solo instruments. My heart nearly stopped.

What I was afraid to even imagine might have happened, had possibly happened. The fumigation might have caused this tragic situation, and the fear intensified about whether Sandra would survive. I fell apart, walked through the dark parking lot with tears streaming down my face, and then tried to calm myself enough to go back inside the hospital.

I found the doctors outside Sandra's room and told them what I had just learned, but they didn't really seem concerned at the time, not feeling her condition and the extermination were related.

I then called the broker with the terrible news. He called the fumigators, and I went back to the house to meet them, praying all the way that somehow, they had found those openings in the wall, had safely and securely covered them as promised. I prayed that there was still some legitimate possibility that the fumigation had not affected Sandra. Sufficient time had passed from the fumigation three days earlier that they could safely open the tented space and look inside the office. To my horror, they found that the openings to those pipes were indeed bare—exposed and open—into and through the wall. They had not been sealed off. They had not done as they promised on the agreement I had signed.

It now seemed very probable that Sandra's condition had been caused by the chemicals. And the added tragedy was that only a few weeks earlier, the deadly chemical that was used, methyl bromide, had been banned from use in California. But the governor of California at the time, Governor Pete Wilson, had waived the ban only days prior to the fumigation, in response to pressure coming from the agricultural and farming businesses. It didn't matter that it was unsafe for the workers in the fields, it killed a bunch of bugs that other chemicals apparently didn't kill. I later learned that part of the problem with using the dangerous chemical in fumigation was that it travels, it does not settle downward but rises and drifts wherever it can through the air, so ultimately it was able to travel into the empty pipes and rise on into the guest house. Its ability to travel, ironically, was part of what made it useful to agricultural farming.

The owner of the little fumigation company was sitting on my lawn in the dark when I arrived back at the house, his head in his hands, obviously also horrified at what had happened. I felt so bad for him that I went over and expressed my sadness and my concern for the situation, as I could see he felt responsible and was just overwhelmed. His company's "manager," the rather macho, arrogant guy who had done the estimate and the inspection and prepared the "careful" instructions for the young workers who actually did the work, overheard me talking to the owner. Later, he stood next to his boss, telling him that I had basically taken responsibility for the tragedy by expressing that sympathy to him. And during the weeks and weeks of depositions that were to follow in connection with a wrongful death suit the family filed, this same man would testify that they hadn't seen the open pipes because a chair was in front of them. There was no chair there except for a loose wicker patio chair that could easily have been moved, seen through, or looked behind.

Sandra's seizures were under control once treatment began at the hospital. But she had not regained consciousness that evening. My daughter Susie went with me the next day to the hospital, and as we sat in the lounge area, I could feel the cold, angry rebukes from her friends who had gathered there.

I understood. This was their friend, a person they loved, and they felt this had happened because of me, because of something that I had caused. I was to blame. I was devastated. It was the worst possible thing I could imagine—that something I had done would cause harm to someone. From the first weeks I was learning to drive a car at sixteen, I was always fearful that one day I might be driving along and some kid would race out of a driveway on his bicycle, I would not be able to stop and would hit him. I imagined this kind of thing happening—or that someone would step off a curb suddenly in front of me. Driving was the first activity I had engaged with in life that held the possibility of accidentally harming someone, and as excited as I was to be learning to drive, that anxiety had never left me. Now here was this moment, something more dreadful than I possibly could have imagined, and I felt the responsibility for it. I was so grateful to have Susie by my side, as we sat in the waiting area of the hospital. I continued to visit every day, praying that somehow Sandra would regain consciousness and all would be well.

Meanwhile, there were helicopters flying over my house, taking pictures of the structures and property, and publishing them in the *Los Angeles Times*, along with articles about the accident. There were reporters at the gate wanting to interview me. They were confronted by a kind neighbor from across the street, who told them I was devastated by the accident and not available for an interview, and that they should leave me alone. That's all he would share with them.

The week continued to be filled with inspectors coming to investigate the guest house, meetings with the insurance claim adjuster from Farmers, and talks with my kind insurance agent Kirby Yale, without whom I never could have gotten through the sad events of the next several months. The first week of Sandra's hospitalization was a maze of my visits to the hospital, and a steady stream of visitors to my house—Sandra's family, more inspectors, and the workmen who had done the fumigation.

The weekend following the accident happened to also be the beginning of the Oscars schedule for that year's broadcast, and I had been hired once again as Choral Director. I had booked the choir and submitted budgets. With rehearsals, pre-recording some underscore vocals to be used in film clips for the show, and a separate scoring session for Billy Crystal's number later in the week, the days were hectic. Then the Oscars orchestra rehearsal and pre-record schedule, always an intense few days, began on the weekend of March 22 and 23, and the week grew more challenging. Inspections and investigations continued at the house along with lawyer visits, so I was back and forth between Capitol Records, the Shrine Auditorium, the hospital, and my home—which was by now not feeling much like a home.

Meanwhile, Sandra remained in the hospital, unconscious. The nurses at the hospital were loving and attentive with Sandra. They manicured her nails, applied makeup to her face, and combed her beautiful blond hair. They tried to make her comfortable. Her brothers continued to visit, and her sister had arrived from Ireland soon after Sandra's hospitalization and was by her side much of the time. I would visit in the evenings and sit by Sandra's bed, softly talking to her—though she remained unconscious—trying to give her courage. "You can come through this, Sandra . . . you are God's child, your life is in His hands, and He will take care of you . . . we all love you so . . . you can come through this . . . I am so, so sorry . . ." and then the tears would come, as I continued to pray that she was hearing me, that my words would somehow give her courage, that she would respond.

The Oscars broadcast was Monday, March 24. On Tuesday morning March 25, Sandra's dear friend Daniel Hughes called to tell me the sad news that the family had taken Sandra off of life support, and she had passed away that evening.

I was devastated. My dear, close friends Carol Lombard

and Barbara Michaels had been talking with me daily through the last couple of weeks and insisted on coming to be with me. Susie and her husband Rick reached out, and Sandra's friend Daniel came by to visit. Meanwhile, the work schedule continued; there was a film call session for Danny Elfman, more inspections at the house, more meetings with the attorney and representatives from Sandra's family. One afternoon I went by my friend Jackie Ward's house for coffee and fell apart at her kitchen table. I just sat sobbing, as she stood quietly nearby until I had exhausted all the tears. We didn't have to talk. My friends Jona and Lee Willis also reached out almost daily and continued to stay in touch through the following months of depositions and legal pursuits. My dear friends were so supportive and kind.

It is interesting how differently reactions and behaviors surface through shocking events such as this. At one point just a day or so after the accident, I was in the guest house while one of the early inspections was taking place, and someone from the attorney's firm hired by my insurance company took me aside. He showed me a place on the bathroom ceiling that they had noticed, where smoke had accumulated, and suggested that perhaps Sandra had been using drugs of some sort . . . meth or some similar drug . . . implying that there may have been a different cause for her condition. This certainly would have made me less responsible. But I cut him off immediately and told him that Sandra had quite possibly lost her life, and I was not going to allow her to lose her reputation and her good name as well. That theory was put to rest.

Another unexpected reaction was from the couple who had just bought my house, which was at that time well into the escrow period. They wanted to talk about renegotiating and reducing the selling price. My broker put that theory to rest as well. I didn't understand the reasoning behind that request, except that they thought the tragedy might get them a better deal. It honestly surprised me, as they'd seemed like nice people.

Sandra's sister and I had become friends, trying to support each other through the painful days, and when the service was planned, she asked me to sing for Sandra's funeral. It was to be at the elegant old Catholic church in the neighborhood, St. Charles Borromeo, on Monday, March 31. I agreed to sing and was touched that she would ask, but expressed concern that I wasn't sure I could get through it without falling apart. The service was a very formal Catholic mass in the high-ceiling sanctuary. I sang from a balcony at the rear of the church, and did manage somehow to get through it. I sang "Pie Jesu," a piece from a really beautiful requiem mass written by Andrew Lloyd Webber for soprano voice and boy soprano. My dear sister-in-law Miriam Sosewitz Clarke played the boy soprano part on the flute. I tried to just focus on the music, and to rise somehow above the tears that hovered just beneath the surface. I was so grateful to Miriam for helping me through that difficult moment. She played beautifully, but it was not easy for her either.

After the service was over and we walked out into the garden through the main entrance of the church, what did we find but, sitting there under one of the olive trees, a man giving an interview to a television crew. The news channel's truck was parked by the side of the road in front of the church and the man, it turned out, was Larry Feldman, the attorney who had been hired by the family in the wrongful death lawsuit. He was giving an interview to one of the local news channels, to bring attention to his case. I found his prank disgusting, but obviously he didn't.

I had only just learned a day or two earlier that Sandra's family had filed the wrongful death suit, and that both the fumigator and myself were the target of the suit, along with the manufacturer of the chemical containing the methyl bromide. Larry Feldman, the attorney, was the same attorney who had represented the families who had sued Michael

Jackson for child sexual abuse. I guess Mr. Feldman thought talking about the tragic death in front of a TV camera outside the church following the funeral would get attention and help his case.

Daniel, Sandra's friend, had called me from his home in Canada a few days earlier, to say that he was coming into town and we needed to meet. Over breakfast, he told me more about the family's suit, because he had gone to the attorney's office with Sandra's sister, her mother, and brothers, had heard the conversation and was realizing that it was largely motivated by her mother and her brothers. He knew the reputation of the attorney, the monetary goal of the suit, and he was concerned.

Following Sandra's service, I had arranged for a reception at Bistro Gardens, a lovely and very traditional, elegant restaurant in Studio City that had a very nice private space for such gatherings. I wanted to do this, but I asked Sandra's sister to hostess the event, lest there be any negative feeling about it in any way among her friends and family. We headed there after the service, and I had also asked my friend Juli Bridges to come with me to Bistro Gardens, so I didn't have to attend alone. I knew it would be difficult to be there, with the group of friends and family who, I believed, still felt I was responsible for Sandra's tragic death. After the crowd thinned, there was an abundance of expensive food left on the buffet table, and I asked the restaurant if they would bundle it up so that I could take it to the homeless shelter I knew of in the area. I had to try to do something good, on that sad day. The staff did pack it up nicely for me, and were sensitive and kind as they loaded it into my car. I delivered it to the shelter, from Sandra and me.

The process of the lawsuit, which morphed into a mediation, turned into weeks and weeks of depositions. The hearings actually extended through the whole year and into the following year. My own deposition was taken, along with the manager of the fumigating company, my real estate broker and others involved who provided technical information about the chemical, etc. One of the young workers, who had been following the written instructions the manager had provided for them, felt so responsible and fearful of reprisal that he fled, returning to his home in Mexico. And the gentleman who was the owner of the small independent company had been so shaken by the accident that he had subsequently sold his company to the "manager," the one who claimed I had apologized for the accident, and whose inspection report left out the open pipes he hadn't spotted because, of course, of that annoying chair.

The hearings that ensued spanned a long period of stress, with hours of tearful drives from my home down the 405 Freeway to Century City, whenever schedules allowed me to attend the depositions. I tried to be there for as many of the other people's depositions as I could, as I wanted to understand and know what others were saying.

The depositions continued all through the year until the following April, when the suit was finally settled. I recently looked at my datebook from 1997 to clarify the dates, details, etc. During that period of time, my work schedule continued to be intense, almost daily and sometimes multiple sessions a day, in addition to SAG and AFTRA board meetings, negotiations committee meetings and the negotiations themselves, a convention in New York in June of the year, visits with family, and loving friends who were trying to keep my spirits up with sharing a meal from time to time. As I look back over the year on those pages, it's amazing to me that I was able to continue functioning. I would not have been able to, had it not been for the kindness and support of those friends. And I suspect that it was a blessing to have the heavy schedule of work as a distraction.

Jack and I had separated in 1993, and we remained friends, but he said to me at one point that if we hadn't had a divorce, this all never would have happened. He would have been present, he would have known about the pipes, etc. This thought was not terribly comforting.

I remember in the midst of the depositions and hearings period, driving home through Hollywood down Fountain Avenue from a session. I found myself trying to emotionally prepare for, and to accept, that if I lost everything—if I lost my home and savings—I would find an apartment in Hollywood some place that would let me keep my dogs, and I'd at least be able to keep on working at the thing I loved. It was hard to think about the possibility that I could lose everything I'd worked for all those years, that my life going forward might be very different, that financial security would be a thing of the past. But I was the luckier one. Sandra was gone. I still had my life, going forward. I tried to embrace the acceptance that life *would* go on, that it would be okay, no matter how things wound up, that life wasn't about houses or bank accounts or neighborhoods. I had friends, I had work colleagues, no one had turned their back on me, and I would make it somehow.

Eventually, the suit was settled. My Farmers homeowner policy, combined with an umbrella policy that I also had, covered my obligations. I am not permitted to share the amounts, but it was ironic that my payment was larger than that of the exterminator's, because I had carried more insurance than they did.

My dear friends Jona and Lee had planned a holiday trip on one of the cruise lines around the time that the mediations concluded, and they urged me to come with them, to just breathe and get a fresh start on life. I decided to do that, and was so grateful for their friendship and their company. It was the first time I had ever been on a cruise ship, and late one night early in the cruise, standing on the little veranda outside my cabin, I tearfully let go of the grief I felt over Sandra's death. Somehow, in that unfamiliar part of the world, in the stillness, I suddenly felt a direct connection with my father who had passed away just a few years earlier, and with my mother, who had passed away about ten years earlier. Surrounded by the dark night, the years disappeared, the distance and dimensions between us disappeared, and I felt their presence as if I could have reached out and touched them. I felt they were giving me their blessing on moving forward with life. My father had always been understanding and forgiving, and I felt his love surrounding me in that still dark night, in the cool air. And my mother, whose side I had stayed by through the darkest times at the end of her life, was there enfolding me with her courage. The universe opened up and I felt its forgiveness and its embrace.

Ironically, at some point in the year or two following the tragedy, I was working on a project that Governor Pete Wilson (you remember him – he had allowed the Methyl Bromide to be continued for use after it had been outlawed...) was there to address the audience on some subject. We were all standing backstage in the wings waiting to do whatever we were there to do, and I realized I was standing right next to Governor Wilson and his wife. I could not keep quiet. I approached him and started to tell him of the tragedy that his decision to allow Methyl Bromide to be in use had caused. And before I could get very far into the story, his protectors on duty stepped up to remove him from the conversation with the crazy lady. I hope he heard enough of it to feel some measure of sadness and responsibility. And I'm glad I didn't get kicked out of the theater that night, or arrested for approaching a state official in a somewhat hostile manner.

That anxiety from my earliest years when I first learned how to drive at sixteen—the fearing that in some unpredictable moment, I might harm someone—made this accident feel like I'd experienced something I had feared all my life. I've never forgotten it, nor the sadness for Sandra, whose life was in the process of blossoming and evolving. I've accepted that there is nothing, was nothing, I could do to change it all. It is painful to write about, and talk about. But it was impactful in my life. My gratitude for the help and support of my friends and family will be forever in my heart. And so will Sandra.

CHAPTER 27
THE LYRICIST APPEARS

I had been writing songs since high school, sitting at the piano scribbling out sketchy notes; and as I told you about in the earlier chapters, Herb Alpert produced me as an artist, a "single" of two songs I had written that was released on Dot Records in 1960. But getting focused on the session singing activities, and being so grateful for the work that was expanding over the years, I really didn't pursue the songwriting for a decade. Then in 1970 I got much braver and did reach out to several of the composers with whom I'd worked on sessions as a singer. I shared some of my songs and lyrics, and just tried to put myself out there as a possibility for lyric writing. One of the composers I reached out to, Dominic Frontiere, liked the material and responded, giving me my first chance to write lyrics for film.

Dominic scored literally hundreds of TV episodes, numerous different series projects from the late fifties–sixties, the most well-known being *The Outer Limits*. He won a Golden Globe for his score for the film *The Stunt Man* and was head of music for Paramount Studios along the way. A project came up for him in 1970, a documentary produced and directed by Bruce Brown and featuring Steve McQueen, *On Any Sunday*. It was about motorcycling, something that Steve was very fond of doing and well-known for within the motorcycling world. Miraculously, Dominic allowed me to take a shot at the lyrics for the main title song, even though I knew nothing about riding motorcycles! I had ridden on the back of one, behind the vice cop I was briefly engaged to during my early UCLA years, but more helpful even than that was the fact that my younger brother Charles at that time was a motorcyclist. So he took me for several rides through La Tuna Canyon, where we could breeze along through the mountain roads, and talking to him, plus the actual experience of riding with him, apparently successfully allowed me to write with some measure of understanding. "On any Sunday, I'm a flyin' man . . ." was one of the lines from the song. It was a thrill to be part of that project, and I did the solo vocal for the main title, along with the background vocals with Ron Hicklin and four other singers. The film has become kind of iconic within the motorcycling community over the years, and just recently I had an outreach from a journalist wanting to do an interview about the writing for the project.

In that same year I also had an opportunity to write an English lyric for an Italian film, *Permette?* staring Marcello Mastroianni. The composer was Armando Trovaioli, and it was a fascinating experience, trying to come up with the lyric that said in English what the film director would trust as appropriate for his Italian language film. The title of the song was "Somewhere, God is Crying" and the phrase that repeats several times throughout the song was "Somewhere God is crying, what is this we've done? Brother love is flying straight into the sun." I was grateful that the composer and the director seemed to be pleased.

The following year Dom was asked to film another independent film starring Elizabeth Taylor and Richard Burton, "*Hammersmith Is Out.*" It was an offbeat kind of plot, and actually never really went any place. In later interviews both Elizabeth and Richard sort of disavowed their participation in the film. But it was fun for us. We wrote three songs for it.

One was the love theme in ¾ time: "Sad little girl in the looking glass . . . who told you wishes come true? They're only beggar's dreams, taking you nowhere . . . fast as they can . . . Once you had dreams worth remembering . . . now you're afraid and alone . . . How far away from hope have you come, and how will you get back home?" set to Dom's beautiful melody.

Then there also was a country song intended to be a source cue, that Dom had conceived of as being the start of a love song sung on the radio in the background. The scene was where two of the character met for the first time, in a bar. He gave me the title "For Openers . . ." But I was in a peculiar mood and decided to find a new twist on that title. It became instead, "For openers, this is the closing . . . 'cause I've cried all the tears I can cry . . . There's nothin' left I can believe in, and there's nothin' to say but goodbye!~"

In 1977 I had a chance to write lyrics for Don Ellis, a wonderful composer very much known in the jazz world, for the film *Ruby*, a drama/horror genre film that needed a song for the end title. The star of the film was Piper Laurie, who wanted to sing the song herself and did so for the end titles.

In 1981 I had another wonderful opportunity to write lyrics, this time with Dave Grusin, the incredible jazz pianist and Oscar-winning composer who scored *The Firm*, *The Graduate,* and *Tootsie* and won his first Oscar for *The Milagro Beanfield War,* but was also nominated for numerous other film scores, including *On Golden Pond*. Dave needed a lyric for a source cue that some children were to be singing on their way into a Catholic church, in the film *Absence of Malice*. I'd worked with Dave as a singer and he knew about the other lyric projects I had done. He wanted a song that felt kind of "old English," and so I wrote the lyric for "Who Comes This Night?" and a children's choir recorded it for the film.

But an even bigger dream came true around that song, about twenty years later. Dave Grusin was involved with the production of the first Christmas album James Taylor recorded, and he called to ask me if I could write a second verse to our song, as the version for the film had been very short, just one verse, and he wanted to submit it to James, to be considered for the album. I did write a second verse, Dave liked it and felt it worked, and we recorded a demo of it one evening at his brother's home studio. We went to dinner afterward at a lovely little Italian restaurant in Brentwood, and when we walked in, the hostess welcomed us warmly, and said, "Oh, Dave, the Bergmans (Marilyn and Alan, the legendary lyricists) are here dining—they will be so glad to see you!" On our way to their table, Dave quietly whispered to me not to say anything about our song and the demo for James we'd just done, because apparently the reason I had gotten to write the lyric for the film initially was because Marilyn and Alan Bergman were out of town at the time!

Dave played the song for James, who loved it, and he included it in that first album and in several other later released Christmas albums. He recorded the song at Capitol Records in Hollywood and was going to record the background vocals and his own lead vocal after Dave had produced the tracks. I asked Dave if I might be able to come to the session and perhaps do some photographs, and he reached out to James, who agreed that I could come. James Taylor had been my musical idol from the late sixties forward, and I was beyond thrilled that this all was happening. I arrived at Capitol Studios on North Vine Street, camera in hand, and walked into the control booth for Studio A. James was seated at the sound control panel, got up when I walked in, and came over to greet me. He extended his hand and said, "Hi, I'm James . . . you wrote a beautiful song . . . would you like some coffee?" That's James—an amazing, sweet guy.

When the CD was finally completed and released, Dave sent me a copy. I can still remember my first time of listening to it in my car, tears of gratitude running down my face.

A bit earlier, in the late seventies while I was still working with Burt Bacharach in concerts, he had an idea about doing an album project where the songs would tell a story of life from a woman's point of view. We met numerous times in his condo on Wilshire Boulevard where he was living and writing then, as he and Angie Dickinson had recently separated. He had reached out to several other woman lyricists as well on the project, and eventually the design of the album morphed less from one particular journey and more into a collection of songs by women lyricists, along with several instrumental pieces. I wrote the lyric for "There is Time," one of the songs included in the album *Woman*, and we recorded the project live in concert with the Houston Symphony, in 1977. I did get to sing the solo on that one, and it was a thrilling project for me to have been a part of. I look at this man, this absolute icon in the music world with hundreds of hit songs recorded by artists all over the world, who somehow thought my words were worthy of his music. I never in my wildest dreams imagined I would have a chance to write a lyric for Burt Bacharach.

CHAPTER 28
THE BACHARACH YEARS

Traveling with Burt was truly one of the highlights of my life, and the opportunity came at just the right time. Though I like to think I've always felt grateful for having had so much good fortune during my years in the business, about eight or ten years into it, I had begun to grow a bit jaded. In the early seventies, the commercials activity was busy, but sometimes it seemed like the people I worked around—the "ad men," the agency guys—were all so terribly impressed with themselves. At that time the jingle business was very much a man's world. The producers, the agency people, the arrangers—all were men. They needed girl singers once in a while of course, but the folks in charge were pretty much all guys. One gentleman, a really very nice producer/arranger, kept outdoing himself with the expensiveness of the wine he would bring for the agency guys, the engineer, and the contractor (all male at that time) to enjoy with him after the session was over. I'm sure when I eventually began to contract in the eighties, I suffered, or appeared to suffer, from feeling a bit of self-importance as well. And even in the early years, where the center of jingle recording happened in Bill Bell's little recording studio off the main streets of Hollywood, I knew I had done well in my community, and I was feeling the glow. But the level going on around me kept it pretty much under control.

Though there were woman contractors in the record session world and even occasionally in the film scoring world, the commercials world was pretty much male-dominated. And in those days, the dollars flowed generously. The great majority of commercials were still done under union contracts, and those contracts required residuals for the airing, the amounts depending upon whether the spots ran during prime time, whether they were running nationally or locally, etc. So if you did a national spot, or a number of national spots, thousands of dollars would pour in. I was doing mostly group work in those days. But a couple of my singer colleagues—one lady, in particular, I remember from a meeting where we were discussing rates, salaries, etc., and I was shocked to learn she was earning in the $300,000–$400,000 range, even back in the seventies. She did a lot of solo work and was a very busy gal.

At the time, the world-famous designer Gucci had a store on Rodeo Drive in Beverly Hills, and one of Gucci's very popular items then was one of his casual designer handbags. The exterior of the bag was a kind of canvas cloth, off-white, with leather handles, and on the fabric cloth was printed the designer's name, Gucci, in rows creating a pattern, all over the bag. One day I saw a copy of that same bag, exact same shape, design, fabric, and handle, but instead of a designer's name, it had "Bullshit" woven into the fabric and printed all over the bag. I couldn't resist buying it, and I carried it everyplace. It was the way I felt about how the people around me were behaving, and it became my mantra. I didn't have the courage to be boldly outspoken, to joke or be a smartass verbally in the studio, nor try to communicate on the same level as Ron, our male contractor, communicated with the guys in the booth. So I let the bag speak for me. (Those to whom the message was directed I'm quite certain never got it.)

Though I was well aware of the good fortune bestowed upon me by being hired for those gigs, it didn't feel fulfilling in a creative or personal way. Most usually, we worked as a small group, two guys and two girls. Solo work happened only occasionally for me in commercials, and so when I had a chance to interrupt the routine that had become for me somewhat taken for granted and go on an adventure performing live with Burt Bacharach, I just grabbed it. It was a chance to do concerts all over the country, singing to people who came to listen and loved what they were hearing, and eventually to travel the world and perform as a soloist with Burt, and it became in my mind merely an expansion of focus, not a total step away from town.

We would have a few weeks in the spring and summer with bookings in Las Vegas at the MGM Grand Hotel and Harrah's at Lake Tahoe, then at Christmas time a return to Harrah's, and at one point we began to do the tent circuit summer theaters-in-the-round on the East Coast. Occasionally there would be concert bookings in other parts of the country, and in the early seventies we did a public television broadcast from a concert in Edmonton, Canada.

On one of the earlier tours, when we were performing music from *Lost Horizons* with an expanded group of singers, another session singer friend Tom Bahler, who later also had great success with his own song-writing, was part of the group. One night after one of the concerts we did in Michigan, we were sitting in the lounge in a big, round booth, Burt, myself, a couple of the musicians, when we noticed making his way through the dining room toward our table, a very strange-looking gentleman, clad in white chef's uniform and pushing a wobbly cart with a huge salad bowl and other cooking accessories. The strange-looking gentleman was wearing a white cap, a mustache, and glasses that covered most of his face, and was rather exaggeratedly bouncing along through the assemblage of booths and tables, doing a very strange little entry dance. As he approached our table, he bowed graciously and announced that he was there to prepare a special Caesar Salad for the Maestro, as a gift from the hotel. He then began wildly tossing the lettuce up into the air, sending it to land everywhere, a shower of crispy greens all over our table, the floor, and the surrounding area. It was then we realized the "chef" was Tom Bahler, up to his usual fun tricks. Happily, Burt was laughing too, as he settled back and returned to sipping his Johnny Walker Red.

Burt also did an Australian tour in 1974, a South American tour in 1977, and a concert tour in the Philippine Islands in 1980, and those international tours were longer than most of our bookings, more like three weeks. We weren't gone constantly, so I could still do my work in town for the most part, but it always took a few weeks upon my return for me to reconnect with Ron Hicklin, my most frequent employer in those days, and Ron would usually not be calling for a few weeks after I returned. And, as referenced earlier, while I was gone and missed sessions, new talent was discovered that eventually replaced me on many accounts. But I still wouldn't have traded those years with Burt for anything in the world.

On the East Coast tent circuit—the summer theaters-in-the-round, some of which I had worked in those earlier years with Nat King Cole—I usually incorporated a side trip visit to see my dad and Dotty in Windham, New York. In those years, Burt performed with a full orchestra and would bring his key players—the rhythm section, the lead solo horn players, the concert master violinist. In Las Vegas and Tahoe it was the house band, augmented by Burt's team. In the east, the orchestras were usually booked specifically for the concerts, again with Burt's key players. The program included Burt's songs, some of the earlier iconic hits, plus some incredible instrumental concert pieces that sort of combined pop/jazz and classical orchestrations. These pieces can be heard on his albums from the seventies.

Burt decided to record the material for the album *Woman* live with the Houston Symphony orchestra while we were on tour. The reality of Burt actually recording a song that I had written the lyrics for, and that I would be singing the solo on with the Houston Symphony was so exciting to me. But I must explain that up until that time, and for all the years that followed, I definitely didn't ever consider myself "an artist." I was part of Burt's team when we traveled and performed, and basically, I was part of the session singer world team when I worked in the studios in Hollywood. It never occurred to me to promote myself as an artist or to advertise the fact that I had written with Burt. It was just one of the gifts that happened along the way. It's a skill—self-promotion—that just was never in my bag of tricks. Maybe if I'd stayed on that pathway that began with Herb Alpert and the Dot Records release, I would have developed that skill along the way. But the work I chose to do all those years, and really, that I was blessed to be a part of, pretty much involved staying *out* of the spotlight. And I like to think that perhaps, instead of the likely five-year career I might have had if I'd been lucky as a recording artist, I instead had a sixty-year career working with some of the most amazing people in our business. I experienced the twists and turns, the ups and downs, the evolutionary changes in our business, and eventually the changes in my own role within it, when I moved more into vocal contracting and lyric writing.

By the time we were working on that *Woman* album, I had been performing with Burt for nearly a decade, the concert vocal group had been reduced from four to three girl singers, and I was doing a lot of solo work with him as well as the group work. Libby Titus, another songwriter who had written one of the songs with Burt for the album, was coming with us to Houston to perform the vocal. Burt called me in my hotel room when we got to Houston and asked if I would try to give Libby some emotional support regarding her performance there in Houston. She suffered from pretty severe stage fright and had gone through some hypnotherapy to try to address it, but she still seemed to him very nervous about the performance. "Can you just try to encourage her, maybe spend a little time with her?" he asked. He also asked me to learn the song, in the event that she just was not able to do it.

I said of course. And I also, of course, was torn because I wanted to be helpful to Burt, I wanted to be a good friend and to be kind to Libby. But on the other hand, if she was too scared to sing her song, I might get to sing it! It was very different from the song I'd written with Burt, longer too, in the version we did for the album, and I loved the musical feel of it. What to do, what to do! In the end, of course, I did learn the song, as Burt had asked me to do, but I also made a special point of spending time with Libby, and I tried to be encouraging. She and I had also done some writing together at Burt's suggestion, but we hadn't come up with anything yet that was a finished product. I decided to be relentlessly supportive to Libby, as I knew it was really something she wanted to try, this live performance before a concert audience. And when it came time for her to step onto that stage, she did a great job with the performance. I was happy for her, and proud, but her hypnotherapist must be given credit for the sudden transformation of confidence as she moved into the spotlight. No one but Burt and myself would ever have known she was nervous.

In the early years with Burt, we performed at the MGM Grand Hotel Showroom in Las Vegas, and then later, on the other side of the strip at Caesars Palace hotel. Melissa Mackay, Marilyn Jackson, Marti McCall, and I worked there many times together, and the group morphed over the years. Ann White later became part of the group when Melissa stepped away, and Jackie Ward also did an engagement with us in Las Vegas. Ann, Marti, and I performed the vocals for the Houston Concert, along with Libby's solo, and we also did the Philippines tour together. At one time Clydie King, a very busy backup singer during the sixties in the soul/rock recording and touring world, was with us on one of the Las Vegas bookings. And another wonderful singer, Carolyn Dennis, was part of the South American tour.

During the Las Vegas bookings there wasn't a whole lot to do during the day except enjoy the pool and the sunshine. On several of the earlier tours, following the release of the film *Lost Horizons* for which he had written the score with Hal David, Burt also added guys to the group, and Jon Joyce, Jimmy Joyce's son, did several engagements with us. In Las Vegas, Jon and I took some great bike rides out along the desert roads. The girls and I would also walk a mile or two to a health foods restaurant we discovered, and in the early days, there was the MGM lion to visit on the lower level lobby of the hotel, where he huddled in his cage, on display in the movie theater lobby for the theater-goers.

Burt's opening acts varied from booking to booking, but two I remember with most affection were Jud Strunk, a songwriter and folky kind of country character performer on the popular show *Laugh-In*, and Anthony Newley, the wonderful British singer-songwriter who collaborated on several hit Broadway shows including *Stop the World—I Want to Get Off* and *The Roar of the Greasepaint—The Smell of the Crowd*. Jud and I became close friends, and I visited his family once in Maine, to look at a house he'd found which he thought I might be interested in purchasing. It was a wonderful old inn, built around 1840, on four acres of land that backed onto a little stream and had just come on the market in North Anson, Maine. Jud knew I loved New England, so he'd been on the lookout for me. I loved it and thought it would be a wonderful place to use as my writing "getaway" in later years, and possibly to have as a bed-and-breakfast one day. It was quite a bargain too, priced at $32,000 at the time! But unfortunately the gentleman I was seeing at the time back home, Kerry Chater, talked me out of buying it. I've forgiven him—it probably wouldn't have been practical, but oh, it was so lovely.

Our other opening act, Anthony Newley—I was in total awe of. Each night during his performance I would stand in the wings offstage, watching him perform. He was such an incredible talent and a very sweet guy. One closing night he had a little gathering in his Las Vegas dressing room, and I and Burt's other singers were invited. That evening I found the courage to say to him, "You must truly love what you do, because you do it so brilliantly!" Tony replied, "Every time I walk on stage it's like climbing a fucking mountain . . ." then proceeded to pour us each another drink and carry on with the evening.

When we did the engagements at Harrah's in Lake Tahoe, I liked to make the trip by car up into the mountains so I would have it available to explore the area, and I preferred staying in a condo in the woods, rather than at the hotel. On one Christmas booking, my daughter Susie and her friend Lisa, both around eleven or twelve years old at the time, came with me, and the hills surrounding us nearby were being cleared to build more cabins. We took a walk one afternoon and came across some big pine trees that had been chopped down as part of the clearance, and lay abandoned on the forest floor. I convinced the girls that we should drag one home, up the hill, to be our Christmas tree and so we did—a huge nine- or ten-foot tree. When we finally got it up to the cabin, we had to figure out how to secure some string from the top of the tree over to the walls in several directions, to keep it from falling over, because of course those chopped-down trees in the woods don't come with a Christmas tree base! But we were proud of our accomplishment. Though I must say, those young girls complained all the way up that hill, so I guess it wasn't such a fun idea for them as I thought it would be—like, an adventure, you know? Like hunting your own Christmas tree, or being a forest pirate on the prowl.

On the East Coast bookings, I always loved being in New England. My grandmother and my father were from New England, and I felt a connection whenever I was there, remembering stories my grandmother had shared. I loved the little towns like Redbank, New Jersey, too, where we played an outdoor stadium, and Westbury Tent Theater, New York.

Australia was our first international adventure, in 1972, and back in the seventies that was a long, long flight! I remember we stopped in New Zealand, just a quick stop to pick up or drop off connecting passengers, but by that time we were only minutes away from our destination. We played Sydney, Melbourne, Adelaide, and Brisbane.

David and I had just gotten married shortly before the trip in a ceremony at a little church up in Solvang. Following the ceremony, there was a dinner reception at Mattei's Tavern, an old stagecoach stop in the adjacent community of Los Olivos. Susie, eleven years old at the time, was my maid of honor, and it was a formal wedding, with a long bridal dress, flowers, and all the family in attendance. It was quite different from my first marriage, the simple ceremony in El Paso near the end of the Ray Conniff tour. David and I thought that the Australia tour would be a very special trip for us to share, so I asked Burt if it would be okay for him to come, and Burt graciously said yes. On that tour, we hung out a lot with my best friend Mark Stevens, Burt's drummer at the time. Mark had a gift for finding the best little restaurants, no matter which town or country we were in. Adelaide, the capital city of South Australia, was a very small, charming little town, very historic-feeling, Brisbane was more sports-minded, and the center of athletic activities. Melbourne was an older, more formal European-feeling city, and Sidney was to be the home of the famous Opera House, which was still under construction at the time and not ready for our engagement. We went out into the countryside one day to visit a wildlife sanctuary, and I still have a darling photo that David took of Burt holding a baby koala bear, both of them smiling into the camera.

Our time in Australia happened over the holiday, Mother's Day, and I called Susie from our hotel in Sidney that day, feeling so sad that I wasn't with her. I wasn't able to reach her by phone, and ended up in tears, sitting on the park bench in a little park nearby. The journey of my work over the years, I realized pretty early on, was one I knew I would have little control over, in terms of schedule. I would either have to show up when asked, or risk losing the connection with that artist, or that account, and the fear was that eventually all the work would just slip away. Freelance work, I suspect in any field, is tenuous at best. I think I accepted that it would take me away from Susie not just for days or evenings, as session work did, but sometimes for several weeks, as the touring with Burt did. And it would have to be all right. It was not always easy, and I know it wasn't easy for Susie.

Finally, as the tour ended and we headed for our flight home from Australia, I remember having such a strong reaction to the sadness—the lost, haunted looks I saw in the faces of a group of Aborigine people we encountered in the airport. On our way to the departure gate, we passed a large group of them, obviously organized for travel together in some sort of "official" way. They were being supervised as they traveled, though exactly what the organization was, the authority supervising them—was not clear to us. It felt like they were being led to whatever their next destination was, but that it was a destination not of their own choosing. We had heard only a bit about the difficulties of their people, their place within their own country during our visit, and I felt the similarity to how the native people of our own country had been displaced, the ownership of their lands usurped by another culture. I was seeing on those faces the pain of a people who had been dispossessed of their land, of their homes, and their country. They seemed lost, they seemed to have given up hope.

I have since read a bit of the history of the Aborigine people. They were the first to occupy Australia, it is believed perhaps 50,000–60,000 years ago. They might be the oldest population of humans living outside of Africa. Through the years they suffered the same indignities of both the Native Americans and the early African American slaves of our own country, and even as late as 1967 they were not all granted the right to vote throughout the country, but state by state. Their people lived in missions or reserves, and their marriages, their lives, were controlled. They were not paid for the work they did, and till the middle of the twentieth century, they were mostly considered wards of the state. Their claim to their rights and to their homeland had become nonexistent. I didn't know these details at the time, but it explains what I felt as we passed by the group in the airport; it explains what I saw in their faces. I will never forget the looks, as if they were still trying to understand, or somehow rise above, what had happened to them.

David and I, as it turned out, separated in 1974, and my session work had slowed to the point that I felt I should sell the house where we lived in Benedict Canyon and find a less expensive place in the valley, maybe Studio City or Sherman Oaks. As I did a bit of house-hunting and learned more about the values of the different communities, I realized I could keep the Benedict Canyon house as a rental, as it was "Beverly Hills postal," a highly desirable neighborhood, and the rent would provide enough income to cover that mortgage, plus part of the payments for the Studio City house. Susie and I stayed in the Studio City house on Ethel Avenue for about three years, in a very nice little residential neighborhood south of Ventura. That's where she met Mitch Ramin, the sweet boy who lived just up the road and who would become the first love of her life. They dated all through high school and through Susie's first year at UC Santa Barbara. When she began tenth grade, she decided to transfer to North Hollywood High, the public high school Mitch was attending. Up until that time she had been going to Highland Hall, the Waldorf school in Northridge where David's nieces and nephew went to school. But the transition was a hard adjustment for her, as the Waldorf method of studies was very different. She decided to return to Highland Hall for eleventh and twelfth grades, and graduated from Highland Hall. She did get to go with Mitch to his North Hollywood High senior prom together, so at least she got to experience a traditional senior prom.

In 1977, I went house-hunting again, as work was steady, we could expand a bit, real estate prices were very reasonable at the time, and my pattern of three to four-year residencies in one place seemed at that point, to oddly have become a pattern of life.

Just before Burt's South America tour came up, Susie and I moved from our house in Studio City to a lovely, larger old Spanish-style home in Toluca Lake. It had once, in its original form, belonged to Janet Gaynor and her husband Adrian. Janet Gaynor was the first actress to win an Oscar, and he was a famous fashion designer for Hollywood films. The house was built in 1928 but had been sold again in the mid-1940s to a doctor, who divided it into three properties. The house I bought in 1977 was actually just the main wing of the original, but it was still 4700 square feet, on an acre of land, and included a three-car garage with chauffeur's quarters attached. The house next door had gotten the original kitchen, the pool, the pool house, and the den. Two bedrooms and a living room were added to that house, and a kitchen had been added to the wing that eventually become my house. It was a lovely old home, set back from the street, and the property backed on to Lakeside Golf Course, which was the rather upscale private golf club in Toluca Lake where the movie stars played in earlier days. Bob Hope's home was a couple of blocks away, but he had built his own golf course on site. Another beautiful old brick English Tudor house around the corner had once been the Bing Crosby home. Amelia Earhart's home was at the end of our street, where Valley Spring Lane dead-ended against the next block where the homes circled around a little lake. It was quite a historic neighborhood. I don't know looking back how I was able to afford this house, but at the time the market was down, and my savings were up, I guess. Also, the floor plan was a bit odd—rather like a train, from the front door straight back past the den, through the living room, through the dining room, to the kitchen, and then up the back stairs to the master bedroom, and back through the hall toward the front entry of the house, and down the stairs. That might have kept the price down a bit.

Burt's South America tour was a wonderful adventure and it was especially wonderful because Susie and I got to experience it together. Because it was to begin shortly after we had moved into the new house, I didn't want to run off for three weeks and leave her in the unfamiliar new setting. So I thought about it, and explained to Burt about the situation, saying I couldn't go on this trip unless Susie could go with me, and sing in the group. She was just sixteen years old, but she had worked quite a bit as a "kid singer" on jingles, she was doing a lot of singing in school, she was writing songs, and she had performed her own song and sung some harmonies with me when I'd done the live weekend performances at The Room Upstairs at Le Cafe Restaurant in Sherman Oaks. We performed there with a small band consisting of my friend Mark Stevens on drums, Kevin Bassinson, my arranger, on piano, Jim Hughart on bass, and my dear brother Jon Clarke playing woodwinds.

I knew Susie could do a professional job in concert with Burt and perform well, and I knew it would be a great experience for her, working with him, learning the material, and singing before audiences every night. Bless him, Burt agreed, and Susie joined the group as the third singer on that concert tour. At the end of our opening night concert in South America, Burt presented Susie with a bouquet of flowers on stage, and thanked her, explaining to the audience that this was her first tour, and saying how proud he was of her. She has never forgotten that.

We played in Rio de Janeiro, Buenos Aires, Caracas, and São Paulo. I remember we had the best steak I've ever eaten in a tiny little restaurant in Caracas, Venezuela. Fortunately, too, Susie had been taking Spanish in high school, so she served as our interpreter when she and I and our friend Richard Kaufman, who was Burt's concertmaster, hung out together. We went up to the top of Sugar Loaf Mountain, a group of us, to see the statue *Christ of the Andes*. Some of the braver folks opted to ride the Sugarloaf Mountain cable car, but I refrained from joining in that adventure. I've always had a thing about heights, especially when it meant being sus- pended in midair hundreds of feet above the ground in a small bucket car. There is a great picture of Burt, featured as ar- twork on the album cover for his *Futures* album, that was actually taken with him inside one of those little bucket cars smiling out through the window, anticipating his own adven- ture in the sky.

In Buenos Aires there were still, in the seventies, tributes of affection to Eva Perón painted on walls and scrawled on buildings. And there were armed guards with machine guns standing on most of the street corners. I had never experi- enced or even imagined anything like that. In São Paulo I bought an oil painting from one of the street artists, and back in Rio when we arrived on our group's bus at the sort of gloomy little hotel arranged by the company who had made all our hotel bookings, Susie, Richard, and I were terribly disap- pointed. So we begged off and said we would pay the differ- ence in a hotel of our choice and manage our own transpor- tation. We took ourselves to the Copacabana Palace Hotel, overlooking gorgeous Copacabana Beach. It was a huge, elegant hotel, very formal, with white columns and huge french windows on all the floors, opening up to view the ocean. It had a very special, rather exclusive restaurant at the time called The Green Door, which I had read about in *Vogue* magazine. So we made arrangements to dine there that evening before the show. Unfortunately, we did not know about the traffic in the city of Rio and though we urged and begged the driver to hurry, we were late for the downbeat! Oh, it was dreadful. Burt was angry, understandably, and poor Carolyn Dennis, the third singer, who had also been late though she got there before we did, was pushed onto the stage with her pink curlers still in her hair.

To make matters worse, I was so nervous and upset that I missed my entrance on a solo I was to sing, and I had to motion to Burt as inconspicuously as possible and ask if we could start over. He turned to the audience and said, "Sally would like to start over," and then sort of banged on the keyboard to restart the introduction to the song again. I wanted to crawl underneath the drum set.

This, by the way, was I suspect a very difficult period for Burt. His amazing success as a songwriter, as a producer of hit songs, and as an artist himself, not to mention appearing on the cover of a magazine as one of the ten sexiest men in the country, had sort of settled down. And at the same time Angie Dickinson, his wife whose career as a film actress had quieted with the birth of their daughter Nikki, experienced a big revival with the TV series *Police Woman,* in which she played the lead role. The series was hot, it was a huge success, and her schedule was heavy with the shooting of the series. I think Burt had fallen into a bit of a depression. One day when I was at the house to rehearse one of the songs we were to perform during that period of time, he was communicating over the phone with his wife through her press agent or someone handling her business because apparently, she was too busy to talk. It had to be a dramatic change in the dynamic of their relationships. So on this South American tour he was having some adventures of his own. He'd connected with a famous race car driver through friends and was out on the road seeing the countryside, such that even Burt himself was late for a performance or two. But on this night, we were the guilty ones, and it was awful. All through the tour, the schedule sort of operated on a different clock, the "South American" clock. Most of the concerts were scheduled to start at ten p.m.

At the end of our last concert, which was held in a large, stadium-type venue, Burt invited me to step over to the piano, to play and sing the song I'd written that he had thought at one time about producing, "Love is a Mirror." Looking back now, as nervous as I am about remembering lyrics, etc. in a performance situation, I can't believe I actually did that. But I did, Burt was an angel to have asked me, and the audience received it very warmly.

A year or so later we did the concert engagements in the Philippine Islands. Susie was by then going to classes at UC Santa Barbara, and couldn't be part of the group at that time, so Ann White joined us. The Philippines was at the time of our visit still under the rule of Ferdinand Marcos and his wife Imelda (the lady of a thousand shoes). We gave three performances there—one in an outdoor arena that was enormous, much like a football stadium, but time and weatherworn and not in stellar condition. The tickets were very modest, just a dollar or so each—which Imelda received credit for having subsidized for the poorer, less advantaged people of the city. All of our engagements were in the City of Manila, and we stayed at the Manila Hotel, a really lovely old historic place. Another of our concerts was performed there at the hotel, with a very high-ticket price and dinner table seating for the upper echelon of Philippine society. And the third concert was at a recently completed new outdoor arena, very much more up-to-date than the first, more like the average places we would have played in other towns. It was, though, a bit uncomfortable to see armed guards again there on the streets of Manila, much like we had seen in Brazil.

Burt told us a story later about how, at the private reception after the performance at the hotel, Imelda Marcos made her entrance to the reception area, serenading Burt as she walked across the room toward him, gazing intently and singing, "The look . . . of love . . . is in . . . your eyes . . . " Oh my. A bit uncomfortable, in the presence of her husband, the brutal dictator.

A year or so later there was one performance back home in Los Angeles that Burt asked me to sing for, just he and I, for a private benefit gathering at someone's home. I had insisted he not pay me, even though he wanted to do so. And the next day I received, as a thank you from Burt, the most beautiful arrangement of flowers I'd ever seen in my life, or to this day. It was enormous—beautiful tall blooms elegantly arranged and mixed with roses, stems of orchid blossoms, and bits of green leaves. It totally filled my coffee table, several feet high and several feet wide. It makes me smile to this day just thinking about it.

Along the way, we also performed live in concert the new material that we had recorded with Burt and that was also included in the albums released during those years—"No One Remembers My Name," "Charlie," and several of the full orchestra jazz-influenced pieces.

I am in awe of Burt's long, creative years of activity. He never stops creating, he continues to write with new collaborators, he has continued to tour and perform in concert into his nineties, and his earlier songs have survived the decades, to be rediscovered by artists of every generation. What a gift it was to have had the years of sharing and experiencing his music. I can shut my eyes and feel the wonder still, of sitting on those stages, surrounded by the live musicians and their sounds, feeling the blue lights all around, as Burt cast a look back over one shoulder, and threw the downbeat for our next entrance.

CHAPTER 29
THE OSCAR MEMORIES

Being involved with the Oscars broadcasts has been another of the very special experiences in my life. In the early years I worked numerous times on the show as part of the choir, and I remember details of one in particular early in my participation, during the years that Johnny Green, a legendary film composer, was the musical director. Mr. Green served in that capacity for seventeen years and also, along the way, won numerous Oscars himself during his film scoring years. This particular year the orchestra and singers were pre-recording some of the production numbers, and we sat on the floor in the hallway of Western Recorders on Sunset Boulevard into the wee small hours, waiting to record the vocals. There were a lot of tracks that didn't involve vocals, and they recorded the show in the order of the program. So Mr. Green, the orchestra, and all of us were there far into the night.

In those days I didn't have a sense of being very personally attached to the Oscars. I worked on the show several times during the late sixties when the event was held at the Santa Monica Civic Auditorium and we were there for the live performances. It was exciting, but it was all so new to me I didn't deeply digest what was going on around me. I mostly just didn't want to screw up in any way.

Later the broadcasts moved to the Shrine Auditorium,

then to the Dorothy Chandler Concert Hall at the Music Center in downtown Los Angeles; most recently they are broadcast from the Dolby Theatre, formerly the Kodak Theatre, on Sunset Boulevard in Hollywood. (In 2012, Eastman Kodak declared bankruptcy, and Dolby Sound Lab exercised their twenty-year naming rights contract and took over the space.)

There were some special times too along the way, before I began to serve as Choral Director. One was in the year 1977, and one of the nominated songs, which won Best Song that year, was the song "Evergreen" from *A Star Is Born*. Barbra Streisand had written the music, Paul Williams the lyrics, and Barbra was to perform it for the broadcast. Bill Conti was the musical director that year, and I was hired by the gentlemen then contracting the voices, Gene Merlino, to sing the solo harmony part that Barbra had sung with herself in the film and on her recording, for one section of the song. I guess the assumption was that Barbra couldn't sing two parts at a time in her live performance.

I was actually very excited at the prospect of doing this, and nervously showed up for the orchestra rehearsal, trying to be as pleasant, respectfully in awe and as inobtrusive as possible, because Barbra was there as well to run through the song with the orchestra. When she realized someone else had been hired to sing her song along with her, she was not too happy about that. She stopped the run-through, quietly had a little chat with the musical director, who had a little chat with the director of the show. The harmony part was ultimately dispensed with, and so was I. Fortunately there were other songs on the agenda, so I still got to work on the show as part of the ensemble, but . . . I'm just sayin', don't mess with Barbra!

Some other special memories—one was the 63rd Oscars Awards broadcast in 1991, and Madonna was performing the song nominated for Best Song, "Sooner or Later," from the film *Dick Tracy*. She had seemed very nervous during dress rehearsal, but she really pulled it together for the broadcast. She also had been in the film in one of the acting roles, and perhaps being that deeply invested in the project made her more nervous. But her performance was terrific, and the song did win Best Song.

Bill Conti held the position of Musical Director for many years on the Oscars, serving in that position for two decades. I loved the concept for the singers that Bill utilized during part of that time, which began the year I had also been hired as Choral Director. He placed the singers in the orchestra pit and we became part of the orchestra. If we were needed on camera for one of the numbers, of course, we worked that out; but basically, we were there with the musicians, watching Bill direct, singing from our microphones in the orchestra pit. A couple of times, depending upon who the directors of the show were and how elaborately they chose to build out the stage, there wasn't room for us in the pit; so once, when the show was done from the Shrine Auditorium, we were to sing from downstairs in the basement, our mics set up in one of the women's dressing room restrooms. I actually knew my way around down there, because I'd sung with the Los Angeles Opera Company chorus when they did the morning performances for the school children at the Shrine Auditorium of *Hansel & Gretel* and *The Magic Flute,* back in my UCLA days. But the sound actually was very good for the voice setup there because of all those old concrete walls surrounding us. We were watching Bill's baton by video hookup.

The night of Madonna's performance we were in the orchestra pit right there in the auditorium at the edge of the stage and could peer over past Bill into the audience seats in the hall. During the broadcast I spotted Madonna and her date for the evening, Michael Jackson, sitting in the front row. Michael was wearing one of his marvelous outfits—a white, rather ornate, military-style jacket and trousers, with white shoes. Michael's jacket had all kinds of gold braid and buttons on it, and he looked *almost* more glamorous than Madonna.

Bill Conti had some wonderful ideas about how to handle the music aspects of the show when he served as musical director. We worked with music cue sheets in front of us that his team of orchestrators had prepared for each of the awards to be announced. All five musical themes from the five nominated productions were written out on our vocal parts. We didn't know which we were to sing, nor did the musicians know which one they were to play, until the winner was announced. And then Bill would give the downbeat, and we would jump in and perform the theme from the winning film as the person who was to receive that award walked up onto the stage.

It was thrilling to work with Bill through those two decades. Even though I had done the show many times during the preceding years working for other vocal contractors and other musical directors, I never felt as intimately involved with the project as when working with Bill. We were there live throughout the evening as the awards were being presented, and the energy and excitement were visceral. There were many wonderful hosts over the years, and Billy Crystal stands out in my memory as one of the very best, most entertaining. Very early in the history of the Oscars, Bob Hope was famous for hosting the show a number of times, and those performances set a high bar, but I think Billy came really close to that bar.

There are other wonderful memories associated with the Oscars, and two gentlemen in particular that I will always associate with the production of the show. One is Gil Cates, whose first year as producer was that 1991 production with Madonna. He went on to produce fourteen Oscar broadcasts in all, and always did a wonderful job of creating a successful show. Gil was a prolific producer and director of film and television, but his dream was to open a theater, and in 1993 he persuaded UCLA to purchase the Geffen Playhouse in Westwood, a historic structure built in 1929 that had originally been a Masonic Affiliates Clubhouse. I remembered the building from when I was a student at UCLA in 1958–1960, when there were student activities there, and later it was used as a showroom for a furniture designer.

The Geffen Playhouse opened its first production in 1995, and one evening I was sitting at the bar talking with Gil at Bill Conti's daughter's wedding shortly after the playhouse opened. He was so passionate about the theater, and asked if I knew about it. I replied yes, and he asked if I had attended a performance there yet. "Yes, of course . . . I'm a subscriber!" Gil reached over from his bar stool and gave me a big hug.

The other gentleman whose involvement was so woven into the Oscars was Michael Seligman. Michael had worked consistently with the production as Executive Producer since the late eighties. He was the guy who really was hands-on, who had to deal with the budget, had to walk through the rehearsals backstage with the presenters and the folks from the Academy, had to make sure that everyone was happy with how things were coming together—the artistic team as well as the business side of things where the bottom line has to be considered. He's the one I always submitted the budgets to, prior to getting the approval on how many singers could be hired, what the schedule was to be, etc.

I can only imagine how important his work on the show has been to him over all these years, how personal it has become. Several years ago, when *Selma* was nominated in 2015 for Best Picture, and the song "Glory," written by the artists Common, John Legend, and Rhymefest, was nominated for Best Song, there was a very emotional performance of the song. It was performed by Common, with John Legend at the piano nearby, and with an on-camera choir, staged on a set created to represent the bridge where the Freedom March was held in Selma, Alabama, as depicted in the film. I was not on camera for that particular number as they had asked for a

Black gospel choir, but was contractor for that and other numbers on the show, and was at all the rehearsals to wrangle the singers, to keep track of the hours, etc. I ended up in tears at the end of that song, each time the number was rehearsed in preparation for the show. That year I also sang as part of a smaller group of on-camera singers who performed with Lady Gaga on a medley of songs from *The Sound of Music*. During the applause, after the number was over, Julie Andrews (who of course was so identified with the song, having performed it originally for the film of the same title), stepped out onto the stage from behind the curtain where she had been watching to surprise Lady Gaga with a hug on camera. Not *much* pressure!

For all the on-camera singers and dancers used that year, Michael gave us, the "non-stars," screen credits—something that is just never, ever done. We were all shocked and delighted, being accustomed in our part of the business as we were to never receiving screen credit for performances in film scores or TV. The folks that provide the porta-potties get screen credit, but not the singers or musicians who perform the score. Occasionally, if music is a significant part of the plot, the musicians might be featured and credited, or if it is an animated feature with a small voice-over acting cast, then they sometimes include the singers because SAG requires that they credit up to fifty cast members.

What a kind, special thing that was for Michael to do for all his Oscars performers.

Another year he gave a post-Oscar party for his production team, including me, and I regretted that I didn't stay very long into the evening, being a bit shy alone at social gatherings. Believe it or not, even after all these years, I'm shy about stuff like that, especially going to those gatherings without a companion. I kind of stand around awkwardly talking to people I don't know for as long as I can stand it, and then I make a dash for the door. I learned recently that Michael had retired from his role with the Oscars and basically from the business, but he will never be forgotten. What a vital role he played in the success of those broadcasts. I was so pleased to run into him on our dinner break from the show this year in February of 2020, as we wandered through the Staples center trying to decide on our dinner restaurant of choice. He was walking with a companion, and they were there to be in the audience. I went over to greet him. "Michael, it's so good to see you!" I said. "I'm still grateful to be here, of course, but we miss you so . . . no one took care of us like you did, and no one handled the production as well as you. It's so good to see you, and I'm so glad I had this chance to thank you again for all those wonderful years!"

We gave each other a hug, and I could see it pleased him, just one more time, to be thanked and acknowledged for his contributions over the years. The projects, the business we are a part of over the years, mean so much to all of us, whether we just show up as part of the crowd, or we are responsible, as Michael had been all those years, for making everything work.

Another one of the memories that stands out among the production numbers done for Oscars over the years was in 2000, when we did an on-camera production number from *South Park*. The song was "Blame Canada" featuring Robin Williams, and I had also contracted the choir for the recording of the song for the film with composer Marc Shaiman. For the Oscars version, we held auditions for the on-camera cast of singers, as character types were needed who would look interesting and fun on camera, but who would also be able to perform the number well musically, and Marc was very involved with those auditions and the performance of the number.

Just a few years ago I was blessed to work again with Robin Williams on the series he did for Fox TV, *The Crazy Ones*, which as it turned out, was to be his last major project.

The storyline was about the quirky head of an advertising agency, the other interesting staff members of that agency, and the adventures they got into with some of their big clients across the world. What a gift it was to have an up-close opportunity to watch this man work. There were several off-camera singing sessions where we created jingles for the agency, and there was one episode where a gospel choir was used on camera. Robin was always so gracious, going out of his way to be kind and to respond to requests for photos, etc. The show only lasted one season, and its cancelation was painful for Robin, contributing to the depression he experienced toward the end of his life. It was absolutely heartbreaking to me when, on the evening news, I heard the sad announcement of his death. It was a shock, and the tears fell as if he had been a personal friend when his face appeared on the screen. But he was so special . . . I had been a fan of Robin's since the first performances I saw of him back in the seventies on the *Mork & Mindy* TV series, but also on every project he had done since. And it was especially heartbreaking because I had gotten to know him just a bit, to witness his humanity, his kindness, and his talent, firsthand. His performances over the years included the obvious gift he had for offbeat comedy, but also for deeply sensitive dramatic performances.

In 2007, the Oscars included an unusual performance especially created by Steve Sidwell, and we singers in the Hollywood Film Chorale became the Sound Effects Choir, providing the sound effects track performed entirely with vocal sounds to scenes edited together by Steve from various films. We became the sounds of rain, car motors, wind, screeching brakes, train whistles, rocket ships. Steve had created something similar for a Honda commercial earlier that year and the 2007 producer of the Oscars, Laura Ziskin, heard it and was fascinated by the idea of doing a similar number for the Oscars.

In 2013, recording artist Adele was one of the guest

performers and sang with a thirty-voice men's on-camera backup choir which I contracted and got to hang with for several days—talk about fun! Imagine being surrounded with thirty handsome, talented guys for several days, catching up over our breaks with several I hadn't seen in a while, and enjoying how much *they* all were enjoying being in Adele's presence. She was such a sweet lady—she tolerated all those selfies the guys insisted on pestering her to take with them. She had just had a baby a few months earlier, and the baby and the nanny traveled with her to Los Angeles and were kept close by during rehearsals. We ran the number musically in a rehearsal space in Burbank, had lunch in the little restaurant on property, and then worked out the final staging on the risers.

The 2013 Oscars was also the year Seth MacFarlane hosted the show. Seth is one of the sweetest, most talented, all-around nicest guys I've ever worked for in Hollywood. I met him working on *Family Guy* and *American Dad*, both his original creations, when they first went on the air. Seth is a lover of music, and in addition to being a fine singer himself (in the Sinatra sense of "singer"), he appreciates and honors quality music performed by live musicians and written by excellent composers. He has always insisted on live musicians when scoring his shows, and before he became one of the busiest guys on the planet, was always present at our vocal scoring sessions. Seth's respect for music performed live rather than on synthesizers, and his belief in its relevance in terms of the emotion it brings to the on-screen production, has been a blessing to the music community here in Los Angeles.

Seth is such an incredibly talented voice-over artist, and he voices multiple characters on his animated shows and does the singing when the character sings. He also enjoyed from the beginning being there to kind of produce or at least give the "ok" for the vocals we would do, wanting to ensure that they conveyed the feel, the character he had in mind, the humor, etc. When he couldn't be present in person, he would call in from wherever he was, and listen over the phone to the final takes before we were dismissed, to give his final approval.

We miss being in his company these days, now that his career has burgeoned in so many directions. I've been able to get up to the Vibrato Grill, Herb Alpert's lovely restaurant and jazz club at the top of Beverly Glen where Seth does his live singing appearances in town several times a year, to hear him and wave hello from my table. But he's getting so popular now that by the time the announcement comes out on Vibrato's calendar, the room is already sold out!

Seth's humor as witnessed on *Family Guy* and *American Dad* is a bit bawdy, to say the least, and his "special material" for the Oscars predictably went, some of it, in that direction. Some of the reviews were tough on him, and it felt at times like the room didn't quite know how to react. But eventually, they definitely got on board.

There was one difficult situation in the pre-records for this 2013 broadcast. Most always over the years, the pre-recorded numbers are done first as instrumental tracks by the orchestra, to get the musicians recorded, as they are a large group of players. Then at the end of the day, the singers come in, to overdub whatever songs need the vocal tracks. So by nine or ten o'clock at night after an intense day of recording, the engineer and crew are pretty much exhausted and ready to go home so they can get back on the job first thing in the morning. On this particular show the orchestra was set up in Capitol Records, Studio A and Studio B, which adjoin and open into each other to create a larger orchestra space, and the musicians were coming back the next morning to do more recording. The day had gone well, the orchestra setup worked well, and Tommy Vicari, the recording engineer, understandably didn't want to break down the orchestra and re-set for the choir, so we recorded standing in two rows in a semi-circle around the microphone, the girls in the front row, the guys behind them, just pushing the chairs and music stands back a bit to create enough space to fit us all in. The response from the booth after we did a take or two of each of the songs was, "Great, let's move on," and finally, "Great, let's wrap . . ." So we did. We never got to hear a playback ourselves, which always makes me feel uncomfortable. Going forward, I would never let that happen again.

The next day I had a call from Michael Seligman, who told me that the producers of the show, Craig Zadan and Neil Meron, felt they didn't hear enough of the guys in the mix balance. I explained that because we were all on one microphone, not on separate microphones as we normally would have been, the vocal track couldn't be remixed to bring up the guys in the balance. It apparently was just in one number, not on all the things we did, that they weren't happy with the sound. Emails started flying about, and I replied that we could easily redo that track in five minutes with microphones on the set when we came in the next day for onstage blocking. I apologized, but explained that we had never been able to hear a playback the previous evening. I also said they wouldn't have to call or pay for a separate session, as we could do it just before our blocking rehearsal.

In a few minutes, another email came through, from Joel McNeely, the arranger who had done that particular chart for the show and worked with Seth occasionally on his live appearances. He later went on to score the live action TV Series Seth created, *The Orville.* Joel was not the Musical Director for the Oscars show itself—that was William Ross—but Joel had done the chart for the song in question. He apparently felt very proprietorial about the one number he was involved with. His email said that he didn't think that the balance was the problem, he thought they needed to "cast younger."

That sent me up in flames. It seemed arrogant and insensitive to me in the moment, and definitely not true. The people I had there (except for myself of course) were young, vital, and very professional singers, and I would vehemently defend their talents and their ability to sound "youthful." I was furious that no one had bothered to let us hear playbacks, and I was offended by his comment. I later got a call from Joel informing me that they were calling in the "*Glee* Choir" to redo the number at Capitol that night. *Glee* was at that time a successful series on Fox that included a lot of very contemporary music, done with layers and layers of over-dubbed vocal tracks. Carol Farhat, Vice President of Fox TV Music, had asked me to oversee the paperwork at the time on *Glee* to be sure things were done properly according to the Fox system, and *Glee* had the highest music budget of any show I'd ever worked on. I reviewed the paperwork from each vocal session and I had never seen figures like that flying past me before. And the singers working on the show varied from week to week. There was basically no such thing as the "*Glee* Choir." IMHO Joel McNeely just wanted to look hip and current to the producers by plugging in the "*Glee* Choir." I honestly thought it was just another chance, in his mind, to show up, do another session, and try to make an impression on the producers and on Seth.

I actually sent Michael Seligman a note cautioning him to watch the billing for that session with the choir and Tim Davis, their contractor/music director. Tim is a sweet guy but was used to an unlimited music budget on *Glee*, which is quite different from how the Oscars music budget works.

Several weeks after the Oscars wrapped and the world had moved on, my phone rang one night. When I picked up the phone, there was Seth MacFarlane. He was calling to tell me not to worry about that pre-record complication, and to say that he was in the booth when we recorded that night and everything had sounded fine to him. He said if the producers wanted the final say on things, they should have planned to be at the scoring sessions. Seth also mentioned that despite the mixed reviews of the broadcast, he had really felt that night that "in the room" the audience was with him. I had felt that too. How kind he was to make that call, and how amazing that it was even on his radar, with everything else going on in his busy life. I was very grateful, and very touched by his kindness.

In 2018, three songs nominated for Best Song were to utilize on-camera choirs: the song from *Mudbound*, "Mighty River," the song "Stand Up for Something" from *Marshall*, and "This Is Me" from *The Greatest Showman*. Each choir was booked separately, as desired by the artist or producer who did the song originally. I was asked to book the "Mighty River" choir, which was requested by Mary J. Blige, the artist, to be "twenty-five percent" diversity, which in this case was rather more "*re*-versity." Originally the producers handling this number had asked me to book a choir like we had used for "Glory," which had been an all-Black gospel choir. But then I learned more about the film and the subject matter, and wasn't sure that I had understood clearly, so I called them back to question and clarify. They said, "We'll get back to you," and then called me back later to tell me that rather than use an all-Black gospel choir, Mary J. Blige requested that "twenty-five percent" of the group be diverse, be other than Black singers. So we had three Hispanic singers, two grey-haired white singers (myself and Gary Stockdale), and two Asian singers. There are so many wonderful singers in our singer community that it's never hard to fill special requests, just hard to choose between so many wonderful, talented colleagues. I'm glad I followed up with that question.

But as I did so, I had to come to terms with the fact that I, along with most other contractors in the business, tend to pigeonhole people, to think of certain people as great for certain things, and not shake that up a bit often enough. The three Hispanic singers were excellent musicians, but I had mostly thought to reach out to them when there was perhaps a Spanish language piece or an on-camera singer described as Latino. On the other hand, the two Asian singers just happened to be first-call singers, very much a part of the session singer community, and worked frequently with me on film score sessions and other projects. I wasn't even conscious of their race, except that when the specific call for "diversity" in this context came up, I did think of them, and was glad I could include them.

This subject has now come up in a much more present way within our community, in this spring of 2020, with regard to the Black Lives Matter movement. It's something that needs to be addressed, and the community is doing so. There needs to be far more diversity in the roles of vocal contractor and within the singers who are called to work on film scoring projects, and the community is working on that. There have been panels gathered on video livestreaming, with a great deal of sharing of stories, and when once again we can all gather in some large room, those of us who've had the privilege of working as contractors hope to do workshops at SAG-AFTRA on vocal contracting, on the process involved, the paperwork, the terms of the various contracts, etc. There have been several excellent Black singer contractors over the years, but it happened that they worked more often in sound recordings, not so much in film and television scoring. The pay rates are better in the film and TV work, and that work also includes residuals.

One of the more personal joys I often experienced from working on the Oscars was that sometimes one of the guest artists was unable to make the orchestra pre-record session and run-through, so I would get to sing the vocal with the orchestra if the artist was a female, for whatever their song was. And for one broadcast, Stephen Sondheim had written the special lyrics himself for his own song "Putting It Together" which was originally from his musical *Sunday in the*

Park with George. Prior to the recording schedule, they needed to do a demo of a song so that Bernadette Peters could work with the new lyrics. The special lyrics addressed the process of putting together the making of a movie, in all its complicated aspects. The pace of the song was rapid, and the words were voluminous. I was asked to do the vocal guide/demo, and got through it, with Bill Conti sitting in the booth looking amused, because I think they sped up the tempo just a bit for the demo, figuring at regular tempo it would feel easier to Bernadette after she rehearsed it at that pace. It was fun, even though I knew *they* knew how much I was struggling to get the words out! I don't know how either I *or* Bernadette ever wrapped ourselves around all those words.

I also got to record two vocals in orchestra run-throughs that Celine Dion would be singing for the broadcasts: for the 1997 show, "I Finally Found Someone," nominated for Best Song, from *The Mirror Has Two Faces;* and "My Heart Will Go On" nominated from the film *Titanic,* for the 1998 broadcast. How lovely it is to have those copies of my own vocals recorded with the incredible Oscars orchestra accompaniment.

I never assumed or expected that the call would come each year to work on the Oscars—that the call to be Choral Director would happen year after year, nor that I was entitled to it. Things change in our business and people have their own teams that they prefer to work with, so I was always happily surprised when, and if, the call came. I have learned that there are fewer disappointments along the way if there are fewer assumptions made. So, best not to assume that the phone would ring at Oscar season. Within the community there are always relationships that develop with composers or arrangers, with musical directors . . . and our projects change and morph along the way, so changes could easily have been made. But the producers must have been comfortable after a few years with my handling of the project, and I was always thrilled to get the call, even in the years when I didn't get that lovely "Choral Director" screen credit. Among the singer community, the singers too were excited to get the Oscars call, and I got to pass along that gift. It's exciting to be a part of that very prestigious event, and a show that everyone in the business looks forward to, for various reasons of their own.

CHAPTER 30
THE HARD-KNOCK SIDE OF LIFE

To be able to make a living at something you love in life is indeed a blessing and a gift. And if that something involves a bit of glamour, occasional interaction with celebrities, and some accolades of your own from the crowd . . . then you might have landed in show business. You undoubtedly have the soul of an artist. That doesn't necessarily mean you *are* an artist, but you definitely want to be, you strive to be. And for most, the journey is challenging, even when it is successful.

But when it becomes intense, or something heartbreaking intervenes, and one begins to see the life with which they have been blessed begin to slip away—some folks can handle it, and some cannot. It takes great courage, in either case. We have all lost friends and loved ones, people that the general public might only know from a distance, by the performances they admire and love. And even from a distance, one feels the pain of those losses. Judy Garland, for example, was forced into the role of celebrity when she was way too young to understand it. Her life became more and more complicated as she had to adapt to situations into which others had placed her. The end of her life was tragic, and because she was a celebrity, the details of her later life eventually became known around the world.

For those of us who have landed, albeit invisibly for the

most part, in that world of show business, those celebrity-type people sometimes become our personal friends as well, if we are lucky. And such was the case with a dear friend I met along the way, who we lost about ten years ago. It is a sad story to share, but it is not untypical of how things sometimes go, and it reveals the complexities of what from a distance, might sound like a perfect life.

I met this friend when she had already accomplished a great deal in her artistic life. She had performed leading roles in the musical theater on Broadway, she had been featured as a guest artist and actress in numerous variety TV shows and films during the fifties and early sixties, she had done night-club appearances, and after the world tour of one of the musicals she performed in had wound down, she settled again back in Los Angeles.

But things slowed down for her, and it was disappointing. I knew of her work, though I didn't know her personally, but I admired her greatly and especially loved one song that she often performed, "My Love Is A Wanderer." She had been a guest, singing that song on the *Danny Kaye* variety TV show when I worked as one of the group singers.

I happened to run into her one day at the AFTRA Credit Union earlier in my career, before we had ever formally met, both of us just standing in line to do some banking. I bravely introduced myself to her and told her how much I admired her work. Her reply saddened me because the disappointment was obvious in her tone. She made a comment about how apparently no one else in Hollywood felt that way about her work.

I didn't see her for probably another decade or two following our brief conversation that day. In the intervening years, her life expanded in other different directions, and in lovely ways. She returned to college, got her degree, and became a therapist. She met and married her second husband, a dear guy, a well-known and highly respected arranger and musical director in the business, and she eventually resumed some of her live nightclub performances. Together, they also began a series of concerts to raise money for AIDS. They enjoyed a life rich with creativity and interesting friends, and they shared many musical events, on and off stage. Their dining table was famous for the most fascinating dinner guests, and one evening I found myself invited somehow, to join the festivities. We had gotten re-acquainted because of a show I worked on with her husband, and the friendship grew.

We became close friends, and when the world itself morphed from the twentieth century to the twenty-first century on New Year's Eve of 1999, they kindly invited me to join them at a little resort out in Palm Desert to celebrate, called Two Bunch Palms. I had recently gone through a divorce that for a time, had become contentious, and it was so sweet of them to drag me along on their getaway. Two Bunch Palms had once belonged to Al Capone, the famous gangster of the thirties and forties, and it had morphed over the years into kind of a naturalistic, rustic resort featuring natural hot springs and massages. It was a peaceful way to welcome in the new year and the new century, which all the world was fearing would include things like online crashes, problems with banking, and anything else disastrous that one could think of.

The three of us had a delightful quiet dinner by candle-light, and as we said goodnight and I was walking back to my little cottage, I came upon a small white dog running about on the dirt path. At first, I thought it was a coyote and was panicked. Then I realized it was in fact a little white dog, and it was limping. Somehow, I got it to come with me into my little cottage, and then I called my friends to ask if they had anything in their room that I could feed it.

They brought over some remnants of their dinner, helped me get the little doggie settled down for the night, and eventually my friend christened the dog "Sweet Pea" for its new name. So, though single on New Year's Eve, I started the new century with a new welcome, furry companion. We made sure that it wasn't someone's missing pet, asking at the front desk if they knew where it belonged, but no one had any information, so Sweet Pea came back home with me to Studio City.

Unfortunately, during the decades when we had not been in touch, and about the time my sweet friend and her husband married, she was also diagnosed with multiple sclerosis. Now, this is where her extraordinary courage enters in. She was able to keep the illness at bay, or at least controlled, with her dedication to holistic treatments, a positive attitude, and watching for new research results and discoveries along the way. But it was a cloud that hung over her life.

In 2002, sadly, her husband passed away, and by that time her illness had become more of a daily presence, and really began limiting what she could do. She continued living alone in their lovely home in the hills between Studio City and Hollywood, and for a time, was able to continue with her own activities, her driving and so forth. She also had taught a class at a cabaret symposium held on the East Coast in the late nineties that I was able to treat myself to, and it was a wonderful experience, and fun to share it with her.

But life was not the same. The golden days were fading. And one disaster after the other arrived to fill the empty spaces. She had loved her husband very much. The fact that he was so entrenched in the celebrity world was nothing more than frosting on the cake, never the cake itself. And she was certainly a diva in her own right, or had been before the spotlight shifted. At least that is how she thought of herself, and indeed, how I thought of her too. I understood what courage and self-confidence, along with the talent, it would have taken for her to do the things she did during her active career as a singer and actress. Auditions for Broadway theater, touring, night club appearances, film and TV acting roles . . . and she did them all.

The illness that had attacked her, multiple sclerosis, for a time had been merely an annoyance. She held it at bay with meditation, careful holistic care and creative activity. She still managed to project the glamorous image that had been so important to her. She shared with me once that even your doctors took better care of you if you showed up eyelash-ed and with regularly scheduled doses of Clairol to hide the grey roots in their offices, or even in the hospital.

But with time, the physical limitations of her world began to close in on her. She couldn't entertain at home without help, and as often as I could be, I tried to be that help. But those evenings fell into place farther and farther apart, and she was not able to fill her table with friends, all of whom had been interesting and brilliant—like one of those dinners you would have in your make-believe world, if you could invite eight or ten favorite people living or dead. Her husband had been brilliantly talented but not wealthy, not like the songwriter who continues to reap the fruits of publishing royalties—just the brilliant man who turned those songs into hits with his wonderful arrangements of them and made Streisand and other artists and writers a few more million. Their lifestyle had been gracious and inclusive, but had its limitations.

When facing disappointments and pressures in life, if a person decides they want out, there's very little anyone can do to dissuade them. And about ten years ago, my friend wanted out.

After her husband died, a string of misfortunes hit her amid financial stresses, one after the other. The glamorous hillside house was threatened by storms, by the mountain slipping away, from the flooding, by the water pipes being ripped apart, by the giant sycamore that fell across the roof. Somehow still, she kept going.

I loved her and I admired her so—she had the ability to be magical. And I tried to be there for her as often as I could, though my own life at the time was filled with work calls and other obligations that had become addictions over the years—Union Boards, and the like. But the quality of her days was changing. Vodka and Ambien had moved in to take the place of the husband she loved and the activities she could no longer do. She was bored, and a few sips of vodka eased the boredom. It took Ambien—and before long, it would take more than just one—to put her to sleep.

Then she began to suffer falls at the house. At first I thought the MS was getting worse, but I was naïve. Friends who read it more clearly knew it was the substances. She even tried AA for a time, but couldn't sustain it. And there were serious injuries. She landed in the hospital four times over the period of about a year, with a broken shoulder and a fractured pelvic bone; each hospital visit required a longer stay in rehab before she could come home. She resisted the use of a wheelchair—had for years—because she feared she'd never be free of it once she allowed that step to happen. But finally, the wheelchair became a fixture.

As the walls of her world collapsed in on her, the best that could be done was that I or one of her other close friends would bring supper up to the house and visit for a while. But her eyelids were always heavy, the words slurred a bit. The caregivers knew they were forbidden to bring vodka into the house, but somehow it arrived. The Ambien—it arrived too, from friends who had prescriptions. Earlier on, the one or two calls I got myself, asking if I could just bring up two Ambien until her prescription could be refilled—I responded to, naïvely. But when I realized what was going on, I lied to my friend. I told her my doctor would not prescribe Ambien any longer because he felt it was addictive and harmful, which of course it is. The requests stopped coming.

The dynamics shifted to another level one evening when I had arranged to take supper up. When I arrived, she asked how long I could stay, and then she sent the caregiver home early. After the woman left, she asked me to pour her a glass of milk and put some vodka in it. I stalled around as long as I could, changed the subject of our conversation, and when she asked the third time, I capitulated and did as she asked.

She ate a few bites of her food, tried to take part in my efforts at conversation, but soon her eyelids fell, and she asked me to help her into the bedroom. Then she told me she would be fine, and would just get herself settled into bed, but would I please bring her a glass of milk, and the bottle of vodka.

"I'm fine, I don't have to rush," I said, "I'll wait till you're all settled in."

I waited for a while in the living room. Then she called and again requested the glass of milk and the vodka. I went back into the room and made small talk for a few more minutes. Then again, the request came.

I was so afraid that if I didn't get them for her, she would try to get up and get them herself and fall again. So, with heavy heart, I marched out to the kitchen. When I bought them back to her, I looked her in the eye and said very seriously "If anything happens to you tonight, it will be my fault . . . " She flashed a look of anger my way and said, "Don't start with the guilt now . . ." Then she calmed down, and I left. As I drove down the mountain, I swore I would never be put in that position again, which meant that she had possibly lost another of the few friends she had left. I felt justified in that moment, and at the same time I felt terribly guilty, like I had abandoned a dear friend who needed me. She had begun to be abusive with the caregivers, and eventually, with some of her oldest friends. Not yet with me, but I knew she had only a few friends left. She called about an hour and a half later that evening, to let me know she was fine, but the words were slipping from her tongue in some strange, almost indiscernible language.

Two days later, she had another fall and a final trip to the hospital. This time no bones were broken, but there was a gash on her face from the sharp edge of a broken vodka bottle, and a huge bump on the side of her head. That was when the talk of leaving began. She told me one day she had decided she was "going to leave the planet next year." I tried on two more visits to propose anything I could think of to help with the boredom—I suggested I could bring my laptop up and we could work on a memoir of her life, which had been really such an interesting one. We tried that several times, but the memories got tangled up in each other, and one day's notes did not match the next.

It gradually became more painful to make those visits. And I had interruptions—meetings out of town that were a few days long, but somehow stretched into weeks. Or work obligations, writing deadlines—whatever I could grab. But the guilt was an ever-present companion.

On the day I had the sad message from her first husband, now a family friend, it had been several weeks since I had seen her. "Sally, it's Howard. I wanted to let you know that our dear friend has been under hospice care at the house for a week or so, and it doesn't look good. If you want to see her, I think you should try to come soon."

I called back immediately, and I was not able to come that day but arranged to come the following afternoon.

The next day I called the house to let them know I was on the way. Another devoted friend, Wendell, answered the phone.

"Oh Sally, I'm so sorry to tell you. She passed away just about a half hour ago."

I tried not to hear the words. The tears started to come. How could I not have been there for her?

"May I come now?" I asked emotionally, "May I still come and just be there with you for a little while?"

When I got to the house, her husband's son, who had had a difficult relationship with my friend but had still tried to be there for her, was at the house. And Wendell, who had answered my phone call, was also still there.

Our sweet friend, her pale skin taut and waxen, her tiny frame so diminished, lay on a hospital bed next to her sofa. Wendell told me that a week or two earlier she had locked herself in her office with vodka and pills, and they had to break in to find her. She had somehow survived that day, but it had so weakened her already weak body that it was truly the beginning of the end.

There could be no more words, no smiles. The music was silenced.

There is an intersection between my house and my friend's, at the top of Laurel Canyon where it crosses Mulholland Drive and continues down to Sunset. It is where I would turn left to go for a visit. It's also the road I travel every time I go over the hill into town, or to the doctor's, or to the studios. I travel that road nearly every day of my life. And I cannot pass that intersection without regretting that I'd not been more present during that last painful period—that perhaps I could have made a difference. For months, I couldn't resist still turning left, to revisit happier memories.

CHAPTER 31
A TOUGH MORNING

The year was 2018. It had been another somewhat challenging morning, with a rushed vocal session that was squeezed in at nine a.m. prior to a ten a.m. musicians' scoring session for a *Simpsons* episode at Remote Control Studios, Hans Zimmer's facility in Santa Monica.

There had been a change in the music team of composers for the show at the beginning of the season, and I was getting used to the new crew, anxious to please them. They, I'm sure, were anxious to please the producers of the show who they were now working for, so perhaps things were a little nervous all around. They seemed like very sweet guys on the few sessions we'd done so far together. And very kindly, they had told me at the end of the first couple of sessions that "we'll be seeing a lot of you!"

We hurried through this last-minute session, singing three or four vocal cues with multiple overdubs which felt rushed, and we normally would have been given a bit longer to perfect them. So I was feeling a little wistful, off-balance, not sure everything had gone well, or that I would be invited back. *The Simpsons* had been such an important part of my life for the last twenty-nine years, ever since I'd sung the main title with Danny Elfman, the composer of the theme, and my daughter Susie. I had worked on some vocals during that first year when

Richard Gibbs was scoring the show. Then in the second season, Alf Clausen was hired as the composer and I was hired as vocal contractor. There were many wonderfully clever, funny vocal cues performed by the singers almost weekly, for characters or the villagers in the town on screen, or for whatever needs came along in the weekly script. Alf created some sensational material with the help of brilliant writers and lyricists, and I truly believe Alf's music helped establish the "sound" of the show.

The producers had recently let Alf Clausen go after twenty-eight years, and this twenty-ninth season had begun with the new team. I suspected, as did many, that the change of composers was largely about the bottom line, about perhaps doing more synth underscores with a younger, less pricey team and not using live orchestra on all the underscoring. I was grateful to still be on the scene, along with Chris Ledesma, the music editor, and Joe Zimmerman, who handled all the "music prep"—the singer and orchestra lead sheets, etc. But we all realized that, as had happened for Rick Riccio, our engineer, things could screech to a halt at any minute. Rick had done the recording engineering for all twenty-eight seasons and had been included with the team for the first couple of episodes, but eventually, because the recordings now took place at Remote Control Studios, Hans Zimmer's facility in Santa Monica, the studio engineer there took over the duty. The shaky feeling this morning, I feared, might be a prelude to another one of those "any minutes" changes. In the rush to get done this morning on time for the strings to begin, the music team had decided to add some synth voices doing the oohs and ahs, something we singers ordinarily would have done. And that, to me, was a bad sign for the future to come.

Alf's creative team had also included Dell Hake, arranger and in later years, conductor, for Alf on the scoring stage, and in more recent years Greg Prechel, who also served as arranger/composer and sometimes conductor for some of the music cues. Alf's son Scott Clausen, who by then had begun to score his own TV projects, also did arrangements from time to time, and Chris Ledesma had begun to do some arranging of cues. Murray Adler, a fine string player, had taken over contracting the musicians after Mike Rubin, Fox Studio's dearly loved contractor for most of their productions, passed away about halfway through the *Simpsons'* unfolding seasons.

This is how the scoring was done through all of Alf's twenty-eight years at the helm, with the blessing, of course, of Matt Groening and Jim Brooks, the producers and creators of the show. Together, we had become quite a closely knit family. Alf and his wife Sally (I eventually named myself "Sally-the-other") would gather at the invitation of the Clausens for holiday dinners and celebrations at Christmastime, and it had become a special tradition indeed.

The news that Alf would no longer be composer for the show had been a shock, not just to us, but to the industry, and very sad for all of us to hear. And of course, none of us knew exactly what that decision would mean for any of us individually, going forward.

The new music team, a band called Bleeding Fingers, was headed by Russell Emanuel, a composer/musician from Australia. The band worked under the umbrella of Hans Zimmer, who is a wonderfully gifted and successful composer himself, but also along the way had added another dimension to his career in Hollywood—he developed a system of incorporating young, aspiring composers into his creative activities, thus working with a team of folks, many of whom went on to establish successful careers in their own names eventually. It gave the young composers an opportunity to learn the craft, to gain some experience, and meet others in the business, and it gave Hans a team of coworkers when schedules got intense. His workplace spanned the globe, literally, as he had roots in Europe, and studios and offices in Santa Monica.

Hans had been hired to compose the score for *The Simp-*

sons Movie when the theatrical features version of the series was produced, and he did an excellent job. I was blessed to work on that project with him as well, to sing and also book the choir. But that decision to use Hans was made after Alf had been scoring the series for close to twenty years so successfully, and to have another composer hired to score the theatrical feature was, I know, very hurtful to Alf. I felt sad for him and somewhat guilty for having been included in the film scoring, but admittedly, not guilty enough to turn it down. I had worked on a number of Hans's early film scores and truly enjoyed working with him as well.

Starting with season twenty-nine, the new team had scored the first couple of episodes primarily with synth instrumenttal sounds, creating an orchestra with maybe a solo instrument or two overdubbed to give it a slightly more "live" effect. Synth vocals had also been used, all of which were a tremendous savings to the bottom line of the music budget. But apparently, the producers were not as pleased with the synth sounds as they had been with live musicians over the years, so for the third and fourth episodes live musicians were plugged back in.

I must share here that there are politics in Hollywood. Yes, it is true. And there are folks perceived as "good guys" and "not-so-good guys." I have always tried to be one of the good guys, though I can't guarantee that others have always seen me in that light. There may be some in town who might not feel that way. It's a very competitive business, and there are so many talented people who never get that chance to be heard or known. Even though we, as contractors, try to do the best we can to be fair, it doesn't always feel that way to those who feel they are on the "outside." And sometimes that "outside" thing happens just because a contractor might not know about a very talented new person out there . . . or a very talented not-so-new person!

At the time of this session, I was well toward the wind-down of my career at seventy-nine, and in all probability, I should just go away and let the new guys take over. But it's not that easy. When you work at something you love for years and years—like fifty or sixty years—it becomes your identity, it becomes who you *are*. And particularly so if you happen to be a single woman, having left three marriages behind, and not looking to try it again. Your work sort of becomes your social life, and your family. So you hang on by your fingernails, because you fear if you don't, you will dry up and just dangle like a spider on its web from one of the rafters. You won't know who you are. No one will remember you. No one will care.

I've worked hard to keep my singing voice in shape, and being asked to perform a couple of solos in 2019 for a tribute evening honoring Lalo Schifrin at Herb Alpert's Vibrato Jazz Club, it helped me feel maybe I was still doing okay, vocally.

When I stop singing, I want it to be because I'm ready, because there's something else, finally, that I want to do, like write more silly little stories or poems and send them off to magazines and literary journals. Maybe even finish this memoir. I don't want it to be because I showed up one more time than I should have and don't sound good anymore.

And to speak honestly, it's hard to experience that change, that wind-down, when the reason is some political shift in the business that happens and suddenly affects our lives. But those things do happen.

So self-doubt lurks just beneath the surface of my psyche, and in this precarious time as far as the future music for *The Simpsons* is concerned, if we're having some bumps in the studio, if things aren't coming together, I fear that it's me. I must be singing out of tune, to their ears. I'm doing something wrong. They want someone younger. And when we feel nervous or insecure, it absolutely affects our performance.

On this morning's session, we were rushing to get the nine o'clock vocals finished by ten so that the string players due to arrive at that time could begin their work. Little problems with the vocals not "settling" into the tempo, as those in the booth conceived it, and seemingly some little pitch problems. I think all the singers on that date were aware of the uncertainty because when you're under pressure trying to do an excellent first take but know you're sort of "on trial," it's hard not to let it affect you.

I had already arrived a little off-balance to begin with, because the young woman who was coordinating the session calls for the new team had sent me an email asking that I send over the names of the singers in advance. They had not asked for this on earlier sessions, so of course my mind started to dart from one paranoid, suspicious thought to the next paranoid, suspicious thought: had the gentleman who was the new musicians' contractor already approached the new team about his own vocal contractor taking over? Had he asked which singers they've been using? Has he suggested that maybe those weren't the best singers they could be working with?

Ah, our own paranoid insecurity does drag us into the darkness. Later, of course, I realized that she needed those names in order that the front desk could clear those people into the building once they showed the proper required identification! But that's how edgy the whole situation had become in my psyche.

We got some of the vocal cues done, but the folks in the control booth decided finally to just skip a couple of the cues that were not yet recorded, in favor of using electronic synth voices oohs and ahs, so they could begin the strings session on time. We could tell there were still problems when we stood around the mic waiting for feedback from the booth. This often happens on sessions, and we also were confident, each of us, that given a few more minutes, we could fix them.

But time was running out—the string players were beginning to assemble in the parking lot, and the crew decided it was time to move on. We filled out our paperwork and tried to maintain a cheerful attitude, but I think the other singers were feeling the same anxiety as I was feeling—was this the last *Simpsons* session we would be doing?

This one situation, this change in composers and musical teams for *The Simpsons*, was a change that affected me very directly, but it was only a part of a much larger change that had taken place in the recording community, has affected the community, and has intensified over the last decade.

The new musician's contractor now handling the hiring of the musicians for the new *Simpsons* team basically *was* the larger change that had taken place in town. He bought his contracting business—the contacts and accounts, as a business—from the musician's contractor in town who had been the busiest and most successful contractor here for the last thirty or forty years. That contractor had always worked with the different vocal contractors when singers were needed on a project, depending upon who the project's composer or studio was preferring to use. But the musicians and singers were always handled separately.

Things had evolved quite differently since the change. The new contractor brought his own vocal contractor in the operations, incorporating vocal contracting with the musicians contracting, and it has basically offered one-stop shopping. So most of the vocal contractors in town had been slightly nudged to the side or pushed out of position altogether. This affected their own work, of course, but also the singers who were most often working for them.

I had experienced changes over the years, just as we all had—new singers come on the scene, new composers, and relationships change and evolve. But it was never as much under one person's control as it had now become. The change created a very different community for the singers, and a different system. It was honestly a bit of a shock, but not totally unexpected, to learn that these changes were now hitting *The Simpsons*. The new contractor had not taken over the *Simpsons* project until the new music team replacing Alf took over, but until that time it was one of very few situations he had *not* yet taken over. And though I was still on board for the *Simpsons* vocals, I knew that things could very likely and inevitably change.

I had initially learned somewhat awkwardly of his replacing Murray Adler a few weeks earlier when I was at one of the previous sessions at The Bridge, an independent recording studio in Glendale. The show had often scored there with Alf, and on that day was scoring with the new team. As I organized the paperwork to hand out to the singers, I realized I had brought out-of-date W-4 forms. Fox Payroll department is very fussy about using only present-year forms. So I went to the nice lady in the office to ask if by any chance, I could borrow five. She replied "Oh yes, the new musicians' contractor just came in and asked me for *fifty* W-4s for the orchestra. So I had to print some!" I suddenly didn't feel so bad, asking for five. So that was how I got news of the "new musicians' contractor." I thanked her for the W-4s and headed for the studio control booth to let them know that the singers were in the lobby, whenever they needed us.

On my way back to the lobby from the control booth, I saw the person who had been incorporated into that musician contractor's business as his vocal contractor of record walking toward me down the hall, headed toward the booth. We greeted each other in the customary friendly manner. He is a good human being, and a very fine composer himself as well, which was his original goal within the business. He hadn't really pursued the goal of session singing. He continued on toward the booth, as I continued back into the lobby.

But my heart sank. I knew how these things worked. This was definitely the political prelude to the new guy's weaving his own vocal contractor into the melody on yet another project in town.

To share a bit of history with you, for the last sixty years or more here in Hollywood in film, television, commercials, and sound recordings work, there have been two separate but equal communities: the musicians who comprised the orchestra performances, and the singers who performed the vocals. The musicians work through American Federation of Musicians contracts and rules, and the singers work under Screen Actors Guild-AFTRA contracts and rules (formerly SAG and AFTRA, two separate unions until 2012 when they merged into one). The two communities functioned separately, and there were various musician and singer contractors who worked within the industry, independent of one another. Composers and studios had relationships with certain contractors they preferred, and the work was spread somewhat evenly, though inevitably politics entered in.

And though it has been sad to lose some of the contacts I had so enjoyed working with over the years—especially most recently *The Simpsons* —in my case the effect of these recent changes wasn't as serious as it was for some. I fully realized I'd already had a wonderfully long ride, one that was destined, appropriately, to wind down at some point. I had to remind myself I had much to be grateful for.

But there are some terrifically talented, personable, and well-informed young singers, capable and experienced, who would have eventually moved into the position of vocal contractor for composers with whom they had worked but now most likely won't, since the process has been so revised. Though some of those relationships could certainly still develop, things are pretty much all handled presently under one roof, and that roof controls the majority of work in town for both musicians and singers. It has definitely become one-stop shopping, and a bit of a monopoly. The offices of the new musicians' contractor are staffed with people who handle audition notifications, calls for demo tapes, contract forms, and other things that in the past were done by the individual contractors in connection with the singer contractor's duties.

The contractors traditionally are people who have worked in the community for some time, have come to know the talents within the community, know who does what well, have learned the various contract terms for all the aspects of the music business, and have sort of floated to the surface. They have either evolved because they somehow established relationships with individual composers or with music departments that trust their abilities. A big part of their job is not only to take care of those people who they work *for*, but also to take care of the singers or musicians who they hire. Their job is to make sure the rules are followed, the payments are correctly made, the conditions are safe, and so on. For this, they get a little extra in their paycheck for their efforts in putting together the right people for the original call. And they keep records in their own files to assure that should the vocals become used for a new project of some kind down the road, they can file the necessary paperwork and the appropriate conversion payments are made. They don't get paid for the additional re-filings, only for the original project.

But the biggest gift they get is that they get to be on those jobs themselves. The rule for the singer contractors is that they also must be a performing member of the group, unless it is a male contractor hiring a women's choir, a woman contractor hiring a men's choir, or someone hiring a children's choir. This is important because they need to be a part of the ensemble, to communicate from the risers into the booth, if there is a problem with the mix in the headphones, if there is an error in the vocal chart, if there is a pitch problem within the room, etc. And they are very much in the driver's seat in terms of who gets to show up for those jobs. As freelance session singers, we do not have agents. Someone tried that about fifty years ago and it didn't work out well, for the singers or that agent. Or, I suspect, sometimes for the sounds of the choir.

I worked for almost twenty-five years exclusively as a session singer on solo and choir sessions for various vocal contractors, before I began to do any vocal contracting myself. By that time I had gotten very involved with my unions, had participated in contract negotiations, knew my community well, and I think (I hope) I did a pretty good job for the composers with whom I've been honored to work, as well as for the colleagues who I was able to include on those many wonderful projects. And I've always tried to take care of the singers I brought into work situations. It's important that those practices continue.

This is how the scoring business works: the process of assembling a recording project—a film, or tv show—begins with a meeting between the producer or the producing studio's music department, the composer, and the musician's contractor. They sit down together and work out the recording schedule, decide what studio should be used, and clarify what the composer's needs are and what dates they will be working. Most all films utilize musicians in a film score but only occasionally also include a choir or voices, so the vocal contractor traditionally was brought in later, and voices added into the schedule as needed, after things had been worked out.

At that initial meeting, the new musician's contractor is now able to say, "If you'll be needing vocals, we can also handle that for you." And his new vocal contractor is plugged in. That person would have been crazy not to accept an opportunity like this. It meant the guarantee of being a part of all of the musician contractor's projects, which were growing to pretty much most all of the scoring work done in town. It meant he would be performing as a singer and contractor whenever vocals were needed on a score for the busy new musicians' contractor, and that he would benefit from SAG payments and residuals on projects going forward.

There were those few rare vocal contractor/composer relationships that endure such things as this change, with one or two composers we'd each worked with closely for some years staying in place. But in most cases, composers are working under a furious deadline and just need to know that such things will be taken care of efficiently. New composers not yet connected to the community were happy to just have things handled, and the new contractor was handling them well for the studios and composers he now worked for.

Just as a brief update: in the two years between this precarious session and the writing of this chapter, I was hired to sing on the Oscars again, I had a chance to contract another film choir for Thomas Newman, did a couple of television projects, and I continued with work for *Family Guy*. So the changes have not yet caused things to be totally over for me. But I am accepting that my work with Fox is most likely to continue drifting off the path, at least for any projects going forward that involve the new contractor and his team. It has been an amazing thirty or so years, and I'm very grateful.

And recently there has been more encouraging news of several of the younger singers in our community outside the one-stop shopping tent having had chances to contract some pretty big major film score vocals, so maybe the process is seeing a slightly more equitable correction in the status quo, and a return to a more diverse and fair marketplace.

CHAPTER 32
FINDING MY WAY HOME

Leaving the studio in Santa Monica that morning in a melancholy mood after the *Simpsons* vocal session, I decided to take the long way home, skipping the drive on the 405 freeway in favor of surface streets. I made my way toward Laurel Canyon, my route through the hills to Studio City where I live. And driving for me, if I wasn't battling traffic on some freeway, was always a somewhat introspective and calming experience. Time to ponder and reflect.

As I drove east along Olympic Boulevard something tugged at me to take a little side trip, since I had the rest of the day free. I drove off-course a bit, turned off Olympic and up into the neighborhood where my mother and I had lived when I was very little, from the age of two or three until about I was about five when she married my stepfather. The little duplex we lived in was on Oakhurst Drive in the modest flatland neighborhood at the edge of Beverly Hills. It was not nearly as chic in those days as it is today, and the duplex no longer exists, having been replaced by a tall condominium development, very stylish and elegant-looking, on the north–south running street that parallels Robertson Drive. Just a block or so away is the corner at Robertson and Beverly Boulevard, where historic Chasen's restaurant used to be. A bit farther south on Robertson Drive, the Four Seasons Hotel welcomes upscale visitors and special celebrity event guests.

I wasn't even sure I could still find the place, the little neighborhood I was looking for. It had been quite a while—decades—since I'd driven through it. But something pulled me back in time, something in me felt it would be comforting to revisit those days on this particular morning. So I headed up Robertson, and when I hit Beverly Drive, followed my nose to the left, toward Beverly Hills proper. In a few blocks, there it was, Oakhurst Drive. I turned and drove slowly along the street, trying to imagine under which elegant clump of expensive condominiums the old one-story duplex bungalow had once stood.

I began thinking about the days when, because of my mother's work singing at the studio on weekly contracts, I had spent most of my time, and had most of my memories shaped, not from the little duplex we shared, but from my time at Mrs. Holloway's house.

She and her husband owned a Spanish-style house at the corner of Arden Drive and Almont Drive, and my mother and I had walked back and forth from there when she delivered me or came to pick me up because it was so close by. So again, I followed my nose slowly along Oakhurst Drive and at the end of the first block, came to Arden, and into Mrs. Holloway's old neighborhood.

In a couple of blocks, there it was. I had not been inside that house for at least seventy years. But there it was, relatively unchanged, in what had somehow still remained a very modest neighborhood within the Beverly Hills zip code. There was something comforting about finding it still there, the small Spanish-style house, one story, its front patio now enclosed with high fencing so that the Spanish styling was almost unrecognizable, and the front door no longer visible from the street. It stood on a corner lot facing Almont Drive, and the land rolled upward on a slight grassy slant to about six feet above the sidewalk. I slowed down, and drove slowly along the side yard of the house, looking for the little narrow stone steps that used to be there, connecting the back yard down to the sidewalk. Some owner, during the seventy-odd years that had intervened since my last visit, had enclosed the backyard with high fencing, so I could no longer peer into the space and see if the fish pond was still there, where I used to watch the huge goldfish swim about. But remarkably, there they were, those little ancient concrete steps. I felt a tug pulling me back through the years, and started to get misty-eyed. (The misty eyes could have been left-over effects from that *Simpsons* session I'd just left). I have clear memories of those little steps still, where I gathered the tiny baby snails that affixed themselves into the crevices. And yes, snails have hung on to a special place in my heart. All these years later, if I walk now through my own garden after dark or along the path to the front door from the driveway and unknowingly step on one, the crunch of their fragile shells is deafening.

These memories filled my thoughts as I continued driving slowly down, past the Holloway's house, searching along the way to see what else might still be there, unchanged. Unchanged . . . that became the theme of the day. I turned the corner on the next block and passed by the house where my friend Helen had lived. I pondered on who might live there now. The house was still there, looking very much the same after all the years, but where was Helen, I wondered.

And next door to Helen's house, Mr. Spencer's house. Thank you, Mr. Spencer, for those little books you made me, those tiny blank pages stapled together. I'm still trying to write those stories.

It's funny how some things stay in your memory as clearly as if you had been there yesterday. Mrs. Holloway's kitchen had a little dinette area that faced onto the front side of the house with one step up, and there was a kind of booth where we sat for breakfasts and lunches and dinners. It was sort of like being in a restaurant. And ruling over the service porch in a threatening manner was Mrs. Holloway's treasured pet; a huge, frightening parrot who spent his waking hours on an open perch, just about at my eye-level or slightly above. I had to walk past that scary beast every morning to get out the back door. The parrot would pick up one leg, as parrots do, glowering at me with his head to one side, curling his claw from the wrist, pulling his feathery elbow up to his side, and just hold it there, threateningly, as if to say, "You make one wrong move, young lady, and I'll tear your nose off!" On some days it almost wasn't worth going outdoors to have to risk passing that bird. I'm sure it wasn't anything personal. Parrots are just like that. So are human beings sometimes.

Checking the time, and realizing I was now driving through a neighborhood no longer part of the log of childhood memories, I reluctantly continued toward West Hollywood, then up into Laurel Canyon and on down to the low hills of home. Somehow, it felt comforting to revisit those memories from long ago, the still-treasured paths; to be reminded of where I came from, and that life is not just all about what might or might not have gone wrong on one particular morning, out of all the mornings in life.

CHAPTER 33
INTO THE WEEDS
(NOT THAT KIND...)

I have been a member of both unions, Screen Actors Guild and American Federation of Television and Radio Artists, since 1961, and my unions have held an important place in my life, and in my heart. The two unions merged into one and became SAG-AFTRA in 2012, and along the way I served on the Los Angeles Board of Directors of AFTRA for about twenty-five years, the National Board of AFTRA for about forty-five years, and the Board of Directors of SAG for eighteen years. I've served as a Trustee of AFTRA Health & Retirement Funds since 1986, continue to serve presently on the AFTRA Retirement Fund as a trustee, and serve as a trustee of the now merged SAG-AFTRA Health fund. During Barry Gordon's presidency several decades ago, I served as National Secretary/Treasurer of SAG, and in the 1970s I served as National Recording Secretary of AFTRA. I have chaired the Singer Committees of both unions, I've chaired the AFTRA Wages & Working Conditions meetings for contract negotiations, and I've served on numerous other committees and negotiating teams. None of these offices or positions, by the way, are paid positions. They are a way for members to assist and to participate in the decision-making and the governance of their union, and to have a voice, however modest, within their industry. So obviously, my relationship with my unions has been a big part of my life.

As happens in the world and in our lives, things change . . . they morph along the way. I don't always love the politics of our union, just as I don't always love the politics of our nation. Politics manage to lie in wait at the core of just about every organization that exists—churches, charitable organizations, communities . . . and unions. And although all the members of a union presumably work in the same business, they do not always view that business in the same way, or see how their union could and should benefit them, within that business.

Unions are under fire right now and have been for some time, sadly. It is my belief that the strength of unions is what created a somewhat more solid middle class in so many parts of our nation. They struggle for survival presently, and when they can function as intended, they take care of their members in ways that no individual worker has the power or influence to do for themselves. They negotiate as a community for fair wages, for health care, for pensions. Both our union pension plans (SAG Pension and AFTRA Retirement Funds have not yet merged) are currently defined benefit plans, which means if you earn enough over the years to qualify for a pension, it is a guaranteed benefit and our plan structure has somehow survived against the corporate pushback, which would prefer it to become a defined contribution plan. That change would mean less responsibility for the plan regarding its growth and financial funding and more decision-making by the participant, as with a 401K plan. I know things have been headed in that direction for a long time out there in the world, but so far, we have been able to maintain the defined benefit structure for our participants in both the SAG Pension and the AFTRA Retirement Funds.

And as to how our unions benefit us through the union contracts: in our workplace, I cannot ever imagine the average non-star actor or singer being able to negotiate residuals for themselves for the future use of their work. I pray that as our industry changes, we will be able to adapt our contracts so that residuals can sustain the members in slow seasons or off-times. Streaming, for instance, pays very differently –much less than the network re-use residuals. But that is the direction of things, and hopefully, with the right people at the helm, the union will adapt and survive. In this time particularly, during which as I write, we are experiencing the COVID-19 virus epidemic, production shut down totally for going on eight months now and will no doubt dramatically affect the amount of production, even when it cautiously resumes. There are new safety guidelines in place that will make production more expensive and more challenging. Somehow, our dedicated union staff has continued to negotiate ongoing contracts, and has been able to process residual payments, and handle other work of the union, with many of the staff working largely from home. And the Health Fund and Pension/Retirement Funds have managed to process pension checks, instigate new pensioners' payments, and carry on. But we recently received notification, with regrets, that some of the staff were being, by financial necessity, furloughed or dismissed from their jobs. So many businesses have fallen on hard times during the COVID-19 pandemic, and our union is no exception.

These are not normal times. And with all my heart I pray that we get through this, that we support our hard-working staff, and we restore the full functioning. But in past years I have gone through challenging times with my union, with its politics, and since this is an intimate chat we are having here, I must share some of my feelings.

As principal singers, one of the "work categories" within SAG-AFTRA, we represent a very small percentage of the total membership, between 2 1/2 and 3 percent. And when the merger was approved, the decision-making regarding the structure of the newly formed organization was decided by committees, then by sub-committees which grew smaller and smaller in number as the details were being resolved. Some of those decisions as to the new structure were political, unavoidably. One aspect that was insisted upon by the predominantly principal actor category representation on those committees was a per capita formula for representation going forward within the officers, the Local and National Boards, etc. Traditionally, the singers have had a higher percentage of actually working members among their category than actors. Therefore, we need input into the negotiations of our contracts, and we need our contracts enforced. Without the representation to accomplish that and make our voices heard, the category suffers.

My experience with Legacy AFTRA over the years was that it was a more democratic organization, and it allowed for representation of all the categories, large and small, on its board, within its negotiating teams, and within the administration of its contracts. But now we are often not even included in contract renewal conversations or other decision-making. Our film scoring work has fled to production sites outside of the country to a large degree because of disagreements between the major studios and the American Federation of Musicians. The studios don't want to pay back end special payments funds to the musicians who play on their productions. Often the back end is where the studio makes up production costs if the film doesn't do well at the box office. My feeling is that with creative thinking, AFM could have worked out some way to accommodate those productions below certain budgets, or below certain gross earnings figures. Nonetheless, the problem still exists, and when the orchestra scoring goes abroad, the choir scoring happens there too, as they just want to record, mix and get it done. This "runaway" production is being done by major studios who are signatories to our contracts, and who theoretically should be bound to those contracts for their post-production, as well as their filming production, to use all union members. But somehow, we can't seem to get this looked at and handled within SAG-AFTRA.

It's a tough one. Once out of the country, unless they are using SAG-AFTRA members, they are not obliged to do the vocals, or any kind of production work, on SAG contracts. "Global Rule 1," which is a rule that says SAG members must be on SAG contracts regardless of where the production is done, benefits SAG actors who are performing the lead roles in productions shot outside the USA. They are often there for weeks, and they are protected by union contracts. But the practicality of a singer traveling to London for a one-day scoring session at Abbey Road—the current hot spot with a lot of Hollywood folks—does not exist. So all this runaway scoring work hovers beneath the radar. In order for us to benefit, we would have to re-locate on our own and then insist on union contracts to cover our work.

My commitment to my union began long ago, when I attended my first AFTRA convention in 1966 or 1967. I witnessed members-at-large, not necessarily celebrities or powerful figures, but delegates elected by their fellow members to attend and represent them at the annual convention, to "speak to power," to actually have an effect. At that first convention I saw journalists and news people I so highly respected— AFTRA's contracts covered daytime network news, the soaps, the GRAMMY, Emmy, and Oscar awards, etc.—pretty much all live TV. A young and dashing Tom Brokaw was there representing the news category of performers at a number of the early conventions. I appreciated and valued their intelligent contributions to conversations from the floor of the convention.

My first convention attendance was in San Francisco, at the height of Haight-Ashbury days, when the fascinating members of the love generation walked the streets, and we tourists ventured there during the free evening hours, hoping to inhale some of the exotic smoke that still lingered in the air. Earlier in the day on the convention floor, an issue had come up during the discussion regarding a vote on approval of contracts newly negotiated. One of the delegates stood at a microphone and asked the man who was executive director at the time (whose name long ago escaped me) a question about a "side letter" that seemed to have set certain conditions of preferential treatment, or perhaps discriminatory treatment to certain of the membership, as a "side deal" to the contract under discussion for approval. The executive stood at the mic before the assembled delegates, self-righteous and indignant, and insisted, "I know of no such side letter!"

The member who had asked the question from the floor replied, "That's interesting, because I have a copy of it right here, with your signature on it . . ." and then pulled it from his pocket. Very soon afterward the untrustworthy behavior of that executive was no longer part of the union, because *he* was no longer part of the union. That demonstrated to me that our union, AFTRA, was truly democratic, that members counted, and that I would have a voice within it if I remained involved, connected, and willing to serve.

Our union is the combination of working members who volunteered their time, and the dedicated paid staff, executives, and attorneys who advise, instruct and guide us through the contracts that protect our work and mandate contributions to our pension and our health plans. Those contracts establish minimums, not maximums, so there is no limit, of course, on what well-known actors can negotiate for themselves on the up side, but there is a *minimum* amount below which no day-player actor, singer, stunt person, voice-over actor, dancer, or background actor can be paid, and those contracts cover theatrical film, prime time TV, network code live TV, sound recordings, commercials, and new media, the contract which now covers streaming and online productions.

A merging of the two unions had been attempted several

times over the decades, but it was always a politically divisive issue. In the eighties, the two unions finally reached an agreement called Phase 1, which at least allowed them to jointly negotiate those contracts where their jurisdiction overlapped, basically in prime time TV and commercials. That process worked quite effectively for several decades. Then another effort was made to approve a merger, but it failed to get the necessary approval vote from membership, and the jointly negotiated agreements continued. However, in 2008 the leadership of SAG and the leadership of AFTRA were at very different places with how contract negotiations were going. The leadership of SAG at that time was very "macho," and the chief negotiator who was brought in from outside the union staff had formerly worked in the professional sports world and was inclined to handle the negotiations as if he was running a Super Bowl team of angry players. AFTRA's leadership at that time was primarily composed of women—the National Executive Director was Kim Roberts, and the National and the LA local presidents of AFTRA were also both women. The disagreements, and what seemed to some the unreasonable attitudes of SAG, finally caused the AFTRA leadership to say, "We're done here." They finalized their contract negotiations separately, approved them by a vote of the membership, and went back to work. SAG instead went on strike. The producers, even after the SAG strike was over, continued for some time to do most of their pilots under AFTRA TV contracts even though the rates were slightly higher, having been settled a year earlier. The producers just didn't want to deal with the leadership of SAG.

But this situation eventually triggered another movement toward merger within the actor community, because their Health & Retirement/Pension contributions were now being divided between the two different union funds, and in some cases, AFTRA covered more of their earnings than SAG and became primary for their health care. Some folks didn't like that, or they were upset that their SAG pension wasn't growing more from their work. Finally, those concerns developed politically to a point in 2012 where a vote was again put before the membership, and this time the merger of the two unions was approved. The next goal, for some, was to then merge the health and pension plans that were attached to each of the merged unions.

For me personally, having two separate health and pension funds has been a great benefit, as I worked enough under both AFTRA and SAG contracts that I earned one hundred percent of my medical coverage over the years, and I was also building two pensions. The SAG pension grew to be the largest, as most of my work, and the highest paying work, was done under SAG contracts. But in the early years, I had built a modest pension from my AFTRA work as well.

Theatrical film and prime time dramatic shows, as well as TV commercials, were all under SAG contracts, and sound recordings and variety TV shows, which I did a lot of in the early years, were all AFTRA contracts. The merged union now administers all contracts, and the health plans have merged into one. We are still trying to work out problems from the merging of the plans that have become apparent since the new plan was put into place, and to fairly balance the division of contributions between the two remaining funds, SAG Pension and AFTRA Retirement, to preserve their strength. Along the way, we realized that certain members had been inadvertently harmed by the merger of the health funds, because they made decisions while under the AFTRA plan that put them at a disadvantage within the changed structure of the new plan's terms. There is a commitment among the Union Trustees to try to address those problems and imbalances, as they surface.

The governmental structure of the merged union is based on proportionate representation. The broadcasters have established a strong committee within the governance which gets the attention of folks because their work brings in a lot of revenue. But for the singers, the dancers, the stunt people—smaller categories—it became harder to make our voices heard. SAG-AFTRA has basically become an actor's union.

Another practice that has really destroyed at least a third of our singer work over the last couple of decades is the nonunion Music Libraries. For independent songwriters and composers, they may be a blessing because those people can negotiate writer's royalties in some cases, depending upon their publishing agreements. But once upon a time if there was a source cue in a scene . . . if someone had a car radio on, or there was music performed in a lounge scene . . . that music was recorded at the time of scoring, arranged by the composer and recorded by his musicians and singers. Years ago I did underscore and source cue vocals for *Murder She Wrote*, *Diagnosis Murder*, *Picket Fences*, *The Love Boat*, *Happy Days*, etc., and all of that music was recorded on union contracts. Now a great deal of that music is licensed from the libraries, and that recording is done nonunion. There is no performance revenue paid to the singers or the musicians when the music is used in film or TV productions. And, as the role of music supervisor became established, that put the search for the right song outside the creative control of the composers. Music supervisors have come to such prominence now that often their screen credit occurs above the *composer's* screen credits.

These changes in our industry were not the purposeful intention of evildoers. They largely represent changes in technology, in the increase of independent productions, and in business model changes. But they have changed the security and opportunities of those who for decades lived by different rules, who have been the performers and artists who brought the music to life but didn't create it on the page. The synthetic samples scoring also has changed the rules, has made live musicians and singers less necessary in many cases.

There are people here in our community of producers and performers, who through their own successes have earned the power to make their own creative decisions based on other than the bottom line, and who do so out of their respect for the power of live music and the artists who perform it. They have managed to keep some scoring here in town, and to keep the few remaining scoring stages up and running. Seth MacFarlane is one of those folks. He himself is an amazing singer with a great love and respect for the tradition of fine music and skilled musicians. He has insisted from the beginning that his two successful animated series *Family Guy* and *American Dad,* and his current new live-action series *The Orville*, are all scored with live musicians, on the scoring stage, most often at Fox's Newman Stage.

The bottom line, I guess, is that eventually we all have to give up control of something and realize that we never had it to begin with. How the union operates is one of those things. It feels like giving up, like letting go of what I suspect has become an addiction in my own life to my union involvement. I have been moved toward that decision in recent years.

On the final day of the third National SAG-AFTRA Convention in 2018, the last convention I attended, where it seemed to me that though the hundreds of delegates were told on the floor of the convention hall that "the leadership of our union is in this room"; in fact it was actually taking place just down the hall in one of the smaller rooms, where a committee of about nine people decided which resolutions should be heard and voted on, which should not, and which should not even ever come to the floor of the convention for discussion. I left that convention feeling like it was time for me to say goodbye.

So I came home, on a sunny Sunday afternoon in October of 2018, from what will be my last SAG-AFTRA Convention. Partly because in my humble opinion I, as a representative of my community, of my singer community, and our contracts— have lost my voice in that room. We have lost much of our collective "voice" as a small category in a union of actors, stunt performers, dancers, broadcasters, and recording artists. I will take the benefits gratefully from my union, and acknowledge that we are helped tremendously by the influence of actors in the business, particularly by the stars who are of course, also members of SAG. So the producers must work with SAG if they want the name recognition of those stars to draw audiences to their films. That has held us in good stead for many years. But unless we can get their attention and make them realize that music is part of filmmaking—that often it is what brings the emotions of the action on the screen to life, that we are part of their union, that we need their attention and their focus for just a moment to try to get things back on track—then we must accept that our landscape has dramatically changed and probably will continue to change. Technology makes so many things possible that couldn't happen during what we now think of as the golden years of our business for musicians and singers.

I have never responded positively to the division of points of view that result in slates for elections within the union, where the politics of the day creep in. In my opinion, there are good guys and bad guys, saints and smartasses on both sides of almost every issue. But like our present political scene nationally, the sides have become so divided that they do not even listen to the facts of what is being proposed, or consider the value in actions before them. They just come down hard on the side of their team. Well, the union has become a similar organization. I'm no longer in the boardrooms, but I'm told by those who are that the division is currently the strongest presence felt in the room. I hope that will one day change.

I think because of my many years doing vocal contracting in addition to singing—which indeed was such a blessing and extended my own career activity by thirty or thirty-five years—I developed along the way, the attitude of "mother hen" toward my singer community. They are a talented, versatile, professional, fun, and loving group of folks, and the hardest part of doing the work of a vocal contractor was making those last couple of decisions to fill the few remaining positions to be hired for a choir or a vocal group. Who needs that job the most, of the many people who are qualified to do it? Who might be falling short of earnings to qualify for their health coverage? Who might I not have been able to include for a while?

I think of us as a community, and that spills over into my union activities. But I came away from that third of the newly merged union's conventions saddened, disheartened, and ready to step away. I have continued to serve in my trustee duties and certainly on the Singer Committee, but on a grander scale, the young singers will have to look at the business landscape and at the union governance structure, and figure out how they can fight to make their voices heard. I am indulging, I know, in shameful self-pity in a way, in terms of the environment at these meetings. I have gotten shut down by the chair on too many occasions, I have found that there is no time or place within the structure to share with that huge gathered body of diverse performers at convention from all over the country what it is we do, why so much of it has gone away, and that we need their help. It is painful to sit in that room and feel like an overlooked outsider. I guess that happens over time with pretty much everyone, in whatever their work world is as things change and evolve.

I suspect that elements of my own life are having some buttons pushed too. Jack, my third husband, and I separated in 1993. I think that after almost thirty years of living life as a single person, feeling out of place at times at social gatherings—feeling like an outsider—is familiar to me in most areas of life. And despite years of therapy, I've failed to shake that sense of "I don't feel like I belong here." So, best I stay home, enjoy the butterflies and hummingbirds in the garden through the window above my computer, and concentrate on writing the silly little stories that are beginning to find homes on the pages of literary journals around the country. I suspect at this point in life that will be much more rewarding. Oh, I shall continue to answer the phone, should it happen to ring, and will arrive on time to a studio whenever I'm invited, as long as I can sing in tune and sound pleasant. (PS -you may remember that male singers, i.e. Tony Bennett...are out there performing well into their nineties. Ladies, however, don't often experience that same privilege). But I am giving up on the political stuff. It ain't my thing any more, and maybe it never was. Though it's definitely habit-forming.

CHAPTER 34
THE SUMMER OF RESCUING BEES

We scooped them out of the swimming pool, Carol and I, one by one, with the dry eucalyptus leaves that had fallen and landed near the coping. You could tell from a distance which ones could still be saved; their little wings beat furiously against the chlorinated water, their little bee feet kicked up toward the sky, their yellow- and black-striped bee backs floated like walnut shells on the sloshing surface of the pool.

We lifted them up and swam furiously to place them on the edge of the deck, so that when they came to enough to realize they were still alive, they would not turn on us. Even the dead bees could sting. The pale white inside skin of my forearm bristled red and painful from just bumping up against one of them in the pool on a day when I had not been cautious.

I was annoyed with my friend Carol at first, because she was so serious about it, so almost obsessed. We spent half our swimming time pulling the hostile little creatures out of the drink. Most of them, groggy and disoriented, crawled along the coping back toward the edge, and eventually fell again into the water. Swiftly we rushed to retrieve them.

On cloudy days it seemed like there were fewer of them, but on sunny days they would swirl in the air around the nest they had built into the backside of the small pool house. We watched them against the dark green leaves of the eucalyptus trees, whirling, darting off, then coming back to circle, circle, circle. They zoomed, dipping low over the water, lifting off, dropping down again, lifting off—-a dance they did until finally the pull was irresistible and they fell into the warm circulating waters, lost and doomed, but for Carol and me.

I can actually remember conversations with those bees. When I was alone in the pool, I talked to them in the same manner I had begun to answer back to the stupid cat clock Carol gave me for Christmas that year as a joke. The clock meowed on the hour and pictures of twelve different breeds of cats spaced themselves around the edge of its face, but the meows were all the same. Because of the bees, I began a whole process of thoughts about fate, about bad decisions, about inevitabilities, about how horrible it must feel to be God.

Then I began to wonder why God didn't do anything about my sweet brother Jon.

God could have stopped all of it. He could have picked Jon up in a giant eucalyptus leaf and carried him to shore, lowering him gently onto the green grass to recover, to gather his strength and move on.

He could have saved us all.

This is the saddest chapter in my life, and in the lives of my dear family. My brother Jon Clarke was one of the most amazing musicians in the music, film scoring, and TV scoring business. And he had the most beautiful oboe tone of any player I've ever heard. More importantly, he was one of the sweetest, smartest, and kindest human beings that ever existed.

Jon was ten years younger than I and by the time he left home to go out into the world, I had gone off to college, had gotten married, and had begun my own work in the world of music. He was an unusually excellent musician at a very early age, his first industry job being to play with Don Ellis's band, at age seventeen. He was too young to legally go into the Las Vegas lounges where Don's band worked, so they had to smuggle him in. He continued on from there to become part of the Loggins and Messina band, playing all the reed instruments and flying about the stage in his moccasins, his fantastic, long, curly blond hair flowing, playing two flutes at a time. On "Your Mama Can't Dance, and Your Daddy Don't Rock 'n Roll," he rocked the hall.

Jon met his wife, Miriam Sosewitz, during his work in the studios on film and television scoring. Miriam also did session work playing flute and was a fine solo flutist. Jon and Miriam had two adorable little boys, and tragically when the boys were only four and seven years of age, Jon was diagnosed with kidney cancer.

He marched bravely through every chapter of his illness, Mimi by his side with the clipboard and medical schedules, and we hoped—prayed—and really believed he was going to be okay. The day after Christmas dinner that first year, with family at my house and tearful goodbyes from his big sister, Jon went into the hospital to have one kidney removed. The surgery went well. I had bought some gold-flecked wine glasses for each of us at Pottery Barn and made everyone promise we'd come back together and bring them along on the following Christmas. We would all gather again, with our gold-flecked wine glasses and celebrate his recovery. It was a tangible symbol, all I could think of to commit us all in my own way and ensure that Jon would come safely through this illness—that we would all be together again.

But shortly thereafter, it was discovered that Jon's cancer had spread to other places in his body. He went through a series of painful radiation treatments at Cedars-Sinai, and I went with Jon and Mimi while he endured his "crown of thorns" as he called it; the "it" being an intricate metal framework kind of thing with sharp prongs on it that held his head perfectly still, in position so that the radiation would only go where it was supposed to, and not into some other area of his brain. But it could not have been fun.

That treatment successfully held things at bay for a time, and Jon and Mimi and the boys relocated full-time to their little home on Kauai, where the boys went to school and Jon switched to a more naturalistic form of treatment. That treatment, however, though it kept him strong, very active, and feeling well for many months, eventually failed to keep the cancer from passing through the blood-brain barrier. The cancer crept again into his brain, and his life ended there on the island of Kauai in 2005. Jon was fifty-four years of age.

The summer that Jon got sick I gained twenty-three pounds. That's a conservative estimate because by the end of August I'd stopped weighing myself. For each pound that he lost, I gained two. Comfort food for anxiety, for sadness, was my drug of choice.

I developed addictions that first year of his illness. I tried anything legal and/or available by prescription to blot out the thoughts that crept into my mind—the gut-wrenching, angry, heartbreaking thoughts that came in the middle of the night mostly, but made intermittent visits throughout the day.

There was plenty that might ordinarily have distracted us from the unspeakable facts of his illness that first year, and there was plenty to rage about, to shout back at the television set about. Only a short time earlier, we had suffered that terrible morning when our nation woke up to the unimaginable images—the smoke, the flames, the cries, the crumbling, plunging concrete, the sirens surrounding the World Trade Center. Following that tragedy, we had the world on our side, and they mourned with us. They lit candles on London street corners, in front of Paris monuments, along park paths in Germany. They would have done anything for us. Then somehow, our president swaggered his way into their collective distain and dying respect and took the rest of us with him. Maybe God was angry about that.

The year of Jon's illness was coincidentally the year of our nation's illness, its perilous escapades. It was the year the guys in Washington sent soldiers marching off to Iraq who were supposed to find Bin Laden, but didn't. And the front page of the *LA Times* gave us new topics each morning to shake our verbal fists at, to take our minds off the business at hand. Jon and Miriam's heavy kitchen table, bearing on its ancient pine surface the generational wounds of hastily placed coffee mugs, of felt marker pens in the hands of three-year-old toddlers and misplaced knife gashes from years of amateur pumpkin-carvings, became the sacred center of our collective anguish. It took our minds off the threat that was at Jon's door, off the fact that his wife and two sweet sons, we feared, would have to continue their journey without him. Instead, we raged at Washington. The family rallied, his dear close friends rallied, and there is still not a day in my life that I don't think of him and miss him. We are blessed, because his music is still floating out there in the world, and when I hear a recording with one of his beautiful emotional oboe solos, my heart smiles.

And of course, the Loggins and Messina days will linger on the sound waves. Jon also played the solo on the main title theme for the HBO series *Six Feet Under*, score by Thomas Newman, and we can still hear that, along with the many other scores he played of Newman's work. Jon was one of the core musicians Tom relied upon, and he loved Tom's work and felt it such a privilege to have been a part of it.

To understand our family, you have to go back to the beginning, to the very beginning. It was a "his, hers, and theirs" family. I know my life would have been very different if my mother had stayed married to my father, and because I loved him so, I often wondered what that life would have been. But then there never would have been Jon, nor Mike and Vickie, from my stepfather's first marriage, nor Charles and Lydia, as Jon also was, the children of that second marriage. I'd never have wanted to have missed my brothers and sisters. And my father, in his very happy later marriage, was the father of two more wonderful brothers, John and Bruce Stevens, and the stepfather of Murray Galbraith, my dear stepmom Dotty's son from her first marriage. So we're all grateful we ended up on the journey together!

But we have all missed and will continue to miss and love Jon, till the end of our days.

CHAPTER 35

THE ELLA AWARDS ADVENTURE

In order to help you understand the impact of the story I'm about to share, I need to explain a bit more about the session singer world. It may sound like, and often is, a very glamorous world to be a part of. And it brings the emotional rewards of knowing you've done a good job, you've performed well—whether it's doing a solo jingle or vocal cue for a film score, singing background vocals on a recording, or being part of a choir in concert or on a scoring stage—or maybe singing a high soprano obligato solo, floating up above the orchestra. But in terms of recognition, that gift is received, for the most part, only from within our own community of musicians, singers, and composers. Most of what we do is uncredited, whether it's a solo main title for a TV series, an emotional solo cue supporting a scene in a movie, or being part of an ensemble. Our individual success—our level of skill and recognition—grows within our own community as we have opportunities to show what we can do as an individual soloist or as part of the highly skilled choral community in our town.

Because of my fortunate decades-long active career here in Hollywood, I've worked with several different generations of singers over the years. Some of the younger singers know me as a vocal contractor or choral director, but they don't know about the other aspects of my career—my solo performances, the lyric writing—or much about my early days in the business. And that's always been fine. I've never been very good at self-promotion, and I thoroughly understood the rules of our game. We show up, do our job, get well-paid for it and for future uses of it, and we for the most part remain invisible.

Back in the early eighties, inspired by the dream of another session singer, a woman who had begun her career in the forties and fifties, singing with jazz bands and in the jazz vocal group The Skylarks, a wonderful charitable organization was established. It came about partly because of Gilda Maiken Anderson's dream, and because Ginny Mancini (the wife of Henry Mancini, who was also a singer and a dear friend of Gilda's), who also shared her dream, had the resources and visibility to turn it into a reality. The organization was called the "Society of Singers" and its purpose was to lend help and support in times of need to those people who could legitimately identify themselves as professional singers, but whose career had fallen upon hard times.

The Society of Singers provided grants and assistance for rent or medical costs and other needs, and eventually, they were even able to purchase an apartment building in Sherman Oaks, CA where they could offer temporary residence. It was a modest building—seven units—but it rescued a lot of folks along the way. And there were some residents there whose names would surprise you . . . even a celebrity with great talent and accomplishments can fall upon hard times. It's the luck of the moment, of the timing, of the events in their own lives.

In the early days, SOS created a special award that also established a source for raising funds. It was called the Ella Award, and it was presented at an annual banquet most often held at the Beverly Hilton Hotel, where record labels, studios, and others in the business could purchase expensive tables, host their colleagues, and be present when the Ella Award was presented, as part of an evening with live entertainment. The first Ella Award was given to (three guesses) Ella Fitzgerald, to honor her long, impressive career. Subsequent awards in the following years were given to Frank Sinatra, Tony Martin, Steve Lawrence & Eydie Gormé, Lena Horne, Rosemary Clooney, Joe Williams, Tony Bennett, Julie Andrews, Plácido Domingo, Barry Manilow, Celine Dion, Elton John, Johnny Mathis, Gladys Knight, Andy Williams, Herb Alpert & Lani Hall, Natalie Cole, Smokey Robinson, and Mike Love. Quite a list!

The Ella Awards began in 1989 and continued every year, with the exception of only a couple of years, until the last Ella Awards event in 2014. I had served on the Society of Singers Board of Directors in the early years, as the organization was becoming established, but my work schedule and the great amount of union activities and involvement later required that I step away.

In 2010, the year that Natalie Cole was honored with the Ella Award, another award was created and added to the ceremony. This was the Voice Award, and it was to be given to one of the many "invisible" singers in our session singer world, the folks who support the stars but rarely step into the spotlight. The first year the Voice Award was given, it was presented to Billie Barnum, a dear, gifted singer who had begun her career in the sixties, had been very much a part of the R&B recording world, later established the group The Blackberries, and continued within the industry as freelance backup and choral singer on many recording and film projects.

It was exciting for us all to be in attendance that evening, to enjoy celebrating Billie, to watch the video that had been prepared sharing the events of her career, many of which most of us hadn't known anything about. It was a special evening, and it revealed more about Billie as a very special person.

In 2011, as the Ella Awards approached, I received a call from the director of the organization, informing me that I had been selected to receive the Voice Award that year, and asking if I would accept it. I was very surprised, and of course, very delighted. She told me that their videographer would be getting in touch with me, and in preparation for the event, would put together a video similar to the one we had seen when Billie Barnum's award had been presented.

I met with the very kind gentlemen who was to create the video over the period of four or five weeks, and we dug through boxes of photographs and memorabilia, deciding what might be most interesting and fun to share. He included still shots from the *Danny Kaye* TV days, shots from Bacharach concerts, the album cover of the James Taylor Christmas Album that my song had been included in, and various other moments and events from over the years.

The evening of the event finally arrived. I had purchased a table for my guests and had invited my family and closest friends. They all knew what was planned for the evening, and shared my excitement about this very special gathering. The event was held at the Beverly Hilton Hotel in the Grand Ballroom, and as I wandered about during cocktail hour, I noticed Jane Fonda, seated with her companion at one of the tables near the edge of the stage. The rest of her party hadn't filled their seats yet, so thinking I wouldn't interrupt anything, I gathered my courage, walked cautiously over, and introduced myself, as unobtrusively as I could. I asked her forgiveness for being so bold as to disturb her at a social evening, and explained that I just couldn't resist doing so because one of my own most special projects over the decades was singing the solo vocal cues in the underscore of *Klute*, the film for which she had won an Oscar. She was kind, not too terribly responsive but acknowledged my greeting. I thought maybe it was okay to approach her, since I was to receive the award and she would hear more about that participation in *Klute* and in other projects later in the evening. The videographer had even included one of my solo vocal cues from *Klute* in the soundtrack of the video.

In an effort to save expenses—and I'll explain a bit more about this later—one of the board members of the organization had volunteered to produce the evening. He was primarily an arranger/composer and would also lead the band on stage. The organization was really trying to keep costs down.

The person who was to present the award and introduce me at the Ella Awards was David White, the Executive Director of Screen Actors Guild and a dear colleague. It was kind of him to take part in the evening. Dinner was served, and then the evening's activities began. After welcoming speeches by the host of the evening, David was introduced and stepped up to the microphone. About the time he began to speak, a production assistant came to my table and led me backstage to a hallway, where sadly, while David was directing all his kind comments about me to my table of friends and family, I was waiting backstage in the hallway, out of hearing range, and missed all the kind things he said.

The young production assistant eventually walked me to the stairs that led up onto the stage, and at the appropriate moment I joined David. He introduced me to the audience and gave me a hug, then we both just kind of stood there. I whispered into his ear, "Am I supposed to say something?" And he whispered back, "I think you are . . ." So I expressed my thanks to the organization, and I shared the thought that came to me, which was that I was particularly grateful to have been able to be the dispenser of "jobs" for my talented colleagues when my work expanded to include vocal contracting in my later years. I had loved making those happy phone calls.

The young production assistant then stepped up and handed me a Crystal Award trophy, and the audience applauded politely, having still no idea who this strange woman standing on stage was. And the evening moved on.

The band played us off. I was numb, in shock. I couldn't figure out what had happened, why they had not played the video. I thought perhaps so many celebrities had wanted to speak in honoring Smokey Robinson that they ran out of time and decided to not include it.

I was barely able to keep the tears from coming, and as I sat back down at the table, everyone also silently wondered what had happened. This would have been, finally, a chance to share the things I was especially proud of, and to feel recognized and acknowledged by my community. I truly was looking forward to sharing some of the adventures from over the years. My family and guests, of course, felt my disappointment. I was able to make it through the evening, and when I got home, I put the award out of sight, thanked my sweet friend Russ Olson who had also shared my disappointment, for his kindness and for the evening, and tried to put it out of my mind.

The next morning, emails started flying from the folks on the Board of the Society of Singers to one another, exclaiming what a wonderful evening it had been, thanking those in charge, etc. I couldn't help it. I replied with a note to all, saying that though I was very appreciative of the honor, I had to share how disappointing it was that the video was not shown—that after weeks of preparing and looking forward to it finally being shared, it would have been helpful if someone had told me in advance that it was not going to be shown.

I had an immediate reply from David Foster, who had served on the event committee. He was terribly upset, felt bad for my disappointment, and insisted that at the next award, my video should be shown. Finally, there was a note from the gentleman who had produced the evening, explaining what had happened, and apologizing. It seemed that because of budget concerns, they had not provided teleprompters to help guide the speakers through the evening. When David introduced me, he was scripted to have said, "And now, if you turn your attention to the screen..." But just trying to make the introduction without the script in front of him, he never said those exact words. The director spoke into the headphones of all those working on the tech aspects of the show and said, "Well, I guess they've decided not to show the video. Let's move on." And that was that.

I eventually got over the painful evening, accepted that I would remain invisible for the rest of my life, and put the lovely Crystal Award on a table in the corner of the living room. But more importantly, I finally realized and accepted that the true and obvious gift of all the stories and details of my life that weren't able to be shared that evening—was that I had lived them all. And that I have truly, truly been blessed.

Just to follow up a bit—as the decades passed from the establishment of the Society of Singers in 1985, and the structure of the music business changed so dramatically, it did become harder to fill the tables at those events, the primary source of fundraising for their charity work. More independent artists were marketed, a less-structured recording world that was not as hands-on evolved, and the major labels no longer purchased one or two tables. And along the way, sadly, the administration of the Society of Singers was turned over to, and mishandled by, a couple of salaried CEOs who took advantage (in my opinion) of the funds available to them, wasting them on office spaces, decorator costs, self-promotion, and their own generous salaries.

The last Ella Awards was held in 2014, and the honoree was Mike Love, one of the Beach Boys. The crowd was smaller, and after the costs of his guests—several tables of family and friends, that were never paid for by him—and the last-minute increase in production costs because of services and equipment Mike Love insisted upon to support his own performance, the evening resulted in an overwhelming loss of about seventy-four thousand dollars in expenses to the organization. A year or two later, S.O.S. had to close their doors and end the Society of Singers. The well-deserved Voice Award at that last event was presented to the Waters Family—Maxine, Julia, Oren, and Luther—wonderful singers who sang on almost every major artist's recording in the sixties and seventies, on film scores and television projects for decades, toured with artists over the years, and still persevere in our business. The video that was created to cover the events of their lives and careers was, fortunately (ahem...) shown. And was wonderful. And I'm glad I was there to join in the celebration.

CHAPTER 36
PANDEMIC POSTLUDE

During the time of writing and editing this memoir, our country and the world were shaken to the core. It's hard to know how the world will be, once we can look back on these days. The coronavirus pandemic, which came to our attention here in the United States in late January/February of 2020 after much denial from the White House, as of early February of 2021 has been an alarming presence for nine months. (Update: ongoing presence into January 2022.) Lockdowns were put in place in March of 2020, once the folks in charge acknowledged that it was serious and had to be dealt with. It was hoped that the rising number of cases would de-escalate, but that sadly has not proven to be the case.

And during that time, when social distancing was so important, and we were mostly at home in front of our television screens, the horrifying images we saw as a nation of George Floyd, the Black man murdered on the streets of south Minneapolis by Minneapolis police officers, inspired demonstrations and protests all over the country, all over the world. Thousands of people, young and old, of every race and every age, marched through the streets. As the weeks continued, more troubling and unacceptable images of violence by police against Black citizens on the streets came to light on our TV and computer screens. Understandable, justifiable emotions continued to inspire more outrage and protests, and at those demonstrations, joined by thousands and thousands of people in the streets, not everyone wore masks. The drama on both levels—the Black Lives Matter movement, and the growing pandemic—increased. Our then-president refused to speak out, except in support of those who defend police violence as acceptable and necessary. He continued to hold huge rallies during the months preceding the November presidential election, and those who attended didn't believe in masks for the most part. Masks became a political issue for some bizarre reason. Our then-president said nothing in these months that accomplished, or expressed a wish for, the coming together of our nation. He spent weeks following his loss in the 2020 presidential election challenging the results—filing case after case charging fraudulent election results but presenting no facts to support the claim. Finally his attempts rose to the level of the Supreme Court, and the justices, including the three he had recently appointed, refused to hear the case.

In the weeks and months prior to the election, Mr. Trump predicted and escalated fear among some that fraudulent voting will have taken place, should he not come out the winner. He postured in those weeks that he hadn't decided yet, should that be the case, whether he would facilitate a peaceful transition or not. Some of us still anticipated his decision with concern, as the inauguration of the newly elected president approached.

Mr. Trump could not give up his campaigning, his public events, his crowds of cheering admirers, even as the virus spread. Wearing masks or not has evolved into a political identity. At one point it was rumored that some of those admirers were paid to show up and sit behind him in their MAGA hats and Trump T-shirts at several of the rallies. And when the TikTok followers managed to enter a million or so RSVPs for a Trump rally and then not show up, as part of a seemingly calculated effort to embarrass him—that is when

Trump began to openly go after TikTok, demanding that it be sold to an American company amid threatens of shutting it down. To me, the connection between Trump's humiliation because of that largely empty rally and his attempt to shut TikTok down was so obvious that I don't understand why there wasn't more public discussion of his efforts and that direct connection.

As months wore on, and the challenges of escalating unemployment, of business closures, of a lack of social inter-action were experienced, we saw another rise in frustration levels. Against all cautions, holiday crowds chose to gather on lakeside beaches, on ocean beaches, and then, as predicted, the pandemic grew.

In late 2020 the downward count of new cases that had begun to happen reversed itself. The many efforts to create a vaccine succeeded in several being approved for use, and another about to be. But the scientists have been so dismissed by our leadership that for some, it is caused a lack of trust in the vaccine's efficacy and safety. This state of affairs has affected lives all over the world. At this moment, myself and my loved ones are safe and well, and blessed to be in peaceful environments, with sufficient food and clean water, with television, and with communication on many levels available. But so many of our fellow beings on the planet are in tragically threatening conditions and it is painful and heartbreaking to see their suffering, even from such a distance.

Refugees are suffering around the world as they try to leave behind one tragic life, only to find themselves in the middle of another. I pray that by the time this book goes to press, we will have changed laws and behaviors related to the racism in our own nation, that we will somehow have begun to help address the imbalance of economic, educational, health, and social conditions all around the world, and that science, supported by governments and citizens, will have created and made available and affordable to all the vaccine that will bring an end to this pandemic that has now firmly wrapped itself around the globe.

Footnote to 2020

It is January 6, 2021. I have just listened, between tears, my heart pounding, to the last three hours of television coverage of the rioting, the violence, the destruction to our Capitol Building, its federal halls and offices, broken windows—the halls of Congress intruded upon—triggered and encouraged by the forty-fifth president, in the hour and a half speech he gave to his MAGA supporters in Washington DC. We have seen the humiliation of our country in the eyes of other nations. We have seen guns drawn in the halls of Congress. We have seen a photo of a renegade, bearded intruder who broke into the office of the Speaker of the House, relaxing with his feet on top of her desk. We heard from the newly elected President Joe Biden, urging Trump to speak to the rioters and calm things down. Then we saw Trump come on camera, and tell his followers in the crowds that yes, they had been cheated, that yes, the election was fraudulent, but that they should go home anyway. I have never, ever seen anything as disgusting, as offensive, as unbelievable as this happening in the sacred halls of our nation. What a sad way to wrap up the old year, or a memoir, or just about anything.

Over the following weeks, the conflict continues in the governmental halls of our nation. Investigations have proceeded, charges have been filed. Cameras throughout the Capitol Building captured faces, voices, threats, thievery . . . their presence and actions cannot now be denied.

And lastly, the tragic beginnings of the attacks by Putin against the citizens of Ukraine on February 24th of this year, 2022, have continued and escalated, to such a degree that charges of war crimes have been made and will be investigated. The majority of countries in the world have come together to try to lend support to the Ukrainians, in all ways possible, short of actions that are believed might trigger an escalation into a nuclear war. There are still at this point in time, those leaders who have not spoken out against Putin's actions, his unprovoked attacks on the civilian people and lands of another nation. I don't understand how that makes sense to anyone, regardless of their politics. We can only hope by the time you read these pages, peace has been restored and those responsible have been held to answer for their actions.

ACKNOWLEDGMENTS

There are many people to acknowledge and thank...some, for their support in the writing of this book, and others, for their support and guidance through the life that this book is about. Two different communities, but I feel so much gratitude for both.

I have always loved writing, and twenty-two years ago, began running off to Iowa City every summer to attend the Summer Writing Festival workshops at University of Iowa in Iowa City, IA. I studied with so many wonderful writers and teachers, and I am grateful for the program itself, and for Amy Margolis who has kept it running beautifully for over three decades now. I hope to return to the streets and classrooms of Iowa City one day soon and dive back into those poetry, play-writing, fiction, novel and memoir workshops once again.

In Iowa I had the gift of connecting in various workshops over the years, with a wonderful mentor, Gordon Mennenga, who has been so kind in offering feedback and comments at every stage of this memoir as it evolved. I am forever grateful to him, an amazing writer himself. He also ran the Creative Writing program at Coe College in Iowa. It was Gordon who encouraged me to finally send out some writings on the last day of one of our workshops, and the first "send" resulted in hearing back the next day that two of my poems were being published in *Hermeneutic Chaos Literary Journal*. Thus began the confidence to continue to submit works from time to time that have landed in various literary journals, both online and in print.

I also want to acknowledge the guidance I received from another wonderful writer and teacher, Laura Munson, with whom I did a workshop in Montana a few years ago. Laura also has given me such helpful suggestions and guidance in the writing of this memoir.

And my gratitude to the wonderful team at Atmosphere Press, who have brought this all to fruition.

The other acknowledgement I must share is for all those amazing people who encouraged me in the early days, who taught me about the business itself and the importance of our performers' unions, SAG AFTRA, AGMA and AGVA. My mother and stepfather, Betty and Tom Clarke, and my father Ken Stevens were all engaged in the music business during my childhood, and shared their own experiences with me, as well as their musical knowledge. And later, my father Ken encouraged me to consider expanding my singing work into the area of contracting voices, which I had always been reluctant to do. I know that this expansion greatly affected my being able to stay active in the business for so long. For that gift also, I owe a huge debt of gratitude to Sandy De Crescent, musician contractor extraordinaire, to Carol Farhat, VP of TV music, 20th Century Fox, and to Tiffany Jones, at Universal studios, for trusting me to handle so many of their projects over the years.

I learned so much from the generation of singers who came before me, who were already well-established when I began working and who were generous and kind enough to include me in early projects, to let me show what I could do, which could lead to getting that next work call.

And that brings me to another acknowledgement. I'm so grateful that my daughter Susie decided to become a "third generation" singer, and that we have been able to share some of these wonderful adventures together. I know it was not the best way to spend childhood as she had to, with a single mother whose working hours were pretty much 24/7 at many points along the way. I wish I could go back and re-do all those early years. Thank you, dear Susie, for your love, for encouraging me to write these pages and get them out into the world before I leave the planet.

I'm so grateful to all the supportive friends, family and colleagues who encouraged me to write about these last six decades of musical experiences, and I'm forever grateful to dear Corey Field, who sipped wine with me on the front porch all through the pandemic days and encouraged me to just get this book out into the world, even if I had to publish it myself.

Spending a life in the music business has truly been like circling a buffet table that's constantly being updated and replenished with the newest dishes and most exotic flavors. I'm so grateful to have received an invitation.

PARTIAL LIST OF FILM CREDITS

102 Dalmations – Singer
50 First Dates – Vocal Contractor
Absence of Malice – Singer/ Lyricist
Abyss, The – Singer/ Vocal Contractor
Action Jackson – Singer
Adam Sandle's Eight Crazy Nights – Singer/Vocal Contractor
Addam's Family, The – Singer/ Vocal Contractor
After Earth – Singer
Airplane! – Singer
Aladdin – Singer
Alice in Wonderland – 1 & II, 1985
Alien – Singer
Alien 3 – Singer
American Flyers – Singer
American Gangster – Singer
American Tail: Fievel Goes West – Singer
Almistad – Singer/ Vocal Contractor
Amityville Horror – Singer
A New Life – Solo Main Title (Sonata #5 for Flute & Keyboard)
Anastasia – Singer
Angry Birds – Solo Singer
Apollo 13 – Singer
Apocalypse Now – Singer
Apocalypse Now Redux – Singer
Armageddon – Singer

At First Night – Singer
Baby Boom – Singer/ Vocal Contractor
Backdraft - Singer/ Vocal Contractor
Bas News Bears – Singer
Bat People, The – Solo Singer
Batman & Robin – Singer
Batman: Mask of the Phantasm – Singer
Batman Returns – Singer/ Vocal Contractor
Beauty and the Beast – Singer
Beetlejuice – Singer/ Vocal Contractor
Behind Enemy Lines – Singer/ Vocal Contractor
Beowulf – Singer
Best Little Whorehouse in Texas – Singer
Big Fat Liar – Singer
Big Trouble – Singer/ Vocal Contractor
Bird on a Wire – Vocal Contractor
Black Cauldron – Singer
Black Nativity – Singer/ Vocal Contractor
Blades of Glory – Singer/ Vocal Contractor
Blown Away – Singer/ Vocal Contractor
Blues Brothers, The – Singer
Bob, Carol, Ted and Alice – Singer
Body Double – Solo Singer
Boys on the Side – Singer
Brainstorm – Singer
Bridge of Spies – Vocal Contractor
Bronco Billy – Singer
Brothers Karamazov – Singer
Brubaker – Singer
Bruce Almighty – Singer/ Vocal Contractor
Buffy the Vampire Slayer – Singer/vocal Contractor
Bug's Life, A – Singer
Butch Cassidy & The Sundance Kid – Singer/ Solo Singer
Butterflies Are Free – Singer
Caddyshack – Singer
Campaign, The – Singer
Casper – Singer
Cats Don't Dance – Singer

Catwoman – Singer/ Vocal Contractor
Charlotte's Web – Singer
Charley Wilson's War – Singer/ Vocal Contractor
Charro – Singer
Chicken Little – Singer
Christmas with the Franks – Singer
City Hall – Singer
City Slickers II – The Legend of Curley's Gold – Singer/ Vocal Contractor
Class – Singer
Coneheads – Singer/ Vocal Contractor
Congo – Singer/ Vocal Contractor
Constantine – Singer/ Vocal Contractor
Contact – Singer/ Vocal Contractor
Coogan's Bluff – Singer
Crossroads – Singer
Cry-Baby – Singer
Dances with Wolves – Singer
Dawn of the Planet of the Apes – Singer
Daylight
Day the Earth Stood Still – Singer/ Vocal Contractor
D2 the Mighty Ducks – Singer
Dead Pool 2 – Singer/ Vocal Contractor
Dead Presidents – Singer/ Vocal Contractor
Deep Impact – Singer/ Vocal Contractor
Detroit Rock City – Singer
Dick Tracy – Singer
Dinosaur – Singer/ Vocal Contractor
Dirty Hairy – Solo Singer
Doc Hollywood – Singer/ Vocal Contractor
Doctor Detroit – Singer
Dr. Zhivago – Singer
Doubt – Singer/ Vocal Contractor
Down with Love – Singer/ Vocal Contractor
Dragonfly – Singer
Dr. Seuss' Horton Hears a Who! – Singer
Dr. Seuss' the Lorax – Singer
Dudley Do-Right – Singer

Duets – Singer
Dutch – Singer/Vocal Contractor
Edward Scissorhands – Singer/ Solo/ Vocal Contractor
Eight Crazy Nights – Singer/ Vocal Contractor
Elf – Singer/ Vocal Contractor
Empire of the Sun – Singer
End of Days – Singer
Epic – Singer
Ernest Saves Christmas – Singer
Evan Almighty – Singer
Evolution – Singer/ Vocal Contractor
Exorcist, The – Singer
Exorcist II: The Heretic – Singer/ Solo Singer
Fabulous Baker Boys – Vocal Coach for Michelle Pfeiffer
Falling in Love – Singer
Fantastic Four – Singer
Family Man, The – Singer
Faster – Singer
Father of the Bride – Singer/ Vocal Contractor
Father of the Bride Part II – Singer/ Vocal Contractor
Finding Dory – Singer/ Vocal Contractor
Flight of the Pheonix – Singer/ Vocal Contractor
Flintstones, The – Singer
Flipper's New Adventure – Singer
Flubber – Singer
Flushed Away – Singer
Forrest Gump – Singer/ Vocal Contractor
For the Boys – Singer
Free Willy – Singer
Frighteners – Singer
Galaxy Quest – Singer
Get Smart – Singer
Ghost Story – Singer
Ghosts – (Michael Jackson, video to theatrical release)
Glimmer Man, The – Singer
Glory – Singer
Glory Road – Singer/ Choral Contractor
Godzilla – Singer

Gone in Sixty Seconds – Vocal Contractor
Good Will Hunting – Singer
Grease – Singer
Grease 2 – Singer/ Vocal Contractor
Great Expectations (1998) – Singer
Guardians of the Galaxy Vol. 2 – Singer/ Vocal Contractor
Greatest Story Ever Told – Singer
Groundhog Day – Singer/ Vocal Contractor
Gunfight in Abiline – Singer
Hallelujah Trail, The – Singer
Hammersmith Is Out – Solo Singer/ Lyricist
Happy Feet – Singer
Heart and Soul – Singer/ Vocal Contractor
Heaven and Earth – Singer/ Solo Singer/ Vocal Contractor
He's Just Not That into You – Singer
High Plains Drifter – Solo Singer
History of the World Part 1 – Singer
Hocus Pocus – Singer
Holy Man – Singer
Home Alone – Singer
Home Alone 2: Lost In New York – Vocal Coach for Macaulay
   Culkin
Hook – Singer
Hop – Singer
Horton Hears a Who – Singer
House on Haunted Hill – Singer/ Vocal Contractor
How Stella Got Her Groove Back – Singer
How the Grinch Stole Christmas – Singer
How the West Was Won – Singer
Huckleberry Finn – Singer
Hunt for Red October – Singer
Ice Age: Continental Draft – Singer
Ice Age 2: The Meltdown – Singer
I Am Legend – Singer/ Vocal Contractor
Incredible Burt Wonderstone, The – Singer/ Vocal Contractor
Incredible Hulk, The – Singer
Indiana Jones & The Kingdom of the Crystal Skull – Singer/
   Contractor

Instinct – Singer
I, Robot – Singer/ Vocal Contractor
In God We Trust – Singer
Inspector Gadget – Singer
Jackal, The – Singer
James and the Giant Peach – Solo Singer
Jay and Silent Bob Strike Back – Singer
J. Edgar – Singer/ Vocal Contractor
Jingle All the Way – Singer
Joe Versus the Volcano – Singer
John Carter – Singer
John Grisham's The Rain Maker – Singer/ Vocal Contractor
John Q – Singer
Joy – Singer
Joyful Noise – Vocal Contractor
Jumanji – Singer
Jurassic Park – Singer
Jurassic Park 3 – Singer
Jurassic World – Singer
Kelly's Heroes – Singer
Killer – Singer
King Kong (2005) – Singer/ Vocal Contractor
Klute – Solo Singer
Lady in the Water – Singer
Ladyhawke – Singer
Last Airbender – Singer/ Vocal Contractor
Last of the Mohicans – Singer
Last Rites – Singer
League of Their Own, A – Singer/ Vocal Contractor
Lean on Me – Singer/ Vocal Contractor
Little Mermaid, The – Singer
Little Nicky – Singer
Little Rascals, The – Singer/ Vocal Contractor
Looking for Mr. Goodbar – Singer
Look Who's Talking Now – Singer/ Vocal Contractor
Looney Tunes: Back in Action – Singer/ Solo Singer/ Vocal
    Contractor
Lost Horizons – Singer

Love Machine – Singer
Made in Paris – Singer
Magnum Force – Singer
Mars Attacks! – Singer
Mars Needs Moms – Singer
MASH – Singer
Masquerade – Singer
Matrix Reloaded, The – Singer/ Vocal Contractor
Matrix Revolutions – Singer/Vocal Contractor
Maze Runner, The – Singer
Meet the Parents – Singer
Meet the Robinsons – Singer
Men in Black – Singer
Men in Black II – Singer
Men's Club, The – Solo Singer "La Vie en Rose"
Mexican, The – Singer/ Vocal Contractor
Mighty Ducks – Singer
Mighty Joe Youns (1998) – Singer/ Vocal Contractor
Minority Report – Vocal Contractor
Miracle on 34th Street – Singer/ Vocal Contractor
Mission: Impossible (1996) – Singer
Money Pit, The – Singer
Mosquito Coast, The – Singer
Mr. Mom – Singer
Mr. Wrong (1996) – Singer/ Vocal Contractor
Mrs. WIinterbourne – Singer
Mulan (1998) – Singer
Munich – Vocal Contractor
Muppet Movie, The – Singer
My All American – Singer
My Favorite Year – Singer
National Lampoon's Christmas Vacation – Singer
National Lampoon's Vacation – Singer
Net, The (1995) – Singer
Neighbors – Singer
New York, New York – Singer
Nick of Time – Singer
Night at the Museum: Secret of the Tomb – Singer/ Vocal
    Contractor

Nightmare on Elm Street, A – Singer/ Vocal Contractor
Nene to Five – Singer
Norbit – Singer/ Vocal Contractor
North – Singer
Oh God II – Singer
Oh God You Devil – Singer
On Any Sunday – Main Title Lyricist/ Solo Vocal
One the Line – Singer
One Night at McCool's – Singer/ Vocal Contractor
Out of Africa – Singer
Pale Rider – Solo Singer
Paradise Hawaiian Style – Singer
Passengers – Singer
Patriot, The – Singer/ Vocal Contractor
Peter Pan (2003) – Singer/ Vocal Contractor
Pebble and the Penguin, The – Singer
Pee Wee's Big Adventure – Singer
Perfect – Singer
Pirates of the Caribbean: The Curse of The Black Pearl – Singer
Polar Express, The – Singer/ Sound Effects Choir Contractor
Poltergeist – Singer
Poltergeist II: The Other Side – Singer
Popeye – Singer
Plainsman, The – Singer
Prep and Landing – Singer
President's Analyst, The – Solo Singer
Princess Diaries, The – Singer/ Vocal Contractor
Psycho III – Singer
Quest for Camelot
Radio Flyer – Singer/ Vocal Contractor
Radioland Murders – Singer/ Solo Singer/ Vocal Contractor
Rango – Vocal Contractor
Ready Player One – Singer
Real Steel – Singer
Red Heat – Singer
Robin and the Seven Hoods – Singer
Rocky Balboa – Singer/ Vocal Contractor
Rocky II – Singer

Rocky III – Singer
Rogue One: A Star Wars Story – Singer
Royal Tenenbaums – Singer/ Vocal Contractor
Rudy – Singer/ Vocal Contractor
RV – Singer/ Vocal Contractor
Salt – Singer/ Vocal Contractor
Santa Clause, The – Singer
Santa Clause 2 – Singer
Scary Movie 2 – Singer
Scooby–Doo – Singer
Scorpion King, The – Singer/ Vocal Contractor
Scream 2 – Singer
Scrooged – Singer
Secret of Nimh, The – Solo Singer
Shaggy Dog, The – Singer
Shark Tale – Singer
Shrek – Singer
Sister Act 2: Back in the Habit – Singer
Sixth Sense – Singer/ Vocal Contractor
Skeleton Key – Singer
Sky High – Singer
Slap Shot – Singer
Sleepers – Singer
Smokey and the Bandit (1977) – Singer
Sneakers – Solo Singer
Snow Falling on Cedars – Singer/ Vocal Contractor
Something Wicked This Way Comes (1983) – Singer
Sound of Music, The – Singer
South Park: Bigger, Longer and Uncut – Singer/ Vocal Contractor
Specialist, The – Solo Singer
Species – Singer
Speed Racer – Singer
Spies in Disguise – Solo Singer
Spider Man – Singer
Spider Man 2 – Singer
Spider Man 3 – Singer
Spy Hard – Singer/ Vocal Contractor
Switching Channels – Singer

Star Trek – Singer
Star Trek Beyond – Singer
Star Trek 1V: The Voyage Home – Singer
Star Wars: The Force Awakens – Vocal Contractor
Star Wars: The Last Jedi – Vocal Contractor
State of the Union – Singer
Stiletto – Solo Singer "Sugar In The Rain"
Stone Boy – Solo Singer
Swan Princess, The – Singer
Swing Kids – Singer
Sucker Punch – Singer/ Vocal Contractor
Suicide Squad – Singer
Superman Returns – Singer
Tale of Despereaux, The – Singer/ Vocal Contractor
Teenage Mutant Ninja Turtles – Singer
Terminator 3: Rise of The Machines – Singer
Testament (1983) – Singer
That's Dancing – Singer
The Fox – Solo Singer
The Little Mermaid – Singer
There's Something About Mary – Solo Singer
Three Days of the Condor – Singer
Three Musketeers, The – Singer
Thumbelina – Singer
Titan A.E. – Singer
Tomorrowland – Singer
Trick 'r Treat – Singer/ Vocal Contractor
That Thing You Do – Singer
Unconditional Love – Singer/ Vocal Contractor
Undefeated, The – Singer
Unsinkable Molly Brown (1964) – Singer
Van Helsing – Singer/ Vocal Contractor
Waiting to Exhale – Singer
War Games – Singer
War of the Roses – Singer
War of the Worlds – Singer
Watchmen – Singer/ Vocal Contractor
What Dreams May Come – Singer

What Women Want – Singer/ Vocal Contractor
Where the Wild Things Are – Vocal Contractor
Who Framed Roger Rabbit? – Singer/ Vocal Contractor
Whose Line Is It Anyway? – Singer
Why Do Fools Fall in Love? – Vocal Contractor
Wild Wild West – Singer/ Vocal Contractor
Wilder Days – Singer
Wolfman, The – Singer
World Trade Center – Singer/ Vocal Contractor
World's Greatest Athlete – Singer
Yes Man – On Camera Singer
Yesterday's Children – Singer/ Vocal Contractor
Your Highness – Singer/ Vocal Contractor
Zathura – Singer

PARTIAL LIST OF TELEVISION CREDITS

Alf TV Series, 1981
American Dad – 2005/2006 Season
American Dad – 2006/2007 Season
American Dad – 2008/2009 Season
American Dad – 2009/2010 Season
American Dad – 2018/2019 Season
Bionic Woman TV Series 1977 2 – Episodes
Bob Hope TV Special
Bold & The Beautiful, The – TV Show
Brady Bunch, The – TV Series
Brave Little Toaster Goes to Mars – TV Episode
Brickleberry TV Series, 2013 – 1 Episode
Burt Bacharach TV Special
Carnival Row TV Series – Episodes 1 – 8
Carol Burnett TV Show
Cleveland Show, The, 2010-2012 – 4 Episodes
Conundrum – TV Movie
Critic, The – TV Show
Danny Kaye TV Variety Show – 1963-1966 – 93 Episodes
Days of Our Lives – TV Show
Daytime Emmy Awards, 1994 – TV
Designing Women TV Show, 1987 – 1 Episode
Desperate Women TV Movie, 1982 – Lyric/Main Title
Diagnosis Murder, 1994-1998 – 11 Episodes
Family Guy TV Series – 1999-2000 Season [Main Title]

Family Guy TV Series – 2001-2002 Season
Family Guy TV Series – 2003-2004 Season
Family Guy TV Series – 2004 -2005 Season
Family Guy TV Series – 2005-2006 Season
Family Guy TV Series – 2006 -2007 Season
Family Guy TV Series – 2007- 2008 Season
Family Guy TV Series – 2008- 2009 Season
Family Guy TV Series – 2000-2010 Season
Family Guy TV Series – 2010-2011 Season
Family Guy TV Series – 2011-2012 Season
Family Guy TV Series – 2012-2013 Season
Family Guy TV Series -2013-2014 Season
Family Guy TV Series - 2014-2015 Season
Family Guy TV Series – 2015 -2016 Season
Family Guy TV Series – 2016-2017 Season
Family Guy TV Series – 2017-2018 Season
Family Guy TV Series – 2018-2019 Season
Family Guy TV Series – 2019-2020 Season
Family Guy TV Series – 2020-2021 Season
Family Guy TV Series – 2021-2022 Season
Father Dowling TV Series – 1990-1991 Season, On-Camera Singer
Frasier TV Series, 1995 – 1 Episode, On-Camera Singer
Futurama TV Series, 2000-2003 – 2 Episodes
Golden Girls TV Show, 1988 – 1 Episode, Solo
Grammys Broadcast, 2017 (Sturgill Simpson)
Happy Days TV Show, 1977-1982 – 25 Episodes
Haunting of Helen Walker – TV Show
How I Met Your Mother TV Series, 2010 – 1 Episode
Huey Long Story: Kingfisher – TV Show
Jay Leno Show
Johnny Carson Show
Kane & Abel TV Show
Last Don, The – TV Mini-series
King of Queens, The, TV Series, 2002 – 1 Episode
Last Tycoon, The, TV Series, 2017 – 3 Episodes
Laverne & Shirley TV Series, 1977-1982 – 6 Episodes
Love Boat, The TV Series
Magnum PI TV Series

Married With Children TV Series, 1992 – 1 Episode
Matlock TV Series, 1986-1990 – Solo Singer
Max Headroom TV Series, 1987 – Voice Over/ A7 Security System
Middle, The, TV Series, 2008 – 1 Episode
Mixed Nuts TV Show
Natalie Cole PBS TV Special
60th Oscars TV Broadcast – Singer/ Choral Director
61st Oscars TV Broadcast – Singer/ Choral Director
63rd Oscars TV Broadcast – Singer/ Choral Director
64th Oscars TV Broadcast – Singer/ Choral Director
65th Oscars TV Broadcast – Singer/ Choral Director
66th Oscars TV Broadcast – Singer/ Choral Director
75th Oscars TV Broadcast – Singer/ Choral Director
77th Oscars TV Broadcast – Singer/ Choral Director
78th Oscars TV Broadcast – Choral Director
79th Oscars TV Broadcast – Singer/ Choral Director
80th Oscars TV Broadcast – Choral Director
81st Oscars TV Broadcast – Singer/ Vocal Contractor
84th Oscars TV Broadcast – Singer
85th Oscars TV Broadcast – Singer/ Choral Director
86th Oscars TV Broadcast – Singer/ Vocal Contractor
87th Oscars TV Broadcast – Singer/ Vocal Contractor
90th Oscars TV Broadcast – Singer/ Vocal Contractor
91st Oscars TV Broadcast – Singer/ Vocal Contractor
92nd Oscars TV Broadcast – Singer
People's Choice Awards
Perry Mason TV Series, 1989 – 1 Episode
Picket Fences TV Series
70th Annual Prime Time Emmy Awards – On-Camera Singer
Quantum Leap TV Show
Red Skelton Hour
Simpsons, The, TV Series, 1989- 2022 – Main Title, 723 Episodes
Simpsons, The, TV Series, 1989-2019 – Main Title/ Off-Camera
    Vocals & End Titles
Smothers Brothers Variety Show
Soul of the Game TV Show
Star Trek 4 TV Series
Star Trek: The Next Generation TV Series

Stedman TV Series
Sinatra TV Miniseries
Taxi TV Series, 1982 – Singer
Three Desperate Women TV Movie
True Blood TV Series, 2008 – On-Camera Singer
X-Files, The, TV Series, 1999 – 1 episode

PARTIAL LIST OF
SOUND RECORDINGS CREDITS

Ron Hicklin Singers

1965
Leroy Van Dyke
The Knickerbockers

1966
Danny Brooks
Jerry Lewis
Hank Thompson
Johnny Sea
Jerry Naylor
Enzo Stuarti

1967
Enzo Stuarti
Vic Damone
Bobby Sherman
Frankie Lane
Goldberg & Levine
The Alan Copeland Singers
Gabor Szabo
Tom Scott
Peter Marshall

Linda Ronstadt
Stu Phillips
Kay Starr
Les Baxter
James Darren
Gary Puckett & the Union Gap
The Billy Vaughn Singers

1968
John Davidson
Bobby Doyle
Sammy Davis Jr.
Ed Ames
Leonard Nimoy
Ron Wilson
Sajid Kahn
Walter Scharf
Randy Hart
Herb Alpert & The Tijuana Brass
Pete Fountain
Barry Richards

1969
Earl Grant
Sajid Kahn
The Checkmates
Bobbi Paris
The Union Gap
Andy Williams
Andy Russell
Jimmy Rodgers
Connie Van Dyke
The big Bounce
Ed Ames
Herb Alpert
Bob Thompson
Lorne Green
Pete Candoli
Burt Bacharach
Neil Diamond
Shirley Bassey
Al Hirt
Johnny Mathis
Liza Minelli
Bobby Vee
Bud Shank
Mark Lindsay (Paul Revere & The Raiders)

1970
Pat Boone
Jerry Fuller
Mike Curb Congregation
Ed Ames
Campus
Mark Lindsay
Paul Hampton
Bobbi Hatfield
Spiral Staircase
Jim Walker

Jerry Wallace
Ken Barry
Charlie Fox (Love American Style)
Bill Medley
Hank Williams, Jr.
Billy Vaughn Singers
Johnny Mathis

1971
The Congregation
Johnny Mathis
The Congregation
Baja Marimba Band
Billy Graham
Ken Berry
Anthony Newley
Lou Rawls
Mel Tillis
Robert Goulet
Ed Ames
Wayne Newton
Hugo Montenegro
Peggy Lee
Jerry Vale
Lalo Schifrin
Susan Hart
Mistic Moods Orchestra
Roger Miller
David Cassidy
Billy-Joe Royal
Stu Phillips

1972
Ray Charles
Sweet Grass
Al Martino
Johnny Mathis

Bobby Vinton
Vikki Carr
Viva
Billy Joe Royal
PF Sloan
Al Martino
Vic Damone
Jerry Fuller
Lost Horizon
Cher
Sony & Cher
Jerry Tawney
Bed Rock
Pebbles & Bam Bam
Austin Roberts
Ranji
Karen Wyman
Lou Rawls
Johnny Mathis
Jerry Fuller
Adrian Smith
Shawn Fillips
England Dan & John Ford Coley
Michael Allen
Hugh Montenegro
Walter Matthau
Lulu

1973
Wayne Newton
Dean Martin
Jim Weatherly
Nancy Sinatra
Tung
Jim Nabors
Bola Sete
Nana Mouskouri
Rodney Allen Pippy

Roberto Carlos
Cher
The Brady Bunch
Robert Goulet
Eydie Gourmet
Rona Barrett
Mac Davis
Alan Copeland
Roger Williams
Don Goodwin

1974
Tony Christie
Vikki Carr
Anthony Newley
Rod McKuen
Ray Conniff
Frank Sinatra
Telly Savalas
Bobby Vinton
John MacNally
Robert Goulet
Rick Lisi
Tom Bresh
Bobby Worth

1975
Johnny Cash
Merv Griffin

1976
Jim Weatherly
John Davidson
Teresa Brewer
Kenny Seratt
Guy Marks
Vickie Lawrence

Jack Fascinato
Mary Lynn
Morris Albert

1977
Tony Basil
Tennessee Ernie Ford
Susanne Klee
Kenny Seratt
Freddie Hart
Sammy Nestico
Ernie Payne
Freddie Hart
Marty Mitchell
Bobby & PJ
Tom Nelson

1978
Shaun Cassidy
Gary Bevison
1979
Cosimo Filane

1980
Johnny Mathis

1981
Mancini Project

1982
Sam Ocampo
Perry La Marca
Placido Domingo

1983
Perry La Marca Singers

1984
Anna Maria Alberghetti
The Carpenters

Other Recording Projects
Elvis Presley (sang)
Michael Jackson (sang/ contracted)
Michael Buble (sang/ contracted)
Harry Connick, Jr. (sang/ contracted)
Frank Sinatra Trilogy Album (sang)
Natalie Cole (sang/ contracted)
Michael Feinstein (sang/ contracted)
John Travolta (sang/ contracted)

ABOUT ATMOSPHERE PRESS

Atmosphere Press is an independent, full-service publisher for excellent books in all genres and for all audiences. Learn more about what we do at atmospherepress.com.

We encourage you to check out some of Atmosphere's latest releases, which are available at Amazon.com and via order from your local bookstore:

The Great Unfixables, by Neil Taylor

Soused at the Manor House, by Brian Crawford

Portal or Hole: Meditations on Art, Religion, Race And The Pandemic, by Pamela M. Connell

A Walk Through the Wilderness, by Dan Conger

The House at 104: Memoir of a Childhood, by Anne Hegnauer

A Short History of Newton Hall, Chester, by Chris Fozzard

Serial Love: When Happily Ever After... Isn't, by Kathy Kay

Sit-Ins, Drive-Ins and Uncle Sam, by Bill Slawter

Black Water and Tulips, by Sara Mansfield Taber

Ghosted: Dating & Other Paramoural Experiences, by Jana Eisenstein

Walking with Fay: My Mother's Uncharted Path into Dementia, by Carolyn Testa

FLAWED HOUSES of FOUR SEASONS, by James Morris

Word for New Weddings, by David Glusker and Thom Blackstone

It's Really All about Collaboration and Creativity! A Textbook and Self-Study Guide for the Instrumental Music Ensemble Conductor, by John F. Colson

A Life of Obstructions, by Rob Penfield

Troubled Skies Over Quaker Hill: A Search for the Truth, by Lessie Auletti

ABOUT THE AUTHOR

In addition to her singing performances and work as a vocal contractor/choral director, Sally Stevens has had her short stories, poems and essays published in: *The Offbeat, Mockingheart Review, Raven's Perch, Hermeneutic Chaos Literary Journal, The Voices Project, Los Angeles Press, Between the Lines Anthology: Fairy Tales & Folklore Re-imagined, Funny in Five Hundred, The Missouri Review* and *No Extra Words* podcast.